Rose, Lisle Abbott

The long shadow:
reflections on the Second
World War era

DATE DUE		
MAR 2 4 1988		

THE
LONG
SHADOW

Lisle A. Rose

THE LONG SHADOW

Reflections on the Second World War Era

Contributions in American History, Number 70

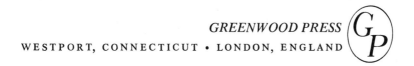

GREENWOOD PRESS

WESTPORT, CONNECTICUT • LONDON, ENGLAND

GP

Library of Congress Cataloging in Publication Data

Rose, Lisle Abbott, 1936-
    The long shadow.

    (Contributions in American history ; no. 70
ISSN 0084-9219)
    Bibliography: p.
    Includes index.
    1. World War, 1939-1945—Diplomatic history.
2. World politics—1945-1955. 3. United States—
Foreign relations—1945-1953. I. Title.
D748.R68   940.53   77-84760
ISBN 0-8371-9892-5

The selection from John W. Aldridge's *In the Country of
the Young* is reprinted by permission of Curtis Brown, Ltd.
Copyright © 1969 by John W. Aldridge.

Library of Congress Catalog Card Number: 77-84760
ISBN: 0-8371-9892-5
ISSN: 0084-9219

First published in 1978

Greenwood Press, Inc.
51 Riverside Avenue, Westport, Connecticut 06880

Printed in the United States of America

10   9   8   7   6   5   4   3   2   1

Contents

Acknowledgments

As is always the case, many people have contributed in many ways to the making of this book. The manuscript has been read in whole or in part by Jon Wakelyn, David Mabon, and Richard Darilek, all of whom have offered valuable suggestions. The essay on postwar United States Far Eastern policy emerged from a paper on the topic which I delivered at Kent State University in March of 1977. I am grateful to Professors Henry Whitney and Lawrence S. Kaplan for the opportunity they provided me to clarify my views on this important issue. I am deeply grateful to my wife for providing me with her professional editorial skills at all stages of the work. Of course, I am alone responsible for all errors of fact or interpretation which may occur throughout these essays, and the views expressed are solely my own.

Lisle A. Rose
FALLS CHURCH, VIRGINIA
August 1977

THE
LONG
SHADOW

Introduction:
The Age of Hitler

FOR A long time we have continued to live off the moral and intellectual capital of a now distant past. Our basic beliefs, judgments, and perspectives continue to be shaped by men long gone.

From the beginning of recorded time, from the beginning, that is, of civilization, men have asked themselves not only who they were but what they were. Man's relation to his fellows, to his economic environment, to his current political system, to his universe, to his god, has preoccupied and perplexed thinkers for centuries. A tradition of fundamental inquiry as diverse as it is rich has characterized the human condition from the start.

But such inquiry has begun to flag in recent decades. Exhausted by the inexorably expanding complexity of modern life, taking refuge in the canons of a new professionalism that decrees all lofty speculation an impertinence, mid- and late-twentieth-century, Western man continues to rely upon his eighteenth- and nineteenth-century forebears for basic clues to an understanding of humanity as a whole. The result has been a growing sterility in both philosophic debate and scholarly discourse. The relationship of criticism to reality is increasingly suspect. Contemporary character and behavior remain tantalizingly blurred and unfocused.

Since the commencement of the mass industrial age some two hundred years ago, popular thought in the West has been shaped by a half dozen great secular messiahs: Thomas Jefferson, Adam Smith, Karl Marx, Charles Darwin, Sigmund Freud, and Adolf Hitler. Jefferson bequeathed us the pleasing image of agrarian, dem-

ocratic man, essentially benign and rational, who, if left largely to
his own devices, would create an essentially static, quite mild, often
invisible, republican political environment of common simplicity,
virtue, and rectitude. Adam Smith propounded a no less engaging
but in some ways more dynamic illusion of economic man, at once
creator and beneficiary of a free-market environment in which mutually offsetting and balanced strivings would inevitably lead to the
greatest good for the greatest number. Only rarely would politics
and the state intervene and then only as impartial umpires to restore
competitive balance and freedom to an essentially self-perpetuating
system.

Jefferson and Smith became the grand architects of nineteenth-
century, bourgeois, capitalistic, quasi-democratic Western Europe
and America. Their genial assumptions about human nature were
the basis for popular belief in the inevitability of human progress,
both material and divine. Reality soon intervened in disquieting
ways. Man proved incapable of restraint, either politically or economically. Jefferson's benign republic was quickly splintered by
partisan strife, often soiled by corruption, nearly torn from its ideological moorings by the pressures of industrialization and urbaniza-
tion, and incessantly wracked by all sorts of internal contradictions
from the issue of black slavery down to the meanest, most persistent
injustices at nearly all levels of society.

Smith's freely running market economy proved equally vulnerable to the realities of human nature. Smith had failed to take fully
into account the ability of the unscrupulous and brutal individual
to master both the means and machinery of production and distribution and the overarching political system which shaped the kind
of industrial system and market economy within which the modern
capitalist would operate.

In many implicit and oblique ways Darwin, Marx, and Freud
each brought fresh and more realistic perspectives to the ongoing
discourse concerning human nature and values. Marx perceived the
many weaknesses and cruel injustices inherent in Smith's economic
system and, implicitly, in classic Jeffersonianism as well. Darwin,
Freud, and their many followers and popularizers, though not explicitly concerned with a detailed refutation of Jeffersonian and

Smithian social criticism, nonetheless sharply challenged the sanguine bases on which that criticism was based.

Marx's response to the callous, exploitative, capitalist system he found about him was to postulate capitalism as but one phase in a historically determined evolution of mankind, an evolution that could only be understood and directed by a revolutionary elite in eventual alliance with an awakened industrial proletariat. But Marx, along with Darwin and his Social Darwinist idolators, introduced a profoundly disturbing element into modern philosophic debate. Violence could no longer be avoided as an ingredient of power and process. Such ruthlessness had decided limits, however. Violence (defined as the "struggle for existence" in the Social Darwinist formulation) was a regrettably necessary element in an essentially humane formulation. Repelled by the many examples of injustice and exploitation around him, Marx concluded that fire could only be fought with fire. Enthralled by the stupendous material and financial achievements of the European and American capitalists in their midst, Social Darwinists embraced the notion that only through ceaseless, anarchic competition could the world exalt its social, moral, and economic superiors while relegating the mass of the "unfit" to permanently subordinate status. If the means were to be violent in both formulations, the ends were not, and the fact that in other hands the means ineluctably corrupted the ends should not blind us to this truth. The end of the Darwinist dream was to be the perpetual victory of some half-conceived and at best vaguely defined oligarchy of incessant overachievers. The end of the Marxist dream was to be the withering away of the state and the establishment of a perfectly running communistic order. Marxists and Social Darwinists alike postulated that out of bloodshed and striving against a morally reprehensible socioeconomic system would emerge an order as basically paradisical and self-regulatory as any model projected by Thomas Jefferson or Adam Smith.

It was left to Sigmund Freud to bridge the chasm between these facile late-nineteenth-century assumptions of progress through violence and our own century's morbid preoccupation with violence for violence's sake. Freud's Vienna—that lilac city of so many dreams—was, of course, Adolf Hitler's Vienna as well, and the dreams that were spawned there proved as sinister as they were light, as vicious as they were frivolous and gay. Vienna was a city of darkness as well as brilliance. If the better cafés and coffeehouses vied with the world-renowned university (where Freud did his most creative work) in supporting and promoting civil life and discourse, the dingy flophouses and tenement areas where young Hitler passed his time in a continually frustrated quest for a life of some meaning spawned their own terrible hatreds and prejudices. As the crushing burdens of late-nineteenth-century life weakened the bourgeoisie, these hatreds and prejudices invaded the middle class, infecting it with the diseased notions of the "Jew banker" and intellectual.

Freud, one of the profoundly civilized men of his time, understood Vienna's divided soul and knew that it reflected the terrible, if generally unacknowledged, division of European thought and society. With rare courage in an age of determined optimism, Freud probed the darkness he found about (and within) him and exposed the growing isolation, estrangement, and meaninglessness of so much of life in the mass social order of his time. His aim, always, was comprehension and cure within the classically rational framework bequeathed by the eighteenth and nineteenth centuries. The attempts to compress and compartmentalize violent impulses through analysis and subsequently to neutralize, if not to dissipate, them by means of therapy were Freud's great gifts to the contemporary world. Exploitation of his environment, mastery of the masses by means of his discoveries, never entered the man's mind. The resurrection and maintenance of his patients' *self*-identity was everything. Freud knew that "man is by nature, at his origins, a killer, and religion is the history of his guilt. Freud aimed to cure man of his guilt and thus to abolish the history of it."[1]

It is only when we come to Adolf Hitler, that symbol of the other, darker Vienna, that the last pretensions to classical humanity are stripped away. Hitler represents a decisive, very possibly irremediable break with the generous assumptions—or at least hopes—about human nature that had been the hallmark of modern discourse to his time. With intuitive genius, Hitler, like Freud, sensed the frightening change in human character that lay at the heart of early-twentieth-century Western civilization. His response to the loneliness, alienation, and desperation that saturated Western life was the concoction of the militant political party and the totalitarian warfare state with their brutal trappings, incessant appeals to pure sensationalism, steadily intensifying dedication to conflict—both hot and cold, foreign and domestic—and, above all, their ubiquitous presence, which sucked dry the public and private lives of the nation, leaving people at once exhilarated and exhausted, aggressive and apathetic. Here is a pattern of power become all too familiar in our contemporary era.

Yet we have been loath to admit the führer to our pantheon of great, modern political artists. We repulse the notion that this product of the Vienna gutters with his gospels of hate, violence, and terror may be the master teacher of our age.* Surely those are not our faces in the faded photographs, the grainy newsreels, of the German people of forty years ago. The Nazi death camps cannot be seriously considered as fit metaphors for our time. Hitler was an accident, a dreadful sport. Assertions to the contrary are merely gushy mea culpas of the weak or the foolish or the sensationalists of our time, of the purveyors of fashionable despair. Our age remains definable by the comfortably traditional terms of economic or ideological conflict, not mere savagery. So we turn away from the survivors of Auschwitz and Buchenwald and Mauthausen; we ignore, when we do not defend, those who perpetrated My Lai and Ben Suc. We do not really wish to listen; we do not want to know.

Nowhere is this attitude better exemplified than in the current debate within American academic circles over national responsibility for that postwar world crisis commonly called the cold war. "Traditionalist" historians defend American policies and behavior from a mixed Jeffersonian-Smithian perspective. America, in Jefferson's words "the last, best hope of mankind," has stood at Armageddon for thirty years, battling the malevolent hosts of international communism on behalf of "liberalism." Revisionist scholars, self-

---

* "In retrospect his life seems like a steady unfolding of tremendous energy. Its effects were vast, the terror it spread enormous; but when it was over there was little left for memory to hold." Joachim C. Fest, *Hitler* (New York: Vintage Books, 1975), p. 764.

styled and otherwise, condemn with equal fervor a cold war America they claim conforms in greater or lesser measure to the Marxist model of a desperate, capitalistic order approaching its final stages of collapse and ruthlessly seeking to stave off the ultimate disasters of chronic overproduction and mass unemployment through the establishment of a global market area.

This century of total war has compromised, if, indeed, it has not banished as irrelevant, the benign images of man propounded by both Jefferson and Smith. Energetic efforts of publicists, apologists, and even a few scholars to the contrary, it is almost impossible to resurrect the notion of the genial, Jeffersonian rationalist in man. As for the system of free-market economics advanced by Adam Smith, twentieth-century warfare states with their incessant demands and regulations have surely put an end to what capitalists themselves had started to destroy as early as the late nineteenth century in their quest for certainty in production, markets, and profit.

But classic Marxism, too, has failed to dominate or satisfactorily explain the course of recent history. If the central fact of the nineteenth century was the industrialization of the West with its accompanying system of expansive, often brutally exploitative, corporate enterprise, which created vast disparities of wealth between the few and the many, the central facts of this century have been (whether Marxists will admit them or not) the incredible expansion of comparative plenty to the Western masses under the capitalist system even as that system itself has been wracked by incessant civil war among its political components.

Marxism has been both a philosophy of materialism and a gospel of successful revolution. But the twentieth century—and particularly the Second World War era that began somewhere around 1933 —has challenged both of Marx's major premises. Materialism, no matter how heavily glossed with spirituality by desperate neo-Marxists, has lost its power to save or persuade us. The urge to accumulate has not lessened; it has steadily intensified under the lash of capitalistic manipulation. But acquisition as an accomplishment in itself has begun to lose its meaning for all but the most poverty-stricken few among us. The more most of us acquire, the more lonely and isolated we become, both from society around us and, more important, from ourselves. We know this, yet we seem powerless to break the cycle and learn anew about ourselves and our condition. As for the prospects for successful Marxist revolution, fashionably leftist critics looking or hoping for the final demise of the capitalist order and the emergence of a new era of beneficence ignore the fact that the ability of the industrial-capitalist system to provide its own ultimate weapons of destruction and to stimulate its own internal crusades of hatred and violence has far exceeded anything its detractors could have imagined. So great has contemporary savagery become that *no* individual, group, or "system" has escaped its awful effects. Thus no individual, group, or system can plausibly maintain or assert the right to be entrusted with the construction of a new order without first reexamining the very premises of behavior and policy. Whether Stalin ever sensed this fact we cannot know. Khrushchev apparently did. American statesmen have begun to acknowledge it and to act accordingly. Recent history has shown us all to be bestial in part if not in whole, the "people," the "masses," no less than the "interests" or the "power elites" who guide or govern or manipulate them.

If we are to undertake a modest reconstruction in understanding, we have to begin with a recognition of the obvious. The chief symbols of our world, East as well as West, South as well as North, are no longer the insatiable capitalist, the brutal foreman, the cowed but restless proletariat inhabiting miles and miles of industrial slums and ripe for revolution. Our symbols have become the faceless soldier, the dispassionate assassin, the distant bombardier, and the fanatical terrorist intoxicated not with a vision of a more humane, better world but simply with his (or her) vision of fire and blood as the solutions to all problems, human and otherwise. Here is man (and woman) the savage, all too recognizable and all too often deferred to in the past forty years out of fear or ignorance or apathy. When we have thus delineated our era, penetrated to its core, we know we remain under the shadow and in the age of Hitler.

Hitler was the generative force, the master orchestrator, the great corrupter, of his—and our—time. His actions, programs, policies, orders, prejudices, and hatreds set the rhythm and tone for at least four decades of history. He and his Nazi henchmen legitimatized three methods to power that had hitherto lain either on the very fringes or beyond the pale of traditional political practice. Grievance and vengeance were elevated to guiding principles of public policy and diplomacy in a great nation state; terror and violence were routinely invoked as solutions to all problems and all opposition within and beyond the state; the totalitarian warfare state was itself idealized as the ultimate expression and final refuge of the lonely, dissociated, emotionally shattered individual searching for meaning and salvation in a chaotic world that had apparently abandoned as irrelevant traditional religious practices, precepts, perspectives, and institutions.

Taken together, nazism's three ways to power constituted a revolution in international life, one whose effects linger today to infect and corrode the domestic political life of many countries even as they continue to poison the course of world affairs. But that is not all. For the impact of Adolf Hitler has extended deep into the private lives of Western men. Willingly or not, knowingly or not, thousands, perhaps millions, have over the past forty years internalized much of the Nazi vision. An intensified contempt for difference and callousness toward others, the enjoyment of random violence or at least acquiescence in its prevalence, the steadily increasing coarseness of rhetoric and thought, the indulgence in cheap and brutal sensationalism in its many guises: all are legacies of the recent Nazi past.

Adolf Hitler was not truly a creator. But he was a sinisterly effective blender of existing trends and a summarizer of long-emerging traits.* A Mussolini might yearn to fashion such a mix as German national socialism under his own Fascist banner, but he largely failed. A Franco might succeed to a degree, but on a scale so comparatively slight as to warrant only passing attention from a later

---

* This latter fact will become apparent to anyone who carefully peruses A. J. P. Taylor's superb introduction to *The Struggle for Mastery in Europe, 1848-1918* (Oxford: Clarendon Press, 1954).

generation. A Stalin might employ the most egregious terror and violence against millions of *kulaks* and later against members of his own party on a grand scale. He might fancy himself, indeed establish himself, as the personification of a secular religious cult every bit as intense in its self-absorption and propaganda as national socialism. Yet there remained always a crucial difference between Stalin and Hitler and the respective movements they led.

Nazism was, as we shall see, a religion of the masses, for the masses, and, in some ways, by the masses. While it is true that the Nazis did set their party off in measurable ways from the people, they provided at least the mirage of a very real leveling in traditional German social relations, as David Schoenbaum has so convincingly demonstrated. Stalinist communism, on the other hand, was a secular religion of, by, and for a sharply defined sociopolitical elite.

These differences in style and personality explain the marked divergence between Stalinist and Hitlerian totalitarianism, which insured that the Russian masses were more insulated from the most debased and degrading aspects of Soviet policy than were their German counterparts under the Nazi regime. Whereas Hitler derived power from his steady development as a mass rabble-rouser and Jew baiter, speaking to and for mass anxieties and hatreds, Stalin came to power, as Bertram D. Wolfe has so forcefully emphasized, through control of the administrative apparatus of the revolutionary movement.[2] Stalin became the *apparatchik* par excellence, the indispensable aide and subordinate to the charismatic revolutionary leadership. It was his very control of the bureaucracy and its files which permitted him unparalleled knowledge of where the skeletons and power and opportunities lay. This knowledge and control permitted him to supplant and then destroy Lenin's more natural emotional, spiritual, and ideological heir, Leon Trotsky. But it was also Stalin's very cold-bloodedness, his dispassionate bureaucratic style of doing things, which kept the mass of his people from being fatally infected with the viruses of hate and blood lust. For when Stalin obliterated the *kulaks* and subsequently waged the Great Terror, he did so with comparative dispassion and lack of emotion; he did not invite the Russian citizenry to partake vicariously of the pornography of violence practiced by the state. Or, to put the matter another way, Stalin *liquidated* his enemies as enemies, granting them and their death a certain, if dubious, measure of dignity. Hitler *exterminated* his enemies as *Untermenschen* deserving no dignity whatsoever. Thus, while both men indisputably became monsters, the one, wittingly or not, shielded his millions of surviving citizens in some measure from the worst of his excesses while the other enthusiastically invited and encouraged his people to indulge their most debased instincts.

Not until June 1941, under Hitler's own provocation, was the Stalinist system forced to change direction and emphasis. The theme of "socialism" was deliberately muted under the impact of the Nazi invasion; the theme of "Mother Russia" battling for her life was emphasized along with stress upon the collective interplay of each and every Russian with his or her government and leadership. And it seems that despite renewal of the purges following the war, this spirit never quite died, providing Stalin and his successors with an inestimably important reservoir of popular support, no matter how grudging, throughout the cold war era.

Thus Hitler proved the master architect of an epoch whose finish is not yet certain. While the tragic effects upon human life of communism and nazism have been comparable, the impact of nazism upon the baser emotions, suggestibilities, and instincts of the human race as a whole has been more profound. Communism, even under Stalin, pleaded some kind of recognizable idealism, however hideously perverted. Hitler transformed man's primal fantasies and lusts into high policy.

Nazism could only flourish in a world of mass alienation and spiritual desolation. Early-twentieth-century Western man found himself deprived of those pastoral roots which Jeffersonianism held most dear. He had become increasingly estranged from his impersonal, often exploitative, capitalist-industrial environment. He had been stripped of his religious convictions and aspirations regarding both this world and the next. By the mid-1930s democracy had been debased in France, its tentative forms obliterated in Japan. It clung exhaustedly to the bodies politic of Britain and the United States where many decent, concerned individuals were certain its days were numbered. Communism appeared stillborn, pent-up, and tearing itself apart within the vast Russian land mass.

If capitalism seemed exhausted, Jeffersonianism irrelevant, and Marxism doomed, the formerly vibrant faith of Western man in Jesus Christ and the elaborate litanies and institutions built around his name had vanished from most lives of consequence. An awesome spiritual void, stimulated only in part by the Great Depression, existed at the center of the Western mansion of civilization. Hemingway summed it up in a phrase: for those of his Lost Generation, good manners had become the substitute for God.* So, of course, had heavy drinking, that real or fancied agent of decent behavior, that barometer of the greatest anguish.

Chaos seemed everywhere, and men and women searched frantically for social myths by which to live. Murray Kempton has reminded us of the stubborn leftist faith of that time.

No man was an island. He could not escape history. If Madrid fell, he fell with it. In his own time, he would know the night of defeat or the morning of final victory. The instruments of his salvation were his to command.

The language of the myth was abstract and collective. Its key words were symbols like "labor," "people," "youth," and "history." It was a language of exhortation, and it was graceless by choice, written on a drumhead, to be read to an impatient army. Those who wrote it assumed that, in years to come, their words would be read by people who would judge them only as the words of the winning side or the losing one. They would be tested by victory or defeat, and not by the judgment of

* The extent to which Christian comfort degenerated to bitter bravado in a still-later generation is reflected in the most celebrated doggerel to emerge from the Indochina war:

Yea, though I walk through the shadow of the valley of death, I shall fear no evil;
For I am the meanest son-of-a-bitch in the valley.

neutrals. The heart of the myth of the thirties was that there were no neutrals.[3]

Kempton, of course, was writing here of the anti-Hitler myth which sent many decent and committed youths to Spain and sent the most foolish or lost souls of that era into the Communist party. This was also the myth which sent a much larger number of people in America into the ranks of Franklin Roosevelt's New Deal, from which they would emerge after 1945 as leaders of that Democratic party that would self-consciously compete with the Communist party of Russia for the minds and hearts of an entire world.

But one can also glimpse in the quietly—or not so quietly—hysterical atmosphere of crisis which Kempton has recalled an opportunity for the contrary preachings and promises of Adolf Hitler. There was not one social myth in the thirties but several, and they all emanated from and centered about a common thirst for new sources of meaning and salvation. If Stalin and Roosevelt and the apparently waning systems they championed still seemed to provide one such source, Hitler provided another. If the Soviet and American leaders (or, more strikingly, someone like Spain's La Pasionaria) symbolized salvation through commitment, Hitler promised salvation by blind immersion: the individual would bestow upon the totalitarian warfare state all his cares, freedoms, hopes, and anxieties, and the state would become the guarantor of his destiny.

Nazism was able to capture the devotion, blind or otherwise, of millions in Germany—and later throughout Europe—because it projected an image of absolute power and omnicompetence. As William Sheridan Allen has written, the Nazi seizure of power across Germany in the spring of 1933 was accompanied by "constant parades and meetings which gave the impression of irresistible enthusiasm and approval. There was the vigor in the economic area which more than anything else seemed to justify the dictatorship."[4] As it was the middle classes of Europe who experienced the greatest trauma, though not, apparently, the greatest hardship, from the depression, so it was the middle class, first in Germany, then elsewhere in Europe, who proved most receptive to nazism.

Yet nazism's appeal cannot be defined within traditional terms of reference. Nazism was a religion* which blended almost satanic charisma with a demonology not of economics, nor even of politics, but of pure and simple pornography.

Nazism was an evangelism of hate. It did not comprise, nor did it ever attempt to project, a coherent body of interlocking perspectives, ideas, or programs beyond those grounded in simple malevolence, revenge, aggression, and extermination. For Hitler, his compatriots, and his countrymen the triumph of the will proved to be the triumph of the will to injure. Nazism was emotional, not ideological. Above all, nazism was nihilistic. Therein lay its deepest

* That Hitler himself, in his more impassioned moments, believed in the essential religiosity of his person and of the Nazi movement is evident from a recollection that stole upon Albert Speer during his days in Nuremberg prison. During the summer of 1936 Speer and Hitler had traveled about Germany and had stopped to picnic by the roadside, where the führer began expounding upon the organizational genius of the Catholic church, which had, among other achievements, permitted peasant boys to become popes from the start. "Believe me, there's a reason the Church has been able to survive for two thousand years. We must learn from its methods, its internal freedom, its knowledge of psychology." Hitler then seemed to denigrate the religious possibilities of nazism: "Rosenberg's fantasies about an Aryan church are ridiculous. Trying to set up the party as a new religion! A Gauleiter is no substitute for a bishop; a local group leader can never serve as a parish priest. The populace would never respond to that sort of thing. If our leadership tried to go in for liturgy and outdo the Catholic Church, it would be completely out of its depth. It lacks the stature. . . ." But then, as the führer continued to contemplate the stubborn power of Catholicism among at least a portion of the masses, his demeanor grew excited and grandiloquent: "The Church will come round. . . . All we have to do is apply pressure to them. And our great Movement buildings in Berlin and Nuremberg will make the cathedrals look ridiculously small. Just imagine some little peasant coming into our great dome hall in Berlin. That will do more than take his breath away. *From then on the man will know where he belongs.* . . . I tell you, Speer, these buildings are more important than anything else. You must do everything you can to complete them in my lifetime. Only if I have spoken in them and governed from them will they have the consecration they are going to need for my successors." Albert Speer, *Spandau: The Secret Diaries* (New York: Macmillan Publishing Co., 1976), pp. 15-16, italics added.

appeal. For those many who had suffered some form of spiritual or ideological death, nazism promised the basest rebirth through incessant, mind-numbing immersion in the often grotesque rituals, pageantries, and fantasies of the folk state.

Nazism was a fervent crusade against that comfortable, bourgeois, quasi-democratic, capitalist world of the nineteenth-century West whose defenders and critics alike—Karl Marx included—placed materialism and material acquisition at the very center of human nature and human striving. Nazism preached not comfort but personal and collective sacrifice, not competition but outright aggression, not revolution against a constrictive order but the establishment of a new all-inclusive order based upon the worship of force as preeminently exemplified by military, not economic, power.

A successful crusade flourishes best when it develops charismatic figures and carefully programed pageantry binding followers and leaders in pack solidarity. Demonology is also essential so that the energies of the movement can be controlled and attuned in such a way as to reinforce further the sense of mass participation and belonging. In terms of charisma and pageantry, the Nazi leadership exhibited a truly evil genius. There was Hitler himself, by all accounts a true Jekyll and Hyde: one moment quiet, unassuming, almost self-effacing, absurdly gallant and deferential toward the ladies, an initially indifferent and fumbling speaker exploring the sense and feelings of the crowd; then, abruptly, the charismatic führer, the self-confident leader of the German people, speaking to them, summoning up all their hatreds, their basest lusts, burning away their anxieties with the rhetoric of grievance and revenge or, in another context, speaking for his *Volk* to other world leaders, voicing their many demands, which were, of course, his demands, in ruthless, nonnegotiable tones. There were the slogans of mass solidarity, the demonically colorful and attractive flags draped in serried rows down wide boulevards or almost touching above the crowded streets of ancient Rhenish and Prussian towns. There were the martial songs, hymns of praise to smash-and-grab power, accompanied always by drums so barbaric that no one who ever heard them could ever forget. There were the organizations, always and everywhere the organizations, culminating (after 1938 at least) either in the Wehrmacht or the SS with their brilliant uniforms, as terrifyingly colorful as the flags. There were the sports and speeches before hundreds of thousands massed in great stadiums or on vast fields. There was always excitement and movement and change and drama and, for those many who lusted after it, a sense of belonging, of kinship. All carefully staged, all carefully orchestrated. A significant portion of the world went a little mad in the thirties and subsequently infected a good bit of the rest with its insanity. Nazism eventually succeeded as a religion of barbarism precisely because there no longer existed any countervailing form to impart a sense of purpose and identity to the life of millions. The evidence is abundant that what resistance to nazism there was, both in Germany and, during the war, throughout occupied Europe, came from those whose secular or spiritual religious values had not been eroded by the many pressures of contemporary life. That there were, comparatively speaking, few such persons speaks volumes about the modern condition and temperament.

But it was in the realm of demonology that nazism reached its highest refinement of savagery. Nazi demonology was grounded in the notion of the folk state. In place of the Christian *aspiration* to salvation and a life of eternal bliss in some otherworldly heaven, in place of the Marxist *promise* of salvation through proletarian revolution and the subsequent withering away of the state, nazism *provided* salvation through the very exaltation of the state and the immersion—forced or otherwise—of each individual in a dual but interlocked pack, the folk and the state. The exaltation of the state became the expression of the collective will and, yes, the saintliness of the folk. The sanctified group, the folk state, by its very definition could do no wrong. But it achieved an even stronger sense of self-identity and self-righteousness because, it was steadily preached, it had *been* wronged. Versailles and the dreadful treaty that it had produced stood as a symbol of national shame imposed on Germany by the rest of bourgeois Europe, and this shame had to be obliterated at all costs.

If, as the Nazis preached, the German folk state was the highest expression to date of the human will, then the preeminence of the German folk state was a moral imperative and the inferiority of all other peoples an obvious corollary. It is well to remember that while the Jew swiftly became the chief target and victim of Nazi malevolence, he was far from the only one. Nazi racial policy and propaganda postulated a world divided between the "Aryan" and a mass of *Untermenschen* that included not only Semites but Magyars, Great Russians, Slavs, Poles, and others. While the Jew was often depicted as the great businessman, the banker, the money lender—in short, the usurious class enemy of solid, middle-class Germany—he was not inevitably so portrayed. Far from it. The Jew and masses of other *Untermenschen* were most frequently and fervently displayed in terms of simple revulsion, of boundless contempt. Time and again, day after day, week after week, year after year, Nazi propaganda invited the peoples of Germany, and later of France, Holland, and elsewhere in Europe, to indulge in their sickest fantasies concerning human difference and depravity. One has only to view some of the films Dr. Goebbels's office turned out on racial purity and impurity to understand this fact: that Nazi demonology was grounded in no economic considerations; it did not truly attract support by reference to any socioeconomic or sociopolitical group. It was, to put the matter simply, a constant incantation of and incitation to the pornography of violence. Here, too, nazism bequeathed much of itself to a later time.

Nazi fantasies about the racial impurities of *Untermenschen*, about an international Jewish conspiracy, and about Jewry and all *Untermenschen* in general must be experienced in some way or other to be believed, as must the corollary, the Nazi mania for racial purity and the completely Aryan physical and mental specimen. Yet while these phantasmagoric obsessions reflected and greatly amplified a prevailing malaise in Western society, they did not create it. In their private lives and public policies, the peoples and governments of the interwar West continued to condone racist practices that had been in existence for decades if not centuries. America's black population continued to languish in that semibondage that had been its lot for seventy years. Millions in Asia and Africa continued to bow down (often literally) before the frequently harsh and corrupt domination of their lands by the representatives of Europe. As for anti-Semitism itself, so respectable had it become in certain quarters by Hitler's time that even now many writers and scholars, gentile and Jewish alike, continue to ponder the haunting question as to whether the expressed inability of Europe and

America to save international Jewry during the Second World War did not mask an unwillingness to do so.

To complete the picture of nazism's pertinence as a powerful, if not universal expression of our time, it is well to recall how popular the "New Germany" was in some prominent circles in the West prior to the holocaust of 1939-45. The New Germany seemed to some the blueprint for tomorrow, a virulent champion of the old, manly virtues of hardiness and sacrifice that bourgeois Europe had softened to the point of disaster. In purely economic terms the Nazi masters had through draconian measures turned a depressed economy and society around, had restored industrial and financial health along with racial and national pride. Labor unions, those banes of the conservative interest, had in the process been broken. Moreover, Hitler had created in the very center of Europe an ideological as well as military and economic buffer to bolshevism. To those chronically stupid—and chronically present—champions of the capitalistic order who would destroy it through adherence to its worst practices and subscription to its most inhumane precepts, Hitler seemed a godsend. As a consequence, he was often flattered as a demigod. The full dimensions of nazism's attractiveness would not become clear until war brought the Wehrmacht flooding across most of Europe, but it is a matter of public record that even a few later opponents of the Hitler gang, including Winston Churchill, expressed some guarded appreciation of fascism, if not the Nazi movement itself, during its earliest days.

As for those British and Continental statesmen charged perforce with doing business with Hitler, one senses, after reading the pertinent histories, biographies, and memoirs of the period, a rising tide of disbelief in the reality of nazism, a disbelief grounded not in folly, as conventional wisdom would all too often have it, but in basic human decency. For a long time, for a fatally long time, Chamberlain, Daladier, Schuschnigg, and the others simply could not imagine that anyone who had experienced the agony and trauma of the 1914-18 trenches could ever seriously contemplate, much less instigate, another such slaughter.

In this context Munich may be seen as an indispensable lesson in the education of liberal opinion. Only when Hitler broke the last compromise democratic statesmen could or would make with him was armed opposition to Nazi aggression at last assured. But Munich proved a lesson too well learned. For the next third of a century it would be ceaselessly invoked in the name and for the cause of the warfare state and the high cold war diplomacy of the West. Thus has nazism shaped our age, often in contrary ways and from various sources. Adolf Hitler was the harbinger, if not creator, of a ferocious life-style which Western civilization had supposedly abandoned centuries before at the close of the religious wars following the schism in Christendom. Aided by the products of the industrial world and its laboratories, Hitler and those who supported, opposed, and succeeded him upon the stage of international politics transformed industrial man into martial man, for whom a life of armed belligerency became an end in itself. The repression and chicanery all too often incidental to the capitalistic system of production and distribution became, in greater or lesser measure, a matter of routine policy in the mid- and late-twentieth-century warfare states. Of equal, perhaps transcendant, importance was the Nazi preoccupation with race which, communicating itself viruslike to vast areas of the earth, intensified and amplified, where it did not resurrect, similarly sick and ancient obsessions in the minds of millions, thus subordinating issues of economic justice to those of human difference.

It has been a long time since 1945. But the geopolitical configuration of our present world was clearly in outline as the Second World War drew to a close. More profoundly, our cast of mind, our habits of thought, our instinctive perspectives, were formed then and remain, a third of a century later, much as they were. A large portion of the world's population continues to dwell in warfare states whose contours are shaped by a weapons culture; terror has become, if not a way of life, at least an expected ingredient of life, private as well as public. Many of us continue to define ourselves by our own grievances. Vengeance will be ours.

There is no longer a comfortable place for us to run. No philosophy, no set of social or political or economic precepts can save us from realization of the brute fact about ourselves. We either are, or have become, predatory animals at worst and higher animals at best, capable of some idealism and limited temperamental improvement. Or we are capable (and this applies to most of us as it did to the German people of 1933-45) of permitting bestial things to be done in our name and ostensibly for our sake rather than run the risk of ostracism from our society, our jobs, our clubs, our friends, our comfortable packs. What was shown to be true of the rest of the world in the 1930s and 1940s was pitilessly exposed to the American people in the 1960s and early 1970s. Long perceived as mankind's final hope, the United States had suffered a terrible fall from grace by 1974, condemned of the mass slaughter of Asia's poor, its constitutional system gravely threatened from within, its generations holding to an uneasy truce after half a decade of bitter conflict. There were no heroes. Those who had condemned the endemic violence, injustice, and brutality in national life frequently did so with equal violence, injustice, and brutality coupled with a striking lack of sophistication. Most distressing of all, though inevitable given the contemporary cast of thought, was the persistence of the we-versus-they syndrome expressed in the notion that if only "the system" could be undone, "the power elite" overthrown, this morally superior group or that ensconced in power or given what it demanded, then the millennium would be at hand. There was little or no thought given to the possibility that the fault lay not so much in those organizational stars which guide our lives and development, but in ourselves—in all of us.

In a figurative sense the American people remained in the year of their bicentennial emotionally and imaginatively amid the ruins of war which the holocaust of 1939-45 introduced into their lives. In the wake of Vietnam and Watergate and all the rest, the most sensitive and aware among them resembled the poor wretches stumbling about the rubble of Berlin during that long ago spring and summer of 1945, sensing a sudden hush, waiting with trepidation for the future, unsure of what would happen next, yet, above all, immensely grateful just to have survived. How this all came about is the subject of the following exploratory essays.

War as Holocaust

1

MEN HAVE always fought and killed one another for a variety of reasons and in a variety of ways. But the term "total war" has a peculiarly twentieth-century application. Never before have humans blended passion and technology so perfectly as to slaughter millions of their fellows and lay waste to such broad areas of their planet.

It is true that the religious wars of sixteenth- and early seventeenth-century Europe were waged with the greatest fury of which the combatants were capable, while warfare in Asia has frequently become an indulgence in pure barbarism. But until the middle decades of the twentieth century, warriors lacked the technology necessary to obliterate not only their fellow warriors, but the societies they represented as well. Moreover, warfare in the ancient and medieval worlds and again in the late seventeenth and eighteenth centuries, while almost a part of the daily fabric of life, was waged for limited, dynastic, or local ends by small, professional, expensive armies whose strategy was as much positional as it was violent. Napoleon with his *levée en masse* and the Union generals of the American Civil War, most notably Ulysses S. Grant and William Tecumseh Sherman in his famous march through Georgia, foreshadowed the age of mass warfare pursued in whole or in part for ideological ends, and the Civil War did indeed introduce the first few, crude products of a rapidly developing industrial society. But not until the Second World War did these factors come together in an exquisite and harrowing blend.

But what of the First World War? Did it not contain all of the elements of emotion, technology, mass participation, and unlimited prosecution necessary to earn the title of "total war"? Not completely. The Great War was, after all, limited to a very narrow geographic area. Except for a few skirmishes in colonial Africa and the Middle East, some intensive political and diplomatic warfare in Palestine and Araby, and some small naval engagements in the Pacific, the boundaries of violence between 1914 and 1918 were confined to the North Sea, northern Italy, Turkey (briefly), and, of course, Europe. Indeed, it can be safely argued that the First "World War" was simply a resumption, admittedly on a far grander scale than ever before, of the intermittent civil war amongst the peoples of Europe that had periodically convulsed the Continent since at least the fourteenth century.*

* Regrettably, Paul Fussell's remarkable study, *The Great War and Modern Memory,* appeared just as I finished this text, and it has proved impossible to incorporate his many fascinating insights satisfactorily. Suffice it to say that while I agree completely with Fussell's assertion that the Great War provided nearly all of the suitable literary images, devices, and assumptions for this century of almost incessant violence, the conflict of 1914-18 remained geographically and therefore psychologically and emotionally contained. Thus perspectives on violence remained limited. While participants of the Great War could later readily perceive a connecting link between 1914 and 1945, or even 1975, and posit the existence of a thirty- or sixty-year war, their perspective was the product of the physically limited combat environment of the western front and was therefore quite misleading as applied to *total* war. This can be seen by recalling one of the many Great War-spawned poems which Fussell himself quotes in another context, Siegfried Sassoon's "Suicide in Trenches":

> You smug-faced crowds with kindling eye
> Who cheer when soldier lads march by,
> Sneak home and pray you'll never know
> The hell where youth and laughter go.

This sharply perceived dichotomy between soldier and civilian, trench and hearth, war and peace, which was such an obvious fact of life in 1914-18, was completely obliterated between 1939 and 1945. Except in the Western Hemisphere, there were no smug-faced crowds during the Second World War: every city, every village, every street, every home, became a real or potential trench.

Nor was the First World War unlimited in the scope of its prosecution. True, the Allies threw a tight naval blockade around Germany, and Berlin at last retaliated with sporadic aerial bombardments and unlimited submarine warfare against the British Isles; these efforts did cause great suffering and hardship among the respective civilian populations, particularly in Germany. But whereas the technological means to wage total war against the enemy's civil population were now available, the will to employ them unconditionally was lacking. The machine gun was never systematically employed against civil populations in 1914-18 as it was, for example, at Babyi Yar a quarter century later. As for that most terrifying weapon of all, poison gas, the Germans could have easily used it against the civil population of Paris at the time when "Big Bertha," the massive artillery piece, was brought within shelling range of the French capital. Three times a week, month after month, Big Bertha sent a few shells into the city. Yet none contained the gas cannisters that surely would have transformed stoical endurance into pure panic. Only the British, at the very end, set afoot plans to launch a thousand-plane bomber attack against Berlin had the war continued into 1919. But it did not, and the airplane, that fearful engine of terror and death, remained a specter to be confronted rather than a tested weapon of war.

Finally, the First World War, for all its fury and for all the hatreds it undeniably generated, was not fought by modern totalitarian governments possessed of all of the modern technological means of mass coercion and propaganda. To be sure, Kaiser Bill and Czar Nicholas, to name the most obvious examples, were avowed absolutists, and the Germans enjoyed the services of a general staff which believed war and military victory to be the highest expressions of human endeavor. Moreover, the war of 1914-18 most certainly did possess strong ideological overtones; one side believed its legitimate aspirations, political and cultural, to have been repeatedly frustrated and mocked and so went to battle determined to obtain righteous vindication, while the other believed, or at least argued, that it was preserving and making the world safe for the expansion of liberal, parliamentary democracy against brutish militarism. Nonetheless, nazism's marriage of an ideology of barbarism to a philosophy of totalitarian government was largely absent from the struggle of 1914-18. War as holocaust came to mankind only in 1939. In the next six years 35 million souls disappeared.* Most of them experienced tribulations and doom so hideous and degrading as to place both their lives and deaths beyond either judgment or martyrdom. They perished miserably in the icy cellars of Stalingrad, on the gray beaches of Normandy, beneath the freezing waves of remote northern seas, in flaming aircraft taking long horrible moments to spin to extinction over Europe or Japan, in the steaming jungles and blasted coral of a dozen Pacific islands. They starved to death in Leningrad or walked to a terrible dreamlike extinction in the chambers and ovens of Dachau, Treblinka, Auschwitz, Mauthausen, and a dozen other extermination camps. They died in the rubble of their homes or in fiery streets in hundreds of towns and cities from Kharkov and Kiev to Warsaw and Dresden, Hamburg and London, Coventry and Tokyo, until at last the two mushroom clouds over Japan brought the bloodletting to a close.

It is well that later generations remember these things, for as the years pass this particular war takes on the romantic cast of all wars. The variety of battle, the heroic deeds, the sense of unity and comradeship among the combatants is told and retold. The terror and the filth, the degradation and the folly, tend to be obscured or to be read as interesting events which no longer have the power to touch our lives. Even this soon after the event, writers as diverse in their approach and perspective as S. L. A. Marshall and Gabriel Kolko all too often conveniently ignore the realities of war. In Marshall's world of combat men never die. They merely "disappear" or are suddenly "gone." In Kolko's world of politics and diplomacy the war never really occurs, but merely serves as a backdrop for the "real" struggle between predatory capitalism and social idealism. But if we do not fully and constantly comprehend what

* Total casualties for the First World War have been estimated at around 10 million, the overwhelming proportion of which fell on the combat troops themselves. The First World War may thus be likened to a kind of provincial tryout or preview in violence to the record-breaking "total war" of 1939-45.

was done, we cannot realize what was lost. And what was lost to the world between 1939 and 1945 in the way of talent and decency, compassion, competence, and simple amiability can never be measured.

The Second World War was a holocaust of unprecedented proportions because for the first time the products of the industrial revolution and the fruits of modern scientific research were applied to warfare on an unlimited scale. In particular, the application of the internal combustion engine to vehicles and aircraft dramatically expanded the dimensions of the battlefield. The tank, with its accompanying armored vehicles, and the heavy bomber, with or without its escort of fighter planes, extended the scope and scale of violence to such an extent that no one was safe from the ravages of war. Advances in other fields of weapons technology, such as microwave radar, long-range submarines and aircraft carriers, magnetic mines, and, at the end, nuclear bombs and rocket propulsion, added frightening dimensions to the force and application of violence. Soldiers and civilians alike were caught up in the swirl of combat; there were no rear areas, no safe havens. Masses of fleeing refugees, often bombed and strafed from the air and shelled from the ground, became as much a part of the landscape in those years as advancing or retreating armies. Millions survived only after losing all those possessions that had once given dignity and dimension to daily life. At the same time that the use of poison gas was tacitly banned from the battlefield by both sides as an unacceptably fearsome form of warfare, it was relentlessly applied by the Nazis to that portion of the European civil population which Hitler and his henchmen felt was either inherently unworthy of continued existence or sufficiently recalcitrant as to deserve pitiless ex inction.

Thus total war came to mean not only unlimited war between soldier and soldier, but also unlimited war between soldier and civilian. The munitions worker, the nurse, the fireman, the clerk, and eventually the enemy's civil population as a whole became as much a target of increasingly indiscriminate violence and death as the machine gunner and the infantryman. So too did the Jew and the Pole and the Slav. From the bombing of Rotterdam in the spring of 1940 to the fire raids against Tokyo and other Japanese cities in the summer of 1945, the cities of the earth—except those in the

Western Hemisphere—became battlegrounds and ultimately charnel houses, while thousands of debased and busy Germans worked
unceasingly to exterminate tens of millions of their fellow Europeans in sequestered death camps. By 1945 the prewar European
physical, social, and cultural landscape seemed nearly obliterated,
while across the breadth of Asia the winds of war had loosed a
great revolt of native peoples against their European masters that
was to prove irresistible. For six long years the men—and women
—of Europe and Asia had incessantly bombed, shot, burned,
gassed, and poisoned each other. When violence at last ceased,
terror, anguish, ruin, and despair remained.

An entire generation of the world's population had been nurtured
on death. Not the death of the genteel bedchamber with the grieving family and the hint of dignity, but the death found in burning
streets and shattered planes and aboard sinking ships, a death
suffused with terror and woe and, doubtless for many, a final relief.
Death, not life, became the norm; survival and a kind of animal
security became the goal of human existence.

The peoples of Europe and Asia responded in strikingly different
fashions to the catastrophe. The First World War had been almost
wholly a European conflict—the first real war in a century. The
violence of its prosecution had been unable to smother the passions
it had engendered; indeed, the violence coupled with a lack of total
victory or utter defeat had fed passion. And so as soon as the defeated—or the humiliated in the case of Italy—had been able to
find a leader who embodied and projected their sense of grievance,
conflict between the victors and vanquished of 1914-18 resumed,
first in the political and diplomatic spheres and all too soon on the
battlefield. Never was a war more impossible to prevent or easier
to predict once Hitler and Mussolini were given free reign after
1935-36. But the violence of 1939-45 was so stunning and widespread that the impulse to act upon national hatreds was completely
burned out of European hearts. Only the surviving Jews demanded
vengeance, but they and their fellow Zionists from Africa and
America were more than content to fight and win political self-
identity in the arid reaches of the Middle East far from the horrors
of the recent past.

The pall of universal destitution which hung over Europe in

1945 and for years thereafter was a sobering restraint on any would-be conqueror. Who wished to rule a desert? Americans far removed from the ruins of the Continent expressed frequent fears throughout the late forties and into the early fifties of a Soviet military thrust to the Channel, but we must presume that Stalin, with much of his own country a wasteland, was more astute than to try something that foolhardy. From 1945 to 1947 Europe lay benumbed in the filth generated by its own violence and lashed by natural disasters such as the Great Blizzard of 1946-47 until a few farsighted leaders, with the help of an untouched and affluent United States, began the tedious and lengthy task of reconstruction amid the rubble.

Simultaneously the Continent found itself at the center of a terrifying new cold war between the victors of the previous hot one. There can be no doubt that the cold war piled fresh anxieties and terrors on a people exhausted by violence and ruin. The thought that any future battle would swiftly culminate in nuclear extinction was an almost unbearable mental and emotional burden. But the European response to this fresh crisis was striking. Running like a brilliant thread through the often tangled weave of postwar European politics on both sides of the iron curtain was the unwillingness of Europe's peoples ever again to barter away their personal and collective destinies to their rulers so as to tempt those rulers to break an always tenuous peace. Although the populations both east and west of the Elbe more or less accepted the rule or leadership of their respective Soviet and American champions, Western Europeans were palpably unwilling to travel too far down the road of provocation and confrontation, while abundant evidence exists that the peoples of Eastern Europe accepted Soviet hegemony grudgingly and that from the late forties on the Kremlin could never count upon their loyalty or support. Stalin and Khrushchev and Brezhnev were frequently restrained—often sharply so—by the challenges of Tito and Gomulka and Dubcek, to say nothing of the workers of East Berlin in 1953 and the people of Budapest in 1956 and Prague in 1968. Thus sullen captives were added to ruined landscapes as factors restraining Soviet appetites during the early and high cold war years.

The people and governments of Britain, France, Italy, and the other countries of Western Europe were no less a restraining force upon American pretensions throughout the cold war era. It is true that the government of France dutifully purged itself of its Communist element in 1947—and suffered grievous, Communist-dominated, industrial strikes for its effort—and that the government of Italy was always receptive to anti-Communist blandishments and support from Washington during the first postwar decade. It is also true that the anti-Russian and anti-Communist sentiments of a significant portion of Western Europeans prior to about 1965 were not the result of docility alone, nor of a passive reliance upon American economic and military power, but stemmed from a sincere fear of Soviet dominance of the Continent and of the malignant influence of native Communist parties in two of the most potentially powerful nations south and west of the Rhine. The origins of NATO were to be found, after all, in the Brussels military and economic pact of early 1948 between Britain, France, and the Benelux countries, which represented an immediate and direct Western European reaction to the Communist coup in Czechoslovakia.

But American policymakers then and for a long time thereafter rather badly misread the motives behind these early European cold war initiatives. Western Europe would undertake a moderate defense of itself against a Communist crusade that would wash away a millennium of political and social culture; it would not arm itself so completely or bind itself so thoroughly to American policy as to tempt either Moscow or Washington into a conflict that would once more make the Continent a vast battlefield and charnel house. Above all, the peoples and governments of Western Europe were absolutely opposed to reviving the specter of German militarism as a counterweight to Soviet pretensions. And in this European disinclination to tease the gods of war and fate through further acts of bellicosity lay the great underlying tension between Washington and the other NATO countries throughout the fifties and well into the sixties.

The memoirs of a score of cold war bound American presidents and policymakers are filled with constant lamentations that Europe never really fulfilled American expectations of NATO military power or completely embraced American fears of Soviet expansionism. But what these men were unwilling or unable to grasp fully was the terrible fear of a revived Germany that filled the minds of an entire generation of Europeans. Beginning with Secretary of State James Byrnes's Stuttgart speech of September 1946, wherein the promise was held out to the West Germans of an early moral, material, and possibly military revival, through the debate nearly twenty years later on a multilateral force, the peoples and governments of Western Europe could never be certain whether Washington in its eagerness to prosecute the cold war successfully might seek to foist German militarism on the Continent. Was Germany reformed? Could she ever be trusted again? A generation that had endured the enthusiastic barbarities of the Nazis could be pardoned if profound skepticism of German intentions endured. A rearmed West Germany, falling prey to militarism and revanchism, upsetting the delicate balance of power on the Continent by seeking sovereign reunion with fellow Germans east of the Elbe, in time would surely usher in the final holocaust. It was a dreadful prospect, and in their determination to prevent German reunification and remilitarization, the peoples of Western Europe were at one with their Communist opponents on the far side of the iron curtain.

Yet American cold war policy seemed so persistently based on a strong, if not united, Germany that resistance to it, either passively or actively, was understandably deemed of prime importance in Western European chancelleries. So the French for years withstood American efforts to introduce German forces into NATO. Paris sought to evade the issue through the device of a "European Defense Community" that would place a supranational army, including some German troops, within the NATO structure. The initiative proved so cumbersome that the French themselves eventually disavowed it. But as a price for finally acceding to the German presence in NATO, the Quai d'Orsay was able to ensure, with British cooperation, that Germany would continue to be prohibited from producing the ultimate weapons of modern war—biological, chemical, or atomic. A decade later conspicuous German interest in a NATO multilateral nuclear force was probably of sufficient influence in and of itself to doom the American proposal in Western Europe.

But even if Germany had not existed to excite European fears of a future war, half a century of real or incipient armed conflict had been enough to create a profound revulsion against militarism that in turn set decided limits on American cold war strategy. Western Europe in 1945 longed not only for peace, but for prosperity and experimentation with new, if still very rough and tentative, programs of social and economic justice. Butter, not guns, fueled and defined the ambitions of many postwar European statesmen and their followers. Thus Europeans seized with far greater avidity upon the promise of the Marshall Plan than upon the necessity of NATO. And they created and shaped instruments of their own—the Organization for European Economic Cooperation (OEEC), the Council of Europe, and the Schuman Plan, to take but several examples among many—with which to exploit the opportunity for material and spiritual rejuvenation which the United States offered in 1947. As one American official later recalled, " 'The OEEC was an amazing institution. NATO has nothing like it. The understanding that was developed there, the real breaking down of national barriers, was unique.' "[1]

By 1960 Western Europe had achieved an astounding material and moral revival, one that would continue throughout the following decade until ultimately it forced a series of fundamental reconsiderations and reevaluations of the world's commercial and financial structure and of the formerly unquestioned dominance of the United States. At the same time the western tier of European nations had undoubtedly moved far to the left, both socially and politically, of where they had been in 1935, and a general optimism had begun to return to daily life. In Walter Laquer's words, "the people as a whole had regained confidence in a society which no longer seemed doomed."[2]

As spiritual and economic strength began to return, a mounting desire once again to act independently of the superpowers could be discerned among Western European governments and citizens. Thus it was that Truman and Acheson, Eisenhower, Dulles, and Kennedy, no less than their Soviet counterparts, found their dreams for a postwar world, molded firmly in their image, increasingly challenged and deflected by reviving ambitions of European statesmen. Adenauer, Macmillan, and, above all, de Gaulle have often proved as difficult for Washington to influence and direct as have Tito, Dubcek, or Ceausescu for the Kremlin. By 1965 at the very latest, Western Europe, now seemingly recovered completely from the holocaust, was demanding to go its own way, to reassess old assumptions, to reexamine old alliances, not in a spirit of armed bellicosity, not with the force of vast armies and air forces behind it, but in a spirit of peace and prideful affluence. Only intellectual life seemed to some observers to have "lost its fervor and distinction." Others, however, saw signs of a rejuvenated sense of social criticism among the young. Youthful critics condemned not only the militarism of the superpowers, but also the boredom and restrictions inherent in modern industrial affluence without, perhaps, fully realizing that wealth and tedium were perhaps exactly what their parents longed to embrace after the multitude of horrors and dislocations of their own youth.

Postwar Europe, then, both east and west of the Elbe, has acted as a critical brake and balance wheel on the pretensions, ambitions, and anxieties of the American and Soviet superpowers, who all too often engaged in cold war with more enthusiasm than either leaders or followers in the two countries possibly would now care to admit. Twice in less than half a century the Continent has been ravaged by mass social violence—the second immeasurably more severe and widespread than the first. Europe will have, if not peace, at least an absence of war and as much of a say in the shaping of global power politics as its various peoples and leaders can obtain. The very scope and scale of destitution during the earliest cold war years and the later yearnings of Europe's exhausted, yet restless population has done much to insure that the often hard and bitter postwar experience has not become prologue to the final solution of the human problem.

Across and below the Eurasian land mass, however, in the huts and villages, jungles and river valleys of Africa and the Far East, the Second World War stimulated rather than exhausted the forces of ambition and violence and hate that had driven twentieth-century man into periodic conflict with his brothers. If the war in Europe was prologue to reconstruction, in Asia it proved a prelude to revolution.

War as Revolution

2

LIKE MANY other emotion-laden terms, the word "revolution" has been debased in our time by repeated and often careless usage. But surely few would deny that the Second World War played midwife to an entire cluster of mass revolts and fundamental changes in the human condition.

International relations were certainly revolutionized by the abrupt, if possibly temporary, disappearance of the nations of Western and Central Europe from their centuries-old positions as the ultimate arbiters of world politics and the equally sudden ascendancy of the United States and the Soviet Union to global preeminence. International warfare was just as certainly revolutionized by the introduction or perfection of an entire arsenal of new weapons that threatened not only to bring human society to an end in any future conflict but also promised to take such a conflict literally out of human hands after the initial push of a button or use of a telephone. Nor was Western society completely immune to the winds of social revolution during the war years. While the studies by Grunberger, Pollenberg, Calder, and even Alexander Werth prove that the necessarily widespread use of woman power ushered in no revolutionary wave in sexual relations, but merely, in Calder's words, exaggerated peacetime trends,[1] and while the same general comment could be applied with equal force to the condition of American blacks, who can deny that the virtual extinction of European Jewry between 1939 and 1945 and the consequent emergence of the state of Israel (peopled largely by immigrants from North

Africa, North America, and especially other parts of the Middle East) has not had a profound impact upon the political, social, and economic life of the world?[2]

Striking as are these "revolutionary" developments—and countless others which the interested student of the war period can readily discern—it is not necessary to twist or dilute the classic definition of revolution in any way to find its seeds embedded in and nurtured by the Second World War. The war, it is true, did not create the great revolt of the non-Western peoples. That can be logically traced back at least four decades and possibly long before. For example, there is powerful evidence to suggest that the Tai Ping rebellion in China between 1851 and 1864 represented the first great revolt against the Western presence and Western influence in an Asian nation. Certainly the long "insurrection" by Philippine nationalists at the turn of the twentieth century was an open revolt against American efforts to continue Western rule over a native population. Francis C. Jones has argued that Japan's victory over Russia in 1904-1905 "greatly stimulated nationalist movements" across Asia.[3] And it is surely beyond argument that the First World War and Woodrow Wilson's lofty—and largely unfulfilled—promise of self-determination for all peoples, to say nothing of the mounting influence of Karl Marx, did much after 1918 to generate native aspirations and clandestine movements for self-rule in much of Asia, if not Africa. But the Second World War at last laid bare, as no other event or development ever had or could, the decline of the imperial West and the assurance of early emancipation for the colonial East and South.

The central fact of the Second World War for countless Asians and Africans was that the imperial powers, France, Britain, and the Netherlands, were partially defeated and some of their citizens incarcerated and shamed for long years by a victorious, colored, non-Western nation—Japan. Japan was not loved by the people of Asia for its achievements. Tokyo's own rule over former Western enclaves was sufficiently brutal and exploitative to assure hatred and contempt. But Japan's early victories revealed how feeble much of the imperial West had become after two years of war in Europe. To hear that France, Belgium, and the Netherlands had been overrun and Britain bombed was one thing to Asians who still saw their colonial masters enjoying imperial perquisites after 1939 in the restaurants and homes of Hong Kong, Singapore, Surabaya, and Saigon. But then to see those masters herded out into the hot Asian streets of 1942 and marched to captivity before Japanese bayonets was something else—and quite shattering. The myth of white rule and Western supremacy, carefully nurtured or carelessly assumed for decades and even centuries, was destroyed in a moment.

Many of the details of Japan's ephemeral rule over Southeast Asia remain obscure more than thirty years later. But enough is remembered or has been learned at least to sketch in the outlines. Tokyo was hobbled from the start by gross ignorance of the region as well as by the contempt which the dominant military and naval figures of the war years held for their civilian colleagues, whose task it was to administer and exploit the conquered regions to the south on a day-to-day basis. The entire thrust of Japanese diplomacy and military strategy in the more than five decades between the first Sino-Japanese conflict and the fall of France in 1940 had been oriented toward northeast Asia, toward Korea and Manchuria, China and Russia.

The tides of war in Europe (which enabled Japan to secure control of Indochina) and in Asia (in which the Japanese military was unable to secure the subjugation of China after five years) almost inevitably swept the Japanese southward and brought them after 1940 into increasing conflict with Britain and the United States. After the American imposition of the oil embargo in July of 1941, assault on Pearl Harbor and a quick, powerful thrust into the mineral-rich regions washed by the South China Sea seemed the only possible choices open to the Japanese government short of humiliating retreat. And so it came to rule a vast area about which it knew comparatively little and which was seething with barely suppressed nationalism. And it is to Japan's credit, however vicious many of her policies and actions were between 1942 and 1945, that she did not attempt to suppress native particularism in Southeast Asia but rather attempted to meet it at least halfway. This is not to say that Tokyo did not have exploitative ends in view. Had the Japanese managed to retain control of Indonesia, the Philippines, Indochina, and Burma, they surely would have demanded that the native governments established there conform to Tokyo's own vague designs for a Greater East Asia Co-Prosperity Sphere. Nonetheless, it is a matter of record that Japan did encourage indigenous nationalist movements in Southeast Asia in a number of ways; Tokyo did fuel, if not kindle, aspirations for freedom and sovereignty.

Japan's most notable gesture came in late November 1943, very possibly in response to the recent Cairo Declaration of the United States, United Kingdom, and China, in which the signatories vaguely committed themselves to work for self-determination for some, if by no means all, of Asia's peoples. A conference was arranged in Tokyo between Japan and four of her puppet or client governments: Burma, the Philippines, Thailand, and Manchukuo. Various anti-Chiang elements in China under Japanese control also attended, as did the Indian refugee leader, Chandra Bose. It was all for show, of course, not for serious bargaining over future relationships. Nonetheless, at the close a joint declaration was issued which pledged everyone concerned to work for Asian independence and to support one another in the common cause. If there was little of real substance that emerged from either the Allied Cairo Declaration or the Tokyo conference, Asia's revolutionaries could nonetheless presume that the interest—if not anxiety—of both sides to win them over reflected changing realities in world power.

For, of course, it was the very devastation of huge areas of Europe, Asia, and, ultimately, Japan itself, which gave such figures as Ho Chi Minh, Achmed Sukarno, Mao Tse-tung, and even Mahatma Gandhi their chance to wrest control of their people's destiny from the weakened grip of Western imperialism or, in the case of China, from a corrupt indigenous regime heavily reliant upon Western sponsorship. The shattered Englishmen, Frenchmen, and Dutch who straggled out of Japanese prison camps in 1945 were no match for the native revolutionaries who seized power with or without the permission of the expiring Japanese at war's end. Nor could European governments, faced with the bitter memories of war and near or total defeat, distracted by the terrible problems of physical and moral, economic and political reconstruction, spare the consistent concentration of power necessary to regain lost colonies. Britain gave way the earliest and with the greatest grace in the Indian subcontinent, although Whitehall continued to cling to Malaya long after it could decently afford to; Holland sought to stave off the inevitable for a time, but by 1950 the Dutch too had realized that their days of power in Java had gone forever; France clung the longest, first in Indochina to 1954, then in even more melancholy fashion in Algeria to 1958. In the process a republic was torn nearly to pieces, to be rescued, if not really saved, by a messianic strong man whose own acumen and stability were not above question.

The great revolt against colonialism by the peoples of Asia and later of Africa will doubtless be remembered as the greatest single event of the twentieth century. Yet until very recently the contours and meaning of the great revolt have been flagrantly misinterpreted and misunderstood in the West, because the cold war has obscured and distorted contemporary Asian, if not African, history. Because the Soviet Union did for a long time aid the Chinese Communists in their successful bid for rule over the most populous nation on earth, because a host of other Asian nationalists and revolutionaries embraced either Marxism or other forms of social and economic radicalism, it was almost inevitable that fearful governments and citizens in the West would argue, then simply assume, that the great revolt had been manipulated, if not created, by the Kremlin for its own nefarious ends. Such an attitude was most understandable in the exhausted and disheartened nations of early postwar Europe, where past imperial glories and prerogatives could be seen vanishing with each passing month and year. To explain the collapse of European rule in Asia as the work of an international Communist conspiracy directed by Josef Stalin and his henchmen was almost irresistible. Yet it is a fact of postwar life that Europeans by and large did reject such a facile thesis. Steeped in the realities of international power politics, sophisticated in outlook, adaptable to the changing tides of world relations, Europe's more perceptive citizens, scholars, and bureaucrats saw the great revolt for what it was and what it portended much earlier than did the Americans, who possessed greater power to advance or retard Asia's nationalistic movements.

It has been suggested that American policymakers came to oppose the more violent manifestations of the great revolt—in Korea in 1950-53 and in Vietnam between 1961 and 1975—because they wished to promote their own sophisticated program for global economic predominance. A far more plausible explanation, however, may be found in the credulous temperament and basically isolationist history and orientation of the American people.

Fashionable historiography of recent years has postulated the emergence of an imperial America at the close of the nineteenth century in response to a voracious capitalistic quest for markets and as a result of the Spanish-American War. Certainly an imperialistic mood seized certain American statesmen around this time, Henry Cabot Lodge and Theodore Roosevelt being the chief exemplars of military and economic expansion. Undoubtedly some business thought became fixed upon the rich prospects of the vast Asian market. Certain religious leaders and zealous proponents of the missionary ideal were irresistibly attracted to the possibility of converting hundreds of millions of "heathen" Chinese to Christ. But, save for the missionary impulse, the imperialistic mood was ephemeral at best.

Paul Varg has demonstrated how frustrating were the efforts of a few American businessmen to "open up" the interior of China to trade. Theodore Roosevelt realized no later than 1908 that America's comparatively modest imperial acquisitions in the far ·Pacific had created more problems than benefits; the Philippines, for example, had already become disturbingly attractive to Japanese expansionists. Subsequent efforts by Taft and Wilson to force the inclusion of American interests into the Western banking consortium in China represented a singular and halfhearted effort to practice the diplomacy of imperialism. John Hay's Open Door policy, if it was indeed instigated by him and not by the British, never became fully operative except in the minds of some historians who insist on forcing a conscious, governing philosophy upon all American policy and policymakers in the absence of hard evidence.

Above all, except for the Philippine Islands, which were promised independence as early as 1916, America built none of the institutions and traditions of European colonialism in Asia. True, small fleets and garrisons were kept in the Philippines and were stationed in and around the international business and residential compounds of China's coastal cities from the turn of the century to Pearl Harbor, but the United States did not build, train, or promote those permanent imperial bureaucracies which were the foundation of British and French rule in Asia. Despite Kipling's call to McKinley's America to take up the white man's burden, twentieth-century America did not send out its best youth to Asian outposts. There was nothing comparable to the Indian civil service or even the debased French foreign legion. Americans in China and elsewhere readily partook of the imperial privileges of the white man where they found them, but American rule over the Philippines, once the deeply racist war against the "insurrectionists" was concluded, was liberal and humane in comparison with French rule in Indochina or Dutch dominance and exploitation of the East Indies.

Given the somber history of American slavery, it would be foolish, indeed, to argue that such comparative imperial mildness and limitation sprang from a national moral superiority. The relative benevolence of American colonial rule seems to have been based rather on its very brevity. Unlike the Great Powers of Europe, the United States had no chronic need to rely upon the raw materials and assured market areas of a vast overseas empire. The enormous territory stretching westward from the Appalachian rim provided a metropolitan resource and market region of apparently inexhaustible extent. Once the costs and burdens of ruling colonial territories of significant extent—such as the Philippines—became obvious, a fundamentally isolationist-minded American government and people began to contemplate liquidation of responsibility.

To the extent that the comparative handful of Americans in Asia and those in Washington charged with Asian affairs were imperialist, they were naive, moral imperialists, committed not so much to economic exploitation as to political and spiritual uplift so that the corner of Asia under their ephemeral control could enjoy the blessings of free government and evangelical religion, American style. This mood was perfectly expressed in its most credulous and popular form by Senator Kenneth S. Wherry of Nebraska, who promised a wildly cheering audience in 1940 that "We shall lift Shanghai up, up, ever upward until it is just like Kansas City."

It was precisely this attitude, coupled with guilt at staying out of the Second World War in both Asia and Europe too long, that prompted American policymakers from Franklin Roosevelt on to embrace Chiang Kai-shek and his already exhausted and corrupt Kuomintang regime as the future democratic bastion of Asia. With

United States aid and tutelage, Chiang's China would become the postwar power in the Far East: a strong, united, and free nation, America's friend and right arm in the western Pacific. Stilwell's heartbreaking experience in China from 1942 to 1944 and the bitter recriminations that tore the United States apart when Chiang subsequently fell before the men of Yenan should have told the Americans how far their dreams had departed from reality.

But, of course, the Americans learned the wrong lesson from their Chinese experience of the 1940s. Credulous, moralistic, wildly overoptimistic, they swiftly became bitterly disillusioned when the horrors of war did not lead immediately to true peace. They searched for enemies without and scapegoats within, and Asia's revolutionaries were immediately labeled as mindless soldiers in the Soviet Union's cold war against capitalism, democracy, and decency. "Godless communism" had triumphed in Asia over the hopes and efforts of those who worked in Christ's vineyards. The great revolt was never understood, Asia's desperate need to rebel against the imperialism of the West was never admitted, and ultimately young Americans were sent into two Asian wars with the word that they were defending the far frontiers of freedom against the forces of darkness. The most morally questionable of Asia's leaders were embraced as unquestioned allies. Only frustration at last caused America to step back, to begin to assess the Asian experience for what it was rather than for what the Americans had thought it was.

It would be as wrong now to romanticize the leaders of Asia's great revolt as it was earlier to condemn them. Ho and Mao and Chou and Sukarno and the rest were bred in a bitter school, and they were far from gentle men. But they led the people of Asia— and by example the people of Africa as well—out of bondage. Their rule was real, the wellsprings of their power indisputable. Europeans began to realize this in the late 1940s and knew it as a fact by the close of the 1950s. America's people and leaders were much slower in grasping this most striking development of the Second World War era, and the price they eventually paid for their blindness was tragic indeed.

The Fateful Weekend: Pearl Harbor and Moscow

3

CONVENTIONAL WISDOM holds that the Second World War began in September of 1939 and that 1942, with its great battles at Midway, El Alamein, and Stalingrad, was the year that doomed the Axis. But conventional wisdom is often wrong, and it is wrong here. As a truly unified, global conflict, the Second World War did not begin until the first weekend of December 1941, and its very inception marked at once the apex of Axis triumph and the beginning of Axis downfall, a full six months before Midway, ten months before El Alamein, and a whole year before the Russian jaws snapped shut around Von Paulus and his Sixth Army at Stalingrad. When Japan chose to widen her Asian aggressions to embrace the entire western half of the Pacific basin at the very moment when Hitler's armies stalled at last in the bitter snows around Moscow, the fierce but localized conflicts in Europe and Asia at last coalesced into a genuine world war, and the Axis fate was immediately sealed.

Crippling strategic and conceptual failures lay behind the simultaneous Axis assaults upon Pearl Harbor and Moscow. Both attacks exposed the limited material and intellectual resources at the disposal of those who ordered them.

The mind of Adolf Hitler has properly intrigued an entire generation of the world's population. Had the man thought out a well-defined policy of internal power and external aggression by the time he wrote *Mein Kampf*? Can that immensely long, boring, rambling, but nonetheless revealing book be taken as an accurate guide to an entire life of mad genius and eventual failure? Or was Hitler merely an opportunist, a master of improvisation and swift exploitation? Did his weak-willed opponents in the West, Schuschnigg, Chamberlain, Daladier, and the rest, provide him by their cowardice with all his opportunities for expansion? Are they in the final analysis as guilty as he of precipitating mankind's greatest slaughter? Was Hitler, in A. J. P. Taylor's phrase, no more wicked than any of the other European statesmen of the 1930s, merely surpassing them in *acts* of wickedness?

Rival assessments of Hitler's character and purpose stem as much, if not more, from observations of the führer's behavior during the war as before it. They arise from a study of his actions during the summer and autumn of 1940, a period that must be considered his greatest moment of decision between the murder of Roehm in 1934 and his own death in the bunker eleven years later. Following his defeat of France, Hitler, like so many successful public men before and since in both democracies and dictatorships, was faced with what we might call a crisis of victory. The crisis of victory occurs when immediate goals have not only been obtained, but have been won so overwhelmingly as to generate problems of their own, while inducing a not unnatural tendency to try to maintain the momentum of achievement. To take but one example from a public life as remote from Adolf Hitler's as it could possibly be, Lyndon Johnson in 1964-66 was faced with his own crisis of victory. Not only had he won a massive mandate to pursue his vast program of liberal reform, but he had won so resoundingly as to dominate a political party which dominated American government and American life. Johnson apparently governed beyond dispute; his task was at once to master and exploit the expectations he had aroused without permitting those expectations to master and ultimately destroy him. A political finesse of the highest order was required, a finesse which it can surely be argued the man did not have. He promised more than he could deliver, and the frustrations he eventually created overwhelmed him and bore him down, leaving behind a sour atmosphere of disillusion and mistrust.

In the summer and autumn of 1940 Adolf Hitler faced a roughly analagous crisis of victory. His policies since 1933, whether based on design or momentary opportunity, had brought him and his embittered and humiliated people unprecedented triumph at little or no cost. The man, his party, and his nation controlled Europe as no tyrant had since Napoleon. In the West, Italy was an ally, Spain looked to Berlin with favor, France was shattered and beaten, two-thirds occupied by German soldiers, the southern third dominated by a regime of willing collaborators. Sweden was neutral; Norway and Denmark were firmly under the Nazi heel. To the East, the Nazi-Soviet pact had led to the partition of Poland; Austria and Czechoslovakia had long since succumbed. Only Britain remained a lonely outpost of defiance, her white cliffs and green fields beckoning tantalizingly across the narrow, blue waters of the Channel during the most glorious summer and fall weather in a quarter century.

Surely now was the time for the Nazi juggernaut to pause, to consolidate its achievements, before seeking new triumphs. Yet Hitler did not pause for any measurable length of time. As early as May 17, 1940, only seven days after commencement of the great assault against Belgium and France in the West, the führer began to speak with some seriousness about a greater thrust eastward; six months later "Barbarossa," the projected invasion of Russia, was far advanced on staff planning tables.

Why? What on earth induced Hitler at the moment of supreme triumph to risk all he and his people had won on an immense gamble in the East? Was it the irresistible dictate of an insane expansionist scheme set forth in *Mein Kampf* and followed with single-minded fidelity from that time forth? Or was it simple opportunism? Or was it a combination of both, or something else entirely which set Hitler on his fatal course? The available record points strongly to a complex mix of design, opportunism, and simple euphoria.

There were, in fact, many compelling reasons—some of them based on incredibly faulty intelligence and reasoning, to be sure—for Hitler to maintain his momentum of aggression in late 1940, to turn his attention eastward. In the first place, Hitler had obliterated only one great power—France—in his astounding thrust to the West. Britain had been thrown off the Continent, but the English remained defiant within their island bastion and well able to sum-

mon the reserves available in their global empire. A year of subsequent German blandishment and bombardment did not break
either the British will to resist or the British power to do so, as the
attack on Dakar and the exploits of the Eighth Army in the western
North African desert (even the disastrous expedition to Greece and
the fall of Crete) amply demonstrated. Moreover, the Soviet historian A. M. Nekrich has recently argued that "the thing that wor-
ried the German fascist leadership most of all was the possibility
of an agreement between England and the Soviet Union."

Such concern was not unwarranted. Although at first glance the
notion of an alliance between bolshevism and Churchillian con-
servatism seemed wildly absurd, particularly in light of the Nazi-
Soviet pact, Churchill in his desperation was not averse to consideration of such a move. We now know from his own pen that the
prime minister repeatedly sought to warn Stalin of developing
German designs on the East, and, of course, once Hitler turned on
Stalin, an Anglo-Soviet alliance swiftly came into being. All this
might appear in hindsight as a self-fulfilling prophecy; had Hitler
not turned on Stalin, Stalin might very well have remained true to
the Nazi-Soviet pact. Nonetheless, Hitler and his generals were
right in not depending upon Stalin's loyalty; disloyal opportunists
themselves, they could recognize a fellow adventurer. And, of
course, Stalin himself gave them ample cause for concern.

It is often conveniently forgotten how unreliable Stalin was as
an ally during the nearly two years in which the Nazi-Soviet pact
remained operative. Those who argue Stalin's fidelity point to his
shock—apparently amounting to near physical prostration for a
time—upon hearing in June of 1941 that German forces had
abruptly appeared on his soil. And the Russians did faithfully live
up to the terms of their trade agreements with Berlin. Paul Carell
has told us of German soldiers crouching in Polish fields just before
dawn on June 22, 1941, waiting the signal to attack while watching
the last supply train from the Soviet zone cross into Nazi territory
laden with goods.

Yet Stalin had proved a disturbingly aggressive partner. Following the fall of France, Russia had annexed the three Baltic states,
and soon thereafter Stalin took Bessarabia and northern Bukovina

from Rumania. In reaction, Hitler carved up the rest of Rumania and forced it into the Tripartite Pact along with Bulgaria and Yugoslavia. When the Yugoslav government subsequently repudiated its forced alliance with the Reich, Stalin announced a formal declaration of friendship with Belgrade, which did not, however, include a Soviet commitment to rush to Yugoslav aid in case of a German attack.

In November 1940 Molotov made a tense visit to Berlin during which he made it clear that Stalin's price for further aid to Germany in her continued war against England would be high indeed, including outright Soviet control of Bulgaria and exclusive Soviet interest in Finland. And Molotov was characteristically blunt. He was told by his Nazi hosts at one point that England was all but finished; soon afterward the RAF was over Berlin in one of its brave but essentially futile early wartime raids. Molotov could not keep his mouth shut, needling his German allies with the remark that if England was really finished, he would like to know what they were all doing in a bomb shelter. This attitude of greed mixed with amused condescension was not likely to lull German sensibilities, and in fact it sharpened Nazi appetites and anxieties. According to Guderian, Hitler was "incensed" by the Kremlin's demands. It can be argued that Stalin was merely instigating a line of policy which he would pursue with ruthless single-mindedness throughout the Second World War and well into the postwar period, namely, the creation of buffer states on his western borders. This is no doubt true, but it is also no doubt true that what the marshal in Moscow interpreted as a legitimate quest for security, the führer in Berlin saw as a series of aggressive acts that had to be cut short.

So for all his breathtaking triumphs, Hitler was not yet master of Europe in the heady days of 1940-41. Indeed, he was not even master of his own house. His ally Mussolini, for whom he seems to have entertained a real appreciation, was proving a troublesome partner. In October of 1940, while on his way to Florence to confer with Il Duce regarding the further conduct of the war, Hitler learned to his surprise and dismay that his Italian ally had declared a private war on Greece. This was unwelcome news, indeed, for Hitler realized that he would soon have to go to his inept colleague's aid, thus expanding the war to the Balkans, further exacerbating Soviet suspicions, and giving the tenacious British yet another opportunity to bring German forces to battle.

But that was not all. "The first result of Mussolini's arbitrary gesture," Guderian has written, "according to what Hitler told me —was that Franco immediately withdrew from any sort of collaboration with the Axis powers. He plainly had no intention of becoming involved in a common policy with such unpredictable partners." In the event, "Italy's unco-ordinated action and mistakes in the Balkans resulted in strong German forces being committed in Africa and Bulgaria, and subsequently in Greece and Serbia. This led to a weakening of our strength in the decisive theatres of the war."[1]

One of these decisive theaters of the war would have to be Russia. For if Hitler could not impose his will and power across the entire Continent—from the Channel to the Volga and possibly the Urals— then he could not be certain of restraining his friends or rationalizing his existing conquests. As an instinctive expansionist he had come a long way—but not yet long enough.

Such were the negative forces propelling Hitler toward war in the East during 1940 and early 1941. There were, of course, powerful positive forces at work also. The Soviet Union in 1940-41 appeared at once potentially rich and practically weak. The Ukraine with its acres upon acres of waving wheat and several major industrial centers beckoned like a temptress. So, too, did the oil fields of Ploesti and, beyond them, Baku. For years Hitler had spoken and written of the vast, inviting East as a playfield for the new super Aryan race and a source of labor for the factories and fields of the Reich. Now, with his west wall against Britain apparently secure enough, it was time to fulfill the promise. Moreover, should the Royal Navy succeed in imposing a firm blockade around the western approaches to the Continent as it had done in the First War, the total resources of the Ukraine and the eastern oil fields would become vital to the future well-being of the German state and its war machine. Certainly the spectacular successes of the U-boat war in the Atlantic made effective imposition and maintenance of such a blockade highly problematical. But in a war whose fortunes were increasingly determined in the laboratory as on the battlefields, who could say how long Doenitz's submarines could sustain the initiative? And Russia seemed ripe for the plucking. Stalin's terrible purges of the thirties, which had shaken the Soviet state to its roots, had not spared the Red Army. Indeed, the two master architects of this potentially formidable force—Trotsky and Tukhachevsky—had both been dispatched by Stalin along with nearly all of the senior officer corps. Morale within the ranks, riddled with watchful party political officers, must have been at rock bottom. Moreover, it was assumed in Berlin and elsewhere that while the Red Army and Air Force were the largest in the world, their equipment was either inadequate or outdated. Certainly the Red Army's dismal efforts against tiny Finland in the "winter war" of 1939-40 seemed to bear out all the contemptuous assessments of Russian military efficiency. Guderian and some others within the Wehrmacht thought they knew better—and events proved that they did—but Hitler and his senior staff officers were convinced that Soviet forces could be brushed aside by the superbly trained and enthusiastic men of Germany, who would then sweep nearly unopposed to Moscow and, if necessary, beyond. "You have only to kick in the door," Hitler told von Rundstedt, "and the whole rotten structure will come crashing down."[2]

Three months after launching Barbarossa, during one of his "secret conversations," Hitler told a circle of colleagues: "The spirit of decision does not mean acting at all costs. The spirit of decision consists simply in not hesitating when an inner conviction commands you to act." Then the führer proceeded to check off, in characteristically rambling fashion, some of the considerations involved in moving east: "I had to foresee that Stalin might pass over to the attack in the course of 1941. . . . The struggle for the hegemony of the world will be decided in favor of Europe by the possession of the Russian space. Thus Europe will be an impregnable fortress, safe from all threats of blockade. . . ."[3]

Barbarossa proved a fallacious decision born as much of blind optimism as of rational calculation. William J. Newman and others have noted how dreadfully narrow was the margin of German military supremacy in 1939-41.[4] So spectacular was blitzkrieg in the West in 1940 that contemporaries assumed a material and numerical superiority on the part of the Wehrmacht that it simply did not possess. At the time of Munich, German military superiority was a reality; less than a year later, when Hitler sent the Wehrmacht crashing into Poland, it was not. The frantic Western democracies were rapidly catching up. The subsequent defeat of the French army once again tipped the balance decisively in Germany's favor, but not so much so that Hitler could afford to fight a war on two fronts. Moreover, he was hobbled to an extent by the very nature of his earlier successes, which had been achieved by bluff and speed, not bloodshed. For all his achievements and popularity, Hitler knew that he did not lead a war-mad people. Indeed, an essential ingredient of Nazi popularity in post-1933 Germany was the restoration of German pride without recourse to war. Sabers had only to be rattled, not used, to obtain cherished ends. Germany did not possess a total war economy in 1936, in 1939, or even in 1941. Not until 1942, in the aftermath of the first terrible reverses in the East and the coming into being against him of the Grand Alliance, did Hitler dare order total mobilization. Indeed, in the wake of the great successes of 1940—even as Barbarossa was being prepared in Wehrmacht planning rooms—Hitler had ordered a tentative demobilization of some units.

Thus when Hitler turned eastward in 1941 he possessed a splendid, but numerically and materially limited, military force and one that had scarcely been blooded in the West. Should the Russian hordes prove stubborn fighters, should "the whole rotten structure" *not* come crashing down, should the superbly trained majors and captains, lieutenants and sergeants, begin falling before Russian bullets, then Hitler and his generals and his people would face an appalling prospect.

And that, of course, is precisely what happened. Stalingrad and after have obscured the fact that the Wehrmacht suffered terrible losses during its first triumphant summer and autumn in the East. The headlong advances across the steppes, the brilliant encirclements, were paid for at prohibitive cost. "There is a uniformity about" German "accounts of the fighting at this time" Alan Clark notes, "which illustrates the German's surprise at finding an enemy who continued to resist long after he had been surrounded." Guderian writes somberly of the "grave and tragic total" of German deaths suffered this first year.[5]

Perhaps in the long run such losses could have been justified and eventually made up by clean victory. But there was to be no victory, largely because Hitler, evidently disconcerted by unexpected Russian resistance, could not make up his mind what he wished to do. Should he capture cities or kill Russians? In initial conception Barbarossa was simple enough. Three powerful thrusts would be launched out of central Poland at Leningrad, Moscow, and the Ukraine. At certain points the tip of each thrust would separate to the right and left in order to encircle and obliterate fixed Soviet defensive positions. Moscow, Leningrad, and Kiev, or perhaps Kursk, would all be captured by winter, bolshevism would be overthrown, the Soviet Union would disappear, Germany would triumph. But stubborn Russian resistance forced Hitler and his generals to pause at key moments in their eastward drive in order to subdue Soviet pockets or face the prospect of powerful, undefeated forces in the rear of advancing columns. Hitler had gambled; he had believed that his mechanized Wehrmacht could easily conquer two of the immutable problems of a Russian campaign—time and distance—while safely ignoring the third—manpower. His splendid forces almost managed to overcome all three at once, but not quite, and the penalty was disaster.

Not until early October were Hitler and his generals sufficiently satisfied that the Russian threat to the rear had disappeared to order the final thrust on Moscow. By this time the Wehrmacht had come within two hundred miles or less of the Kremlin; it had slaughtered literally hundreds of thousands of Russian soldiers and captured and enslaved many hundred thousands more. Indeed, at this late date in the campaign the Germans for a brief time outnumbered the Russians in front of them. But four months of desperately wearisome campaigning had left men and machines worn to the nub. The final advance began with a foreboding that grew steadily as temperatures dropped, snow began to fall, the first Siberian troops appeared before the struggling Nazi columns, and the dreaded T-34 tanks emerged suddenly from within woods or behind hills or half-ruined buildings.

The superbly trained and disciplined Wehrmacht nonetheless pushed stolidly on through the cold and blizzards of the Russian winter, dwindling as it advanced. Machines froze and broke; divi-

sions were decimated by chill, stomach disorders, and death. By
the first week in December the German army had closed up to a
semicircular arc only twenty to fifty miles from Moscow, and some
patrols claimed to have seen the Kremlin spires looming in the gray
distance. But the confident, swaggering hordes of summer had been
reduced to numb exhaustion. Now the *Stavka* ordered up its vast
mass of Siberian reserves, and suddenly between December 5 and
8 it was all over. As the Siberians advanced wave upon wave
through the wind and snow, the once-splendid German forces
shattered and splintered and threatened to fall completely apart.
"Despair gripped the German foot soldier and a trembling paralysis
afflicted his commanders. . . ." Only Hitler's stand-firm order, Clark
believes, saved the Wehrmacht from utter obliteration.[6] It painfully
regrouped, hung on, and then retreated slowly, sullenly, in disciplined fashion, to hastily prepared winter quarters. It would try
again when the sun and mild winds of summer reappeared. But
never again would it see, or claim to see, the Kremlin spires. Ahead
of it lay days and weeks and months and years of retreat, despair,
defeat, and death.

As German boys fought frantically through the snow to escape
the onrushing Siberians in front of Moscow that fateful first weekend of December 1941, halfway around the world a Japanese naval
force neared balmy Hawaii on its own mission of death. A sense
of desperate purpose, less intense perhaps at this moment than that
felt by Hitler and his soldiers but just as real, gripped Japanese
hearts. For the attack on Pearl Harbor was the culmination of two
years of steadily mounting "hostility born of long frustration and
growing anxiety."

For nearly two decades the viciousness of the "sneak" attack on
Pearl Harbor precluded serious question in both the United States
and Japan as to possible American provocation of Japanese militarism.[7] Recently, however, a number of American scholars, writing
under the cloud of our morally and politically questionable involvement in Vietnam, have sought to revise conventional wisdom on
the origins of the Pacific war. They point to Cordell Hull's distaste-
ful diplomacy of morality toward a Japan bogged down in a humiliating adventure in China (not unlike America's later "lost crusade"

in Indochina). They stress the Roosevelt administration's imposition of drastic economic sanctions in 1940 and 1941, culminating in the freezing of all Japanese assets in this country, which were palpably designed to force Japan either to renounce her entire imperialistic adventure on the Asian mainland or to launch a hopeless war for imperial if not national survival. They emphasize Roosevelt's unwillingness to meet and negotiate with Prime Minister Konoye in late summer 1941, the last possible opportunity to resolve mutual antagonisms short of violence. One of them, Bruce Russett, has gone all the way to argue explicitly what others have assumed implicitly: that Japan offered no clear and present danger to American interests or security in the vast Pacific region during the first two years of the Second World War.[8]

Where then does the burden of responsibility for Pearl Harbor lie? With Japan or with the United States? Russett has been bold enough to pose the question properly, and so we may begin by asking (1) whether Japan did indeed pose a clear and present danger to the United States in 1940-41, or (2) if she did not, whether the American government and people were right in *thinking* she did, for we must never forget that history is not only what happened, but what people think happened or thought was happening.

That the United States drove Japan to an act of desperation at Pearl Harbor can no longer be denied. Paul Schroeder has argued forcefully that prior to July 1941 the United States was moving slowly but perceptibly toward fulfillment of two realistic goals: splitting Japan off from the Axis partnership and limiting or stopping her advance southward. But on the verge of this triumph, Japan foolishly forced Vichy France to surrender military control of Indochina, thereby placing the Philippines and British Malaya in unprecedented strategic danger, and a suddenly aroused American government, press, and people abruptly burdened the warlords of Tokyo with a third and completely intemperate demand: total withdrawal of Japanese forces from the entire Asian mainland and Japanese abandonment of the four-year-old "China incident." "Through her single-minded pursuit of this unattainable goal, the United States forfeited the diplomatic victory which she had already virtually won."[9] Schroeder's assertion seems to resolve both basic questions to be asked about the origins of the Pacific war. Although Japan may have *at one time* posed a clear and present danger to American interests in the Far East, that danger was in the process of liquidation through diplomacy when the United States allowed emotionalism to take precedence over reason. Perceiving the Japanese threat as greater than it was because of Japan's foolish incursion into Indochina, Washington upset the diplomatic balance and mounted an economic and diplomatic offensive against the Japanese of such force and character as to induce a mood of desperation in Tokyo that made war inevitable.

But was the situation as simple as all that? Were the Americans wrong in reacting as they did to the latest example of Japanese aggression? Was it not only diplomatically disastrous but morally reprehensible to call Japan to such impulsive account? Or had relations between the two countries deteriorated so steadily over so long a period of time that the American reaction was, in the contemporary world context, inevitable?

Historians, even those as capable, careful, and responsible as Professor Schroeder, generally operate from a premise of dispassion, which they define as rationality, and from an assumption that war is invariably avoidable simply because it is by nature so cruel, immoral, and unforgivable, no matter who wages it. Thus they approach almost any study of an approaching war from the perspective of avoidability. They dwell in book after book, article after article, on why the war came when it did. But statesmen and politicians deal with the world as it is, which includes passion, emotionalism, fear, anxiety, and distaste. Until Hiroshima presumably made such thinking unthinkable, their perspective has frequently been: Let us avoid war as long as we can (otherwise known as "keeping the peace"), *but*, if it must come, let it come. This is not to say that Roosevelt maneuvered the country into Pearl Harbor so that he could leap into the crusade against Hitler. It is simply to say that FDR and Hull and Henry Stimson and a great proportion of the American press and public after mid-1941 believed, as Schroeder has noted, that war was preferable to *any* further appeasement of Japan.

If we turn the historian's traditional question—why did war come when it did?—around and ask why peace was preserved as long as it was, we may get close to the reality of the coming of not only the

Pacific war of 1941-45 but of all wars. It can be argued that according to its lights, America preserved the peace with Japan as long as possible, that Japan in fact had come to pose a clear and present danger to American security by 1941, and that the United States responded ultimately with measures that were calculated to resolve the situation with Japan short of war if possible, but by war if necessary.

Of course, war could have been avoided in 1941; of course, Americans could have decided that no matter what Japan did in Indochina or China or anywhere else in Asia, she presented no clear and present danger; of course, peace could have been maintained longer, perhaps permanently, if Japan had herself finally curbed her expansive impulses. But peace could have been preserved in 1941 only if Americans had thought differently than they did. The kind of world that an overwhelming majority of Americans wanted to see established in 1941 precluded the kind of appeasement diplomacy that would have kept the peace. Forty years of steadily mounting hostility and prejudice between the two countries, capped by Japan's sudden rush into Indochina in the context of steady aggression in Europe by Tokyo's newest ally, Nazi Germany, guaranteed an end to American forbearance.

As early as 1907 tensions between Japan and the United States had reached alarming proportions. Washington was increasingly fearful of Japanese designs upon the Philippines, our most important but also most weakly garrisoned colonial possession. The following year the Great White Fleet made an ostentatious call on Japan as part of its round-the-world cruise. In Tokyo, meanwhile, animosity toward the United States was rising for a number of reasons. There was some feeling that Theodore Roosevelt had taken advantage of Japanese military exhaustion to mediate an end to the Russo-Japanese war of 1904-1905 on terms far more favorable to the Czarist regime than it deserved. More immediate and infuriating was the vicious treatment accorded Japanese nationals and particularly Japanese schoolchildren by labor organizations and governmental bodies in California. The effort of the San Francisco school board in 1907 to segregate Japanese children raised an understandable and legitimate cry of outrage in Japan and gave Roosevelt one of his more uncomfortable moments in the White

House. The situation was poorly resolved by a Japanese promise to limit future migration to the American West Coast. Japanese fury at the blatant racism of the American neighbor across the Pacific was rekindled at Versailles, where Woodrow Wilson ultimately refused to fight for an antiracist clause in the League of Nations charter. Were the Americans always to look upon Japan with amused contempt and condescension? This was too much for a proud and brave people to endure.

During this same era American suspicions of Japanese aspirations grew rather than diminished, reflected as they were in a steady effort to delimit or at least deflect Japanese expansionist appetites away from American property. The Taft-Katsura, Root-Takahira, and Lansing-Ishii "agreements" and the Four Power and Nine Power Treaties signed during the Washington Naval Conference of 1922 all represented efforts by American statesmen to establish a firm and enduring balance of power and interest in East Asia and the Pacific. Japanese bellicosity, symbolized most blatantly by Tokyo's outrageous Twenty-one Demands on China during World War I, created a very real if temporary crisis in Japanese-American relations. If in the early years of the twentieth century American racism was never subtle, Japanese belligerence was seldom restrained.

By 1930 matters had become so tense in the Pacific that one sensational publicist, Hector C. Byewater, could write a rather popular novel entitled *The Great Pacific War*, which was to begin in the very near future when Japan would successfully and suddenly bomb the Panama Canal while the bulk of the American fleet was in the Atlantic. By this time, too, it was becoming clear to American officials that Japan had no intention of abiding by the Washington conference agreements on nonfortification of Pacific island holdings, that Tokyo was busily building bases in the Marshalls and Gilberts while the United States continued to station token naval and military forces in the Philippines and kept the midocean outposts, Guam, Wake, and Midway, virtually unfortified. Officials in both Washington and Tokyo had long since formulated plans for a Pacific war between the two countries, and young officers on attaché duty in the two capitals during the twenties and early thirties routinely wished each other good-bye with the hope that they would not meet again to say their final farewells over gunsights in midocean. Thus even before the Manchurian incident, powerful currents of antagonism and anxiety had developed in both countries.

As is well known, Japan, suffering deeply from the effects of the worldwide depression of the time, began a decade of expansionism in Asia with the abrupt and unprovoked conquest of Manchuria by the Kwantung army in 1931. What is perhaps less well known is that this act reflected, among other things, the emergence of the military as a critical—and ultimately decisive—factor in Japanese domestic politics. Throughout the 1930s, largely by and through abrupt spasms of violence, the army moved to subvert civil government at home in order to pursue an expansionist policy abroad. The army's motivations were many and complex. It wished to allay the constant threat of national weakness caused by overpopulation on the one hand and by a fatal paucity of natural resources on the other. It wished to overcome what it believed to be a long-standing humiliation and neglect of the warrior class by civil government. It was determined to wrench control of national life from a civil bureaucracy and industrial plutocracy—known as the *Zaibatsu*—which seemed to be rapidly leading Japan away from her rural, agrarian roots and traditions toward an urban-industrial system of vast exploitative and repressive potential.

In fact, army unity foundered on the issue of the bureaucracy and the *Zaibatsu*. A fervent group of younger officers, following what they termed *Kodaha*, or the "Imperial Way," wished simply to obliterate both the industrialists and bureaucrats. Their more sophisticated and experienced senior officers, the *Toseiha* or Control Group, wished merely to subvert the bureaucrats and *Zaibatsu* to military will. As early as 1932, the *Toseiha* employed, or at least permitted, the *Kodaha* group to come close to terminating independent civil government, then frustrated the young fanatics sufficiently to provoke them in February 1936 into a brief but violent storm of blood and terror that destroyed them as an effective political force. But the triumph of the *Toseiha* signaled not moderation but further expansionist adventures. For all their fanaticism, the *Kodaha* had been as intent upon domestic reform as on foreign adventure. After 1933 the *Kodaha* preached respite and consolidation of gains in Manchuria and north China in order to hasten and assist reform at home. It was the *Toseiha* who sought to still or subvert domestic reform through incessant overseas expansion that would provide the safety valve necessary to deflate such pressure. Thus the triumph of the *Toseiha* after 1936, together with the steady frustration felt by the navy because of its ostensible second-class status vis-à-vis the United States and Great Britain, provided the rationale and impulse for years of steady aggression in Asia.

Manchuria in 1931 was followed by the brief invasion of Shanghai the next year and by steady pressure on north China, which culminated in July 1937 in the Marco Polo Bridge incident at Peking, the spark that ignited a furious eight-year war between China and Japan. To sober observers it soon became obvious that this was a war neither side could win. China was simply in no condition and never had been to strike effectively at Japan. Japan in China proved to be as frustrated as Hitler in Russia; she simply did not command the human and material resources to conquer the vast territories of the foe. Month after month, year after year, Japan expanded into the void. She conquered the rich coastal cities, moved inland to rape Nanking, drove millions of pathetic refugees into the hinterland, sent swarms of bombers over remote Chungking to terrorize the cowering government of Chiang Kai-shek. All that a determined and ferocious but essentially limited military-industrial power could do to achieve victory was done. The result was failure. Harassed by Communist guerrilla forces in the north, unable to bring Chiang's armies to decisive battle, Japan had bogged down badly in China by the time Hitler sent his legions into Poland in September 1939, bringing Europe to war once again.

During this period the American response had been both unprecedented and ineffectual. Washington's response to the Manchurian incident had been the so-called Stimson Doctrine of January 1932, in which the Secretary of State announced his country's determination not to recognize any changes in the global status quo effected by force. A month later, in his publicly released Borah Letter to the chairman of the Senate Foreign Relations Committee, Secretary Stimson eloquently restated America's total opposition to aggression and hinted that the United States might abrogate ex-

isting naval agreements. Having vaguely rebuked and mildly threatened the excitable militarists in Tokyo and Manchuria, and having
for the first time aligned his nation, however tenuously, with the
League of Nations and its policies, Stimson flatly refused to go any
further either in terms of threat or alliance. Japan's leaders were
thus led to the not unreasonable conclusion that the United States
vigorously opposed their actions but would do little to stop them.

The reaction of Roosevelt and Hull to the outbreak of the Sino-
Japanese war in 1937 was little better. Chiang was sent some trucks,
but the total amount of United States loans to China prior to September 1940 was under $50 million. Indeed, as Schroeder has
noted, up to 1937 at least, Japan was generally regarded in this
country, though not by this government, as a friendly power despite
her incursions abroad and the increasing militarization of her life
at home.

The dramatic shift in American public attitudes toward Japan
began soon after the outbreak of the Sino-Japanese war. Since 1931
Japan had pursued her objectives in China with relative care and
prudence. Manchuria had been so swiftly detached that world
opinion had not had sufficient time to crystallize in a firm anti-
Japanese mood. The subsequent infiltration and subversion of north
China had been accomplished with sufficient *strategic*, if not rhe-
torical, caution as to keep world attention lulled. Following the
Marco Polo Bridge incident and the commencement of outright
hostilities, however, Chiang refused to let the Japanese play out
their strategy of piecemeal conquest. Late in 1937 Chiang sent his
best divisions marching toward the Japanese settlement at Shanghai, hoping to provoke a reaction that would alarm world attention.
The Japanese stupidly accepted the challenge, and for several
months Chiang's forces held them pinned against Shanghai until
at last Japanese ground, air, and naval superiority battered the
gallant Chinese to pieces.

But the Kwantung army had been lured to the heart of China.
It had no choice now but to try to finish off the Kuomintang. Frustrated at being so hoodwinked, infuriated at Chiang's unwillingness
either to fight a decisive battle or to capitulate, Japanese forces reacted with pure and indiscriminate barbarism. Barbara Tuchman,
a scholar not normally given to purple prose, later asserted that "A

self-defeating ferocity accompanied" the Japanese troops "like a hyena of conquest, growing more ravenous by what it fed on." From Shanghai, Japanese forces swept westward down the Yangtse Valley, their troops and airmen indiscriminately bombing, shooting, raping, and pillaging in an orgy of horror. "Nanking fell in circumstances dreadful even for China."

Determined to make an example of the capital that would bring the war to an end, the Japanese achieved a climax to the carnage already wrought in the delta below. Fifty thousand soldiers hacked, burned, bayoneted, raped, and murdered until they had killed, by hand, according to evidence witnessed and collected by missionaries and other foreigners of the International Relief Committee, a total of 42,000 civilians in Nanking. Groups of men and women were lined up and machine-gunned or used alive for bayonet practice or tied up, doused with kerosene and set afire while officers looked on.

Chiang's fervent hope for an awakening of world opinion was partially realized. Shanghai and Nanking suddenly "made the world China conscious. . . . Journalists flocking to the drama and richly nourished twice daily at Chinese Government press conferences reported tales of heroism, blood and suffering. China was seen as fighting democracy's battle and personified by the steadfast Generalissimo and his marvelously attractive, American-educated, unafraid wife."[10]

However frightening China's agony, however deeply hated Japan became in this country as elsewhere, Nippon was not perceived as a direct threat to American security as a result of the Sino-Japanese war. Had Japan confined her attentions to the East Asian mainland above Indochina, it is highly doubtful that relations between Tokyo and Washington would have deteriorated so swiftly. But in September 1940 the Japanese committed an act of such apparent and direct hostility toward the United States that their behavior could no longer be dismissed as of no consequence to national security. On September 27 Japan adhered to the Tripartite Pact with Nazi Germany and Fascist Italy. With a single signature the government in Tokyo had apparently aligned itself wholeheartedly with that Nazi conspiracy and aggression which since 1938 had gobbled up one European nation after another by fraud or force and had finally imposed a world war upon the craven democracies of Western Europe. Moreover, Tokyo's sudden alliance with the European warmongers seemed the culmination of a whole series of sinister Japanese moves over the previous three months.

By June 10, 1940, Hitler had stricken the imperial powers, France and Holland, from the list of independent nations. In Tokyo covetous glances were quickly focused upon the fabulously rich French and Dutch possessions in Southeast Asia. But the expansionists still had to contend with an apparently powerful clique of moderates, including, it would seem, the emperor himself. The expansionists, however, had two things going for them at this time: first, the inability of the current Yonai government to come to some terms with Washington and London over the "China incident," and, second, the stunning success of Hitler and Mussolini in Europe. With British and American attention riveted on the European drama, Japan was apparently presented an unprecedented opportunity to forge her long-contemplated Co-Prosperity Sphere in East Asia. In July the ineffectual Yonai government was practically overthrown by the army, and a new administration was forged under the nominal leadership of Prince Konoye.

Konoye was no fire-eater; the army did not intend that a fire-eater lead Japan at this moment. But Konoye quickly accepted Hideki Tojo, prominent among the army expansionists, into his cabinet as war minister and then proceeded to blunder badly in nominating Yosuke Matsuoka as foreign minister. Matsuoka was, in the words of one respected student of prewar Japanese history, "very much the Japanese counterpart of Ribbentrop," that is to say, self-assertive, conceited, garrulous, and wholly oriented toward fulfilling a goal of national expansion. A fervent believer in the creation of a Greater East Asian Co-Prosperity Sphere under Japanese aegis, "Matsuoka appears to have been confident that he could make use of the Axis Powers while not committing himself too fully to their side." Japan would be well advised to follow a course roughly parallel to that of the Soviet Union, taking advantage of German victories in Europe to descend upon the Asian possessions of France, Holland, and Portugal. Britain surely would soon be crushed by Hitler; the United States would then stand alone, threatened by both Japan in the Pacific and Germany in the Atlantic, and would be reduced to paralysis or frantic continental defense. Such was the rosy view of the future held by Matsuoka, Tojo, Navy Minister Yoshida, and even Konoye in the promising days and weeks of 1940 following Germany's triumph in the West. And it was this view that propelled Tokyo into proposing Japanese adherence to the Axis alliance immediately following Hitler's triumphant sweep across northwestern Europe.

The Tripartite Pact, which was announced to a world at war after several weeks of intensive negotiation, confirmed all the worst suspicions about Japan held in Washington and London—and understandably so. The pact seemed aimed directly at the United States—appearing to promise that if America moved either in Asia or Europe, the three Axis powers would immediately band together against her. Moreover, Japan was not obligated immediately or directly to move against Great Britain but could be expected to reap the Asian fruits of a successful Nazi invasion of British soil. Finally, and most ominous of all, the pact specifically stated that the existing relations of the three powers with the Soviet Union would in no way be jeopardized by their adherence to the pact. This meant that when Hitler unilaterally chose to move against Stalin the following year, Japan was not obliged to aid him. Having suffered some fearful drubbings from the Russians in the north Manchurian border area during the still little-known Russo-Japanese war of 1939, Tokyo was in no mood to subject her armies to further adventures against the Bolsheviks, especially when all of the incredibly rich Southeast Asian area lay ready for the taking.

Certainly the pact was a triumph of sorts for Japanese diplomacy, and it did constitute a warning to the United States to stay its hand in both Europe and Asia. Yet how clear a warning was i ? As F. C. Jones has pointed out, much of the language pertaining to mutual aid was vague, and Japanese negotiators successfully resisted specific commitments to counter future United States moves in either Europe or the Pacific. Nor, it must be stressed, can the pact in any way be interpreted in retrospect as a "blueprint for aggression"—collective aggression—by the Axis powers against democracy's crumbling citadels. It represented, in fact, an effort by both Nazi Germany and Japan to limit and localize the ongoing wars in Europe and Asia both geographically and politically until such time as one or the other or all the Axis nations together chose to expand the dimensions of conflict. Although it was never stated, a geopolitical assumption underlay all of Axis diplomacy in August and September 1940: that both America and Russia possessed the strength and position to turn the existing peripheral wars on the Eurasian land mass into a true world war unless they were dealt with properly and at the right time. For the Axis cause to succeed— whether collectively or individually was never exactly defined—it was mandatory to control the pace and timing of aggression. If at all possible, the Soviet Union and the United States had to be kept out of the war until each could be suitably dealt with at the pleasure of the Axis.

But, of course, the Axis powers simply outsmarted themselves. By its very existence the Tripartite Pact instantly created the very conditions it was meant to forestall. If the pact did not represent a blueprint for immediate aggression, it certainly seemed so to anxious Western bureaucrats and peoples during the dark days and weeks immediately following the swift collapse of all of northwestern Europe to nazism. Hitler now stood on the Channel; the following June Japanese soldiers brazenly marched into French Indochina. When would Axis aggression stop? How far would it extend? Would British power be exhausted and American power nibbled away by ever-continuing Axis expansion? Prudent officials in both Washington and London, charged with defining and defending respective national interests, cannot be blamed, even from the perspective of nearly four decades, for placing the most pessimistic interpretations upon both German and Japanese policies. Perhaps, as some historians have recently asserted, Roosevelt should have met with Konoye in the summer of 1941 after further Axis moves in both Europe and Asia had brought the United States and Japan to the brink of war in the Pacific. Konoye seems to have realized by this time that both the feckless China venture and the aggressive spinoffs into Southeast Asia were bringing Japan closer and closer to a fate that must be avoided at all costs. But years of expansionist militarism had generated their own momentum, and by this late date no one in Tokyo could really stop it. FDR was undoubtedly quite correct in assuming that little of positive benefit but much disillusion would result from the certain breakdown of a Japanese-American summit.

Yet if Japan, through adherence to the Tripartite Pact and subsequent aggression in Southeast Asia, set in motion a chain of events that led irrevocably to the great Pacific war with the United States, it is equally true that Tokyo did not have the resources, and knew it did not have the resources, to prosecute that war to ultimate victory. Here was one of the twentieth century's tragic ironies: a nation committed to militarism, to expansion, to the total warfare state, yet so ultimately weak in comparison to its aspirations as to demand more than it could ever realistically hope to attain. To apprehensive Americans in the early months after Pearl Harbor, Japan seemed a colossus. But the handful of realists in Tokyo who had not succumbed to the general euphoria created by the incredible early victories never forgot the precariousness of their country's position.

Japan's weakness and strategic and tactical timidity with regard to the Pacific war were clearly reflected in air and naval planning. Pearl Harbor was a desperate gamble, not a calculated act of aggression. Serious planning for the raid did not really commence until the latter half of 1941, and even then the carrier fleet sent to bomb Hawaii had orders to turn back at the last moment should the Nomura-Kurusu mission to Washington bear unexpected fruit. This is not to deny that the new Tojo government in Tokyo was neither bellicose nor confident; it was assuredly both. Konoye had been restrained; Tojo, though desperate, took the opposite tack. And at least one later Japanese writer, Masanori Ito, bitterly condemns the navy for capitulating to Tojo's and the army's pressure. Earlier in 1941 Konoye had asked Admiral Yamamoto whether there was a chance for national victory in a war against Britain and the United States. "I can raise havoc with them for one year," Yamamoto replied. "After that I can guarantee nothing." But no such comparable advice was given to Tojo. "The Navy not only failed to object to war, it failed also to point out that defeat for Japan would be inevitable in a long drawn-out conflict." Years later Vice Admiral Tomiji Koyanagi would write apologetically that the navy was "gradually dragged to war."[11]

But nothing could have prevented a Japanese-American war after Japan's takeover of French Indochina in July 1941. And behind this incident lay the shadow of Japanese aggression in China itself. By the eve of Pearl Harbor, China had become America's Poland. Liberal opinion in the United States had come to regard the embattled land as another outpost of decency and innocence locked in frantic struggle with a predatory aggressor. Japan could not disengage from the China quagmire as American officials now demanded without the severest loss of face and influence in that Asian world whose destiny Tokyo so ardently wished to shape. Washington felt, rightly or wrongly, that spreading Japanese aggression could be strangled only by stopping the flow of essential war materials from the United States, including precious oil. An aroused American press and public asserted that to continue supplying such materials to an aggressor power was to abet aggression. Who could or can contest such a point in a world at war? Yet curtailment of these supplies left the Japanese with only three choices: national humiliation, an early collapse of the industrial and military order, or a sweep south and west to seize the mineral-rich imperial holdings of the Americans, Dutch, and British which lay in a broad arc from the Philippines to Java, Malaya, and Sumatra. The attack on Pearl Harbor was designed to shatter the American Pacific fleet (the bulk of the U.S. Navy remained in the Pacific, despite growing tensions and isolated battles with the German submarine fleet in the Atlantic) and thus gain time for Japan to consolidate her hold over the western Pacific.

But it is Japanese planning—or lack of planning—*after* Pearl Harbor that most strikes the historian's attention as he seeks to resolve the question of Japan's threat to the United States in 1941. To put the matter simply, Tokyo developed no serious plans to meet the menace of a furious, revengeful United States after Pearl Harbor. Indeed, the Pearl Harbor raid itself was a greater fiasco than it seemed for many years. In the first place, Tokyo had not intended to "stab America in the back" at Pearl Harbor. As is now well known, delivery of the declaration of war was to precede the Hawaiian attack by thirty minutes. The slow fingers of an inexperienced typist, combined with the ignorance of envoys deliberately uninformed of the attack, upset the delicate timing and created a tragic myth. Hours later, out in the Pacific, exultant Japanese fliers returning from Pearl Harbor begged to be allowed to return for further strikes. The American fleet was in flames, the aircraft shattered and broken on their strips. But vast oil reserves remained, and some of the fliers, at least, were aware that the American carriers had not been caught at their berths, as had been hoped and expected. Had the oil reserves at Pearl Harbor been destroyed in a subsequent Japanese attack, the American carriers then in midocean might well have run out of fuel to lie crippled and stranded until the Japanese could have found and dispatched them at will. But there was to be no second assault. Admiral Nagumo, in command of the Japanese carrier strike force, was unwilling to risk turning what seemed splendid triumph into unnecessary disaster by remaining in the area any longer. The American carriers could be anywhere. There would be many further days to fight, he told disconsolate airmen cryptically as he turned back toward Japan.

For the next four months the Japanese navy allowed itself to become an appendage of the army as it advanced through Southeast Asia and the islands of the western Pacific. No effort was made to maintain pressure on the American fleet either in midocean or near the enemy shores. Available accounts of Japanese thinking and action in this crucial period reveal a government, nation, and military increasingly blinded by easy victories over forlorn garrisons and determined not to undertake hard thinking about enemy intentions or capabilities. Indeed, it is difficult to escape the impression that Tokyo hoped the American problem would just go away after Pearl Harbor. There was so much to conquer and consolidate; it was too much to plan seriously for an early American menace.

The first jolt to this ostrichlike approach to strategic planning (which in some respects resembled Hitler's attitude toward Britain as he turned eastward in the spring and summer of 1941) was the Doolittle raid on Tokyo in mid-April 1942. Thereafter, Japanese strategists at last felt compelled to face the American problem, to clarify long-standing assumptions and impulses. What they concocted, of course, was the fatal plan for the seizure of Midway Island. Discussion of the battle of Midway is beyond the purview of this essay. But the strategic and tactical assumptions behind the Midway assault and the atmosphere in which the proposed invasion was planned reflected the limits, at least for a time, of Japanese aspiration in the Pacific.

Successful seizure of Midway did not assume further advances in the mid- or eastern Pacific area. Midway was to be the climax of a larger, hastily devised, Japanese plan—first revealed and partially blunted in the Coral Sea only a month before—to develop a "ribbon defense" at midocean. Japan would seize and fortify island outposts in the Aleutians, at Midway, and in the Solomons. Behind this line Japan would exploit as rapidly as possible all the many riches of her new western Pacific and southeast Asian empire. America would find Hawaii, only a thousand miles from a Japanese-held Midway, untenable as a forward fleet anchorage and would be forced back to the California coast. For some years, it was assumed, an ever wearier United States would batter itself to pieces attempting to puncture the ribbon defense. But a rapidly expanding, increasingly powerful Japanese nation and fleet would contain or repulse such assaults until in a decade or so the United States, exhausted, disheartened, and weakened by the loss of such essential commodities of war as the rubber and tin of Southeast Asia, would sue for peace and an acceptance of Japanese domination of Asia and western Oceania. With Hitler still in firm control of all Western Europe, a new global balance of power would have been struck between the Axis powers and their enemies.

The miscalculations inherent in such a scenario are staggering to contemplate from the perspective of thirty-five years. That the United States would in time supinely submit to the implications of Pearl Harbor was simply too much to expect of any nation. That the United States could not obtain or develop artificially the necessary materials of modern war was too much to hope from the most advanced industrial nation on earth, one capable of endless inventiveness. Finally, to assume that *Japanese* resources were sufficient to defend effectively a belt of ocean six thousand miles long while simultaneously exploiting and keeping in permanent subjugation the vast empire behind it represented an incredible act of faith.

In fact, from the beginning the folly of the Japanese vision was apparent. During the war games conducted on the flagship *Yamato* in May 1942 it was clear that the extensive tasks assigned the superbly trained but numerically few warships and pilots in the Midway effort were beyond Japanese capabilities. The same ships and men would have to subdue an island and defeat a small but powerful enemy fleet almost simultaneously. The games showed this to be impossible. The umpires simply changed the rules and results to make it possible. Japanese ships ruled sunk in an early phase of the operation were arbitrarily resurrected to reappear in later battles. Seldom in military history have plans been so shaped to meet the demands of dreams. Only through the greatest series of blunders imaginable could the United States have lost the battle of Midway. Such blunders were not forthcoming—indeed, the U.S. Navy had broken the Japanese code and knew of Japan's every move. A shattered Japanese fleet, shorn of its finest ships and best pilots, reeled back across the Pacific in defeat and disgrace.

Midway restored for a brief time the balance of power in the Pacific, and soon American war plants and training camps tipped it the other way, obliterating the effects, but never the memory, of Pearl Harbor. For Japan the Midway debacle was inherent in the Pearl Harbor attack. Did Japan represent a clear and present danger to the United States in 1941? The answer is yes and no. As an aggressor nation that had allowed itself to fall into a political and military morass in China, as an avowed ally of other aggressor states in Europe, as a militarist society that seemed increasingly incapable of self-restraint and increasingly unpredictable in mood and intent, Japan by mid-1941 had become a clear and present danger—an outright menace—to whatever peace and stability and independence remained in the fragile and shaky world of East Asia. For half a century the United States had been an intimate part of that world as conqueror, imperial tutor, commercial exploiter, and player (however naively) of the regional balance of power. American interest in the area, both material and above all spiritual, had focused upon China. Not to have opposed Japanese aggression there (and in Indochina), not to have aided China, however minimally, would have represented a cynical betrayal of those ideals and self-interests which Americans cherished. Roosevelt and Hull sought to avoid the implications of Japanese behavior for many months until Japan's apparently limitless designs became all too clear. Had Roosevelt and Hull permitted Japan to do in East Asia what Britain had earlier permitted Hitler to do in Central Europe, the country and the Allied world of 1941 would surely have never forgiven them. The president and his secretary of state would have joined the ranks of the despised "appeasers" of Munich infamy, and Roosevelt's ability to govern would surely have been gravely imperiled.

But Japan just as certainly did not represent a direct military threat to American security in 1941. In comparison to the United States, though not to Britain by this time, Japan remained a second-rate industrial, naval, and military power. To be sure, the Japanese fleet was large and efficient. But even after Pearl Harbor it did not attain the quantitative and qualitative superiority necessary to carry out its nearly insuperable tasks. Had Pearl Harbor not occurred, had a Pacific war somehow been avoided and Tokyo not pushed so vigorously or quickly out into midocean and down into Southeast Asia, then it is difficult to see how Japan could have substantially threatened basic American security interests in 1941 and for some years thereafter anywhere but in the far western Pacific, where such a threat had existed for forty years without bringing on war.

America thus chose to invite war in late 1941 for essentially emotional, psychological, and idealistic reasons. Committed to a vision of a free, democratic China that did not exist even in embryo, sincerely dedicated to a comparatively liberal personal and public life-style at complete variance with the predatory totalitarian systems of Europe and Asia, the American government and people (or at least a majority of the people, if public reaction to the Japanese oil embargo is any indication) concluded in mid-1941 that aggression could no longer be tolerated in silence or deference; a diplomatic and economic line had to be drawn. In drawing that line, the Americans drew themselves inexorably into the Second World War. Six further months of hesitation and planning and ever dwindling hope ended in a day of infamy.

So within the space of seventy-two hours during the first weekend of December 1941 the war of 1939-45 was transformed. Hitler's failure before Moscow assured the survival—and the eventual triumph—of the Soviet Union, while Japan's simultaneous folly at

Pearl Harbor at last brought the United States into the conflict as a full participant.* The 1939 resumption of Europe's ancient, fitfully prosecuted, civil war abruptly melded with Japan's decade-old aggressions in East Asia to produce at last that Second World War which has dominated and determined the course of international life for the past third of a century.

---

* One of the great unanswerable questions of the Second World War is *why* Hitler gratuitously declared war on the United States four days after Pearl Harbor. Speculations on the reasons for this act of lunacy would fill a large book. The facts remain (a) that Hitler was in no way compelled to enter the Japanese-American war by the provisions of the Tripartite Pact and (b) that no documentation has been found detailing the führer's motives for doing so.

Grand Strategy

4

SO THE storm of fire and blood swept over much of the earth. The Axis nations continued to be rushed along by their own impulses for total security, for the attainment of a magical line which their enemies could not cross and behind which they could perfect their metropolitan power bases to a point of invincibility. Insecurity is ever the fate of aggressors. Their careers generated by anxieties and shaped by a successful search for rationalized hatreds, aggressors are ceaselessly tormented by always receding, always beckoning symbols of impregnability. Neither the German general staff, nor the führer, nor the militarists in Tokyo ever had plans for total world conquest. But understandably it seemed that way to their enemies, because the Axis leaders were bewitched by ever-more-distant goals of safety. (It must also be remembered that the scope of Nazi aggression and commitment was twice widened in 1941 by the follies of Mussolini and the incompetence of his armies in the Balkans and North Africa.)

Hitler had at first seemed to have the Urals in mind as a final security goal of the Third Reich—at least in his lifetime. After the repulse at Moscow, he scorned suspension of further offensives, the creation of a static Leningrad-Kiev-Odessa defense line, and development of the vast European empire at his feet. He insisted on striking deep into the oil-rich Caucasus as soon as the winter snows of 1941-42 had disappeared, and to screen this forlorn thrust he sent the Sixth Army pushing south and east to its ultimate doom in the icy, corpse-strewn streets and cellars of Stalingrad the following winter. Thereafter, the führer was briefly prevailed upon to assume a defensive strategy in western Russia, but with the coming of the summer campaign season in 1943, he found resumption of a limited attack strategy irresistible. The result was the battle of Kursk, the greatest armored conflict of its time and a decisive defeat for the Wehrmacht. "The battles for the Kursk salient cost Hitler half a million men and when they failed all possibility of avoiding total defeat had gone."[1] The Wehrmacht commenced its long, stubborn, melancholy retreat to the gates of Berlin.

The militarists in Tokyo felt similarly impelled to fatal over-extensions. In the half year following Pearl Harbor they sent their fleets and armies storming across East Asia, humiliating the handful of Westerners still there, creating unprecedented opportunities for native nationalists. By April the Japanese fleet was even making a brief and successful foray into the Indian Ocean, Burma was rapidly crumbling, India seemed ripe for conquest as well. By June of 1942 Nazi armies were deep in the Caucasus, Rommel seemed about to sweep through Egypt and all of the Middle East, and it appeared distinctly likely to a still largely powerless Allied world that Nazi soldiers moving east through Iraq and Iran might well shake hands with Japanese boys pushing westward from Burma and across the north Indian plain. Then, indeed, would the Axis control all the Eurasian land mass, its Middle Eastern bridge, and its north African periphery in a broad swath from the North Cape of Norway to Rangoon and New Delhi, to Hong Kong, Shanghai, and Tokyo.

If the Axis war machines defined the geopolitical scope of battle, their enemies responded in kind. Between 1942 and 1945 military considerations consistently dominated grand strategy. Revisionist historians, of course, have argued otherwise. They assert that the war was essentially a political and economic struggle—at least after the Axis tide had been turned by mid-1943. But the record does not bear out the contention. (Regrettably, many of the revisionists have chosen to rewrite the record to accord with their ideology. The confusion of dream and reality is not confined to military minds alone.)

Allied strategists could have followed one of three paths. They could have elected to wait, to hold the line with minimum resources until the vast industrial power of the United States and the manpower of the Soviet Union could have been fully utilized in a single rush to victory. There would have been no peripheral fighting, but rather two coordinated (if possible) direct assaults. The Nazi heartland in Europe would have been smashed by simultaneous invasions from East and West. This would have been followed by a direct assault on Japan. In both cases the gamble would have entailed a rapid thrust through enemy forces, creating such demoralization as to induce quick surrender. If in hindsight this strategy seems so foolish as to be dismissed out of hand, it should be remembered that prewar American policy in the Pacific was based on just such considerations. Until Pearl Harbor rendered it meaningless, American planning for a Pacific war assumed a fleet sortie from Hawaiian waters and a decisive engagement with Japanese warships somewhere in the Marianas or Caroline archipelagoes, after which the great Pacific war would be over. A short war, in other words, the dream of nearly all military men throughout history. Even later, in Europe in 1942-44, a number of British and American military people clamored first for a strict husbanding of all resources so as to insure a successful, cross-Channel assault in the West and later, when once on the Continent, for a pencil-like thrust on the German heartland, stripping the existing broad front of as many supplies, arms, and men as possible. Although always rejected as a dominant strategy, the victory rush beguiled some Allied military thinkers throughout the war. (Montgomery, of course, *was* given a brief chance in October 1944 to try a thrust across the Rhine and the north German plain to Berlin. It failed at the start in the streets of Arnhem.)

An alternative which could have been applied to the rush-for-victory strategy was to fight the war exactly as revisionist scholars claim it was fought—as a political conflict in which the anti-Communist and imperialist interests of the Western powers were given consistent precedence over final defeat of the Axis enemy. Pursuing such a well-defined policy, Washington and London would have had to run the risk of casting the ever-suspicious Soviet ally back into Nazi arms. Lend-lease shipments to Russia would have had to have been carefully rationed and severely curtailed, if necessary, so as to regulate as much as possible the Communist advance through eastern and central Europe. An *eastern* Mediterranean strategy would have had to have been pursued with vigor; Anglo-American armies would have fought not only in Sicily and Italy but in Greece, Albania, Bulgaria, Yugoslavia, and Rumania as well. Above all, Churchill's impassioned plea for a thrust through the Ljubljana Gap —the "soft underbelly" of Europe—would have been heeded, and even had it not been, the combined chiefs would surely have ordered Eisenhower to try for Berlin in the spring of 1945. In the Far East, operations in the central Pacific would never have been undertaken. Instead, Anglo-American forces would have worked against Japan from the Southeast Asia Command or from MacArthur's head-quarters in Australia so that a step-by-step reconquest of the former western colonies, Burma, Indochina, Indonesia, and the Philippines, and of China as well, would have preceded any implementation of plans for an invasion of Japan. Had Anglo-American planners truly believed in 1941-45 that "international communism" was a threat comparable to that of nazism—and could they have sold this assumption to their war-weary peoples or ignored public opin-ion as some revisionists have claimed they consistently did—then the war would have been planned and fought far differently than it was.

Allied generals and statesmen chose instead to follow a third course in their prosecution of the war. In a crusading mood, de-fined by a sense of outraged virtue, soldiers and civilians embraced the war as the single, overriding reality of their time—the trans-cendant "given" of their era. Reason had failed, goodwill had failed, appeasement had failed, persuasion and warnings had failed. Now military victory, not economic advantage or political or ideologi-cal gain, dominated strategic thought. Such dedication to the pros-ecution of total war and the unconditional surrender of the enemy explain at once the comparatively intelligent quality of Allied stra-tegic planning and the utter ruthlessness with which growing Allied military power was applied. This is not to deny the influence of political considerations upon grand strategy. Such considerations were never beyond the calculations of the leadership at both the Kremlin and Downing Street.

But throughout the war America, Britain, and Russia *did* pursue a common strategic pattern in which political considerations and developments were shaped and defined by the accelerating rate of conquest, not vice versa.

From the outset Soviet planners found themselves in a uniquely advantageous position. Their problems were tactical and logistical, not strategic. Unlike the British and Americans, the Soviets shared the Eurasian land mass with their Nazi enemies. The Nazis had directly invaded Russia along a broad front of land; they could be beaten and pursued into their own heartland the same way. Nor was there any need, as there was with Hitler, to defend an enormous circular periphery from a host of enemies, East and West, while extending constant succor to an ally of increasingly doubtful value.*

Thus, from the beginning the Russian military task was comparatively simple: trade space and men in European Russia for time and weapons and the mustering of still more men. The industrial plant was moved beyond the Urals in one of the epic hegiras of modern times. The Nazi assaults of 1941-42 were barely contained. At last the Soviet high command unloosed carefully husbanded forces and spectacular new weapons (the T-34 tank, ground-to-ground rockets of demoralizing effect, popularly known as Stalin Organs, and efficient aircraft with competent pilots) to brush aside the last, faltering Nazi thrusts at Stalingrad and Kursk before turning to a constant offensive, summer and winter. Tactically, the Soviet high command utilized the methods of armored warfare first proposed and developed by such earlier theorists and practitioners as Liddell Hart, de Gaulle, Guderian, and Rommel. The Nazis found their own tactics of "lightning war" and rapid envelopment and entrapment by armored columns now turned against them.

---

* It is interesting to speculate on the course of events had Japan returned the favor which Hitler had done Tokyo by declaring war on the United States. Had the Japanese declared war on the Soviet Union late in 1941, forcing Stalin to tie down large contingents of the Red Army in the Far East, it is entirely possible that Allied victory in Asia might have preceded that in Europe. Or, alternatively, that the Soviet Union would have collapsed. But until the final weeks of the war Moscow and Tokyo felt sufficiently preoccupied elsewhere to retain an uneasy peace.

War on the *Ostfront* was incredibly savage from the first, but its fury increased rather than stabilized with time. For the Germans the pattern became one of retreat and hold until the Soviets mustered their supplies and rested men and vehicles for the next thrust, then retreat and retreat again until Soviet pressure ceased for another brief spell and new lines could be built, only to be overrun in the next avalanche of Russian steel and fire. And as the Red Army advanced across the Ukrainian and White Russian steppes into Poland, Czechoslovakia, Hungary, and even Germany, the soldiers found appalling evidence again and again of what the Nazi death squads following behind the Wehrmacht had done to the native peasant and urban populations. Terrifying recollections of earlier sufferings and death of loved ones in the first desperate months and years of the Nazi invasion were now compounded by evidence on every hand of German destruction and atrocities, and a deadly mood against all things German swept through the Russian columns.

German soldiers soon sensed that death was preferable to capture and fought all the more desperately. To crack German resistance as swiftly and ruthlessly as possible, Soviet generals, it is alleged, often threw their men against the Nazi lines with suicidal fury, filling the soldiers with vodka, then hurling them out onto the battlefields with officers at their back under orders to shoot anyone who turned about. Nazi minefields were neutralized swiftly by marching Soviet columns through them.* Thus did the entire *Ostfront* from the gates of Moscow to the gates of Berlin and everywhere in between become a gigantic killing ground, a vast thousand-mile swath of scorched earth and shattered cities.

While Nazis and Soviets staged the longest and bloodiest single battle of the Second World War, British and American strategists were facing a different set of problems while incurring mounting Russian suspicion that the West really meant to stay off the Continent until national socialism and communism had done each other to death. How could Anglo-American armies best and most

* The German novelist Theodore Plevier alleges that this practice was common also in the Wehrmacht during the early years of the Russo-German war, with the difference that Nazi commanders only utilized personnel from convict battalions.

quickly engage substantial enemy forces? How could Anglo-American power be brought directly to bear against the Nazi enemy prior to a massive Western engagement of German forces?

The initial solution to the first question had been Winston Churchill's. From the beginning he was determined to throw what forces he could against the Nazi and Italian enemies wherever and whenever possible. Given Britain's precarious position and Hitler's domination of the Continent during the eighteen months between the fall of France and Pearl Harbor, such a strategic decision was unwise at best and foolhardy at worst. It led to the debacles at Mersel-Kebir and Dakar in 1940, which certainly made the task of anti-Nazi Frenchmen far more difficult, and to the catastrophes in Greece and Crete the following year. Churchill's further decision to strip the British Isles of virtually all mobile armor in order to seek a final desert victory in North Africa was a most desperate gamble, which came off only because The Few managed to keep at bay the threat of a German invasion of Britain through domination of the skies over Kent. Churchill's effort after Dunkirk to maintain Britain as a viable military and political opponent of Nazi Germany through repeated displays of national bulldog courage no matter how futile (as in Greece) was a very near-run thing. It required great spirit—but also the greatest good luck.

With American entry into the war in Europe, the scope and scale of strategic planning in the West immediately expanded. As in 1917 the United States seemed to possess an inexhaustible reservoir of men and materiel. But such an assumption proved false. American factories could and did produce mountains of goods from tanks, B-17s, battleships, and carriers to chewing gum, hosiery, and Coca-Cola—the latter three items apparently of equal value to the former. But the United States did not possess a limitless pool of manpower. Unlike 1917-18, the United States was now fighting a truly global war. Pearl Harbor inevitably wrenched American attention toward the Pacific, and ultimately three-fifths of the total national effort would flow to the areas south and west of Hawaii. Moreover, the United States found itself inevitably an air and naval power, and these respective services, both traditionally demanding young men of higher quality than the infantry, required enormous personnel drafts. Finally, the Great Depression itself continued to cast a sickly influence over national life. Medical boards were shocked to discover the low physical state of millions of young Americans called to the draft in 1941 and 1942. The result of all these factors was that the U.S. Army in the Second World War was comparatively small—and comparatively old (averaging an age of twenty-six years).

American strategists soon decided that Hitler would have to be defeated in the West by an American army (in conjunction with British and Canadian allies) of only ninety divisions. Firepower and the mobility of the vast armored forces being provided by America's factories would replace mass and volume.

No one, not Churchill, not Roosevelt, not Marshall, not Alanbrooke, or anyone else, denied that eventually the small but seasoned British and Canadian forces, joined by the emerging American army, would strike at the heart of Nazi Germany by a cross-Channel assault. But the problems facing Anglo-American planners were far different from those facing their Soviet counterparts. Britain had been thrown off the Continent in 1940; America had never been there in this war. To reenter the Continent successfully, and in such a forceful way as to avoid becoming bogged down in a resumption of that static trench warfare that had defined the First World War, would require the most exquisite calculations and timing. Dieppe proved that. This reconnaissance in force undertaken by British and Canadian commandos (and a handful of American rangers) in August 1942 was almost a complete fiasco. Much of the invasion fleet, small as it was, lost its way, and many troops were landed under the muzzles of German guns. Command coordination ashore and between ship and shore ranged from chaotic to nonexistent. Casualties were appalling, and the force, or what remained of it, had to withdraw as best it could. If this was a rehearsal, what promise did a full-scale invasion have? Dieppe seemed to confirm British fears that an early lunge into France, without the most careful preparation and training, could only lead to total disaster.

Nonetheless, Allied armies could not be allowed to molder awaiting the proper moment to attempt one great rush to victory. As Churchill cried out to Marshall in one of his more impassioned moments, "Muskets must flame!" And so a peripheral strategy came into being, aimed at nibbling away at Axis strength along the southern fringes of Fortress Europe—in North Africa, Sicily, and Italy —until Allied strength in England was sufficient to guarantee a successful cross-Channel assault and lodgment in France. Characteristically, the peripheral strategy of 1942-43 was the result of compromise between the British and American staffs and their respective chiefs. The Americans were never totally happy with the peripheral strategy and were frequently reduced to a state somewhere between disgust and despair at what they believed was their British cousins' determination to carry it far beyond the point of effectiveness. And one suspects from their published memoirs and diaries that the British always feared to take the great cross-Channel leap. It is far easier to withdraw an army from the Continent—even under the appalling conditions of Dunkirk—than to land one successfully. Dunkirk had been a traumatic experience. No British leader or group of leaders could successfully plead to either his people or his conscience for absolution if the bloodbath of 1914-18 or the degradation of Dunkirk should come once again. So beneath their vociferous declamations that, of course, they viewed a cross-Channel attack as the culminating enterprise of the European war, Churchill and his generals felt great unease. Would it not be better to mount an assault on the Dodecanese or attempt a thrust through the Ljubljana Gap or even an invasion across the Bay of Bengal before the great leap? Increasingly exasperated Americans deflected these flights of fancy, knowing full well that such enterprises would strip the invasion of France of what was absolutely essential yet in chronically short supply: troops and landing craft. With Pacific commanders insistently claiming masses of both, the invasion of France would be run closely enough.

So the British got their way early, and the Americans got their way late—but not too late. In November 1942 a small Allied force invaded western North Africa and in conjunction with Montgomery, whose long-delayed offensive at El Alamein had begun on October 23, succeeded the following spring in finally crushing Rommel. In the interim American forces had been badly bloodied at the Kasserine Pass, and the cocky Yanks learned how frighteningly good the German soldier was. The lesson, like the beating, was absorbed, and the spirit and competence of the American soldier, both initially low, improved markedly. The invasion of Sicily came in the summer of 1943, followed by the easy invasion of Italy at Salerno, then the nearly disastrous effort to outflank German forces by an assault at Anzio, further up the western Italian coast. By the end of 1943 Anglo-American forces seemed bogged down in the endless mud and rain and hills and mountains of southern Italy.

But planning and buildup for the cross-Channel assault continued. North Africa, Sicily, and Italy had toughened the staffs and soldiers of the Allied armies. There could no longer be any excuse for postponing the great crusade in Europe past the coming summer.

But despite the gathering storm of Allied might, the reality of Allied power seemed and was minuscule. Prior to the invasion of Normandy, Allied armies had engaged no more than eleven German divisions in their peripheral probes of the Nazi empire; the Soviet had engaged over ten times that number for two years. The probing, suspicious questions and taunts from the Kremlin continued unabated. When could help—real, measurable aid above and beyond the bits and dribbles of lend-lease materials brought into Murmansk by the inhumanly courageous men of the Arctic convoys —be expected?

The Kremlin was not alone in asking this question. From the first day of the war, and particularly after Britain had been forced off the Continent, Anglo-American strategists and statesmen had continually pondered how best to bring what power they possessed to bear directly on the German heartland. The answer was at hand: air power, the massive bombing of enemy cities and factories. Zealots argued that air power alone could win the war, if not in 1943, as one of them maintained, at least eventually, without the terrible expenditure of blood and treasure entailed in a direct assault on *Festung Europa*. Proponents of air power have consistently overstated their case for a half-century. But in the fearful days in Britain after Dunkirk and in the United States after Pearl Harbor, they seemed the only persons able to deliver an early promise to strike the enemy hard, strike him often, and strike him at home. Thus the RAF's Bomber Command and the U.S. Eighth Air Force quickly sprang into frontline status in the European war between 1940 and 1944.

But the final triumph of strategic bombing did not come at once. In the period between Dunkirk and Pearl Harbor, Bomber Command courageously but incoherently raided Germany and the Continent. By mid-1942, with the Eighth Air Force still slowly collecting in England, Bomber Command's defenders were themselves on the defensive. The prewar assumption that "the Bomber will always get through" had evaporated. No British fighter plane possessed the range to escort the Wellingtons and Blenheims to their targets and back, and nearly three years of war had amply demonstrated the vulnerability of bomber aircraft to flak and fighter defense. If Bomber Command was to retain its position as the foremost strike force in the British arsenal, if it were not to be swept from the skies, then it must exploit all climatic and natural advantages. Daytime flights over the Reich were suicidal. Bombing could only be done at night.

But nighttime precision bombing had demonstrably proved impossible. The difficulty of following terrain, even with the crudely built and mounted radar sets of the time, the omnipresence of industrial smog over the great manufacturing cities of western and central Germany, the variability of climatic conditions, to say nothing of the ever-present searchlights, flak, and fighters which made every flight, in Edward R. Murrow's memorable phrase, "a kind of orchestrated hell," absolutely precluded precision work. Earlier estimates and assumptions that a given target had been "blasted" or "clobbered" proved wildly optimistic. Bomb dropping within a five-mile radius of a given target was considered phenomenal.

It was at this point, in the summer of 1942, that Professor F. A. Lindemann, the personal scientific adviser to Winston Churchill, circulated his top-secret memorandum on the strategic bombing of Germany to a select group within His Majesty's government. Lindemann demanded with extraordinary intensity a new policy of "area bombing." No longer would Bomber Command's efforts be directed at a single industrial target or even a cluster target of factories. Now

bombing must be directed essentially against German working-class houses. Middle-class houses have too much space round them, and so are bound to waste bombs; factories and "military objectives" had long since been forgotten, except in official bulletins, since they were much too difficult to find and hit. The paper claimed that—given a total concentration of effort on the production and use of bombing aircraft— it would be possible, in all the larger towns of Germany (that is, those with more than 50,000 inhabitants), to destroy 50 per cent of all houses.[2]

As is so often the case in modern government, the fate of Lindemann's proposal was linked to an ongoing bureaucratic struggle between Lindemann's own faction of courtiers around the prime minister and an "out-group" composed of Sir Henry Tizard, chairman of the Aeronautical Research Committee, and his followers. The Lindemann paper went to Tizard and his people, who studied the supporting statistics and concluded "that Lindemann's estimate of the number of houses that could possibly be destroyed was five times too high." Indeed, one of Tizard's younger colleagues, the brilliant scientist P. M. S. Blackett, argued that Lindemann's estimates were inflated at least sixfold. But by this time, as C. P. Snow has noted, "Bombing had become a matter of faith." Britain herself had suffered the blitz, Bomber Command was the only service arm even remotely capable of striking the German heartland at this time, millions of pounds had already been expended on its behalf, and to deny the Lindemann strategy would be in effect to deny any further role of significance to strategic bombing.

Immediately the Tizard faction found itself a highly unpopular minority. Bomber Command's newly appointed chief at this time, Arthur "Bomber" Harris, was a vociferous and effective exponent, a truly pugnacious warrior at a time when pugnacity was profoundly valued. Thus, "The Air Ministry fell in behind the Lindemann paper. The minority view was not only defeated, but squashed. The atmosphere was more hysterical than is usual in English official life; it had the faint but just perceptible smell of a witch hunt. Tizard was actually called a defeatist. Strategic bombing, according to the Lindemann policy, was put into action with every effort the country could make." Blackett later echoed Snow's indictment. He, too, had spoken with Lindemann in the summer of 1942 and found Lindemann obsessed with the bombing offensive "to the almost total exclusion of wider considerations." To Lindemann bombing "seemed the one and only useful operation of the war." Lindemann "even suggested that the building up of strong land forces for the projected invasion of France was wrong. Never have I encountered such fanatical belief in the efficacy of bombing."[3]

Men seldom become monsters or embrace a potentially monstrous policy gratuitously. Lurking behind Lindemann's assessment and its acceptance lay the horrible vision of another stalemate in the West on the scale of 1914-18 should Allied forces succeed in landing in France. The First World War had literally eviscerated an entire generation of French and English young men. Anything, any policy, that could avoid a repetition of such horror had at least to be tried.

Nonetheless, it is difficult, if not impossible, to speak dispassionately of the Allied air effort during the Second World War. As it evolved, first in Europe, later in the terrible fire-bomb raids over Japan, it probably accounted for the deaths of more people, more civilians, than any other form of barbarism practiced between 1939 and 1945 except for the Nazi extermination program. Snow, himself safely cast out of the strategic bombing decision by his adherence to the Tizard faction, admitted years later:

It is possible, I suppose, that some time in the future people living in a more benevolent age than ours may turn over the official records and notice that men like us, men well-educated by the standards of the day, and often possessed of strong human feelings, made the kind of calculation I have just been describing. Such calculations, on a much larger scale, are going on at this moment in the most advanced societies we know. What will people of the future think of us? Will they say, as Roger Williams said of some of the Massachusetts Indians, that we were wolves with the minds of men? Will they think that we resigned our humanity? They will have the right.[4]

From the beginning the "area bombing" offensive against Germany carried out by the RAF's Bomber Command was an appalling, pitiless war against the citizenry. Ever more savage means were employed to break civilian morale, culminating in the terrible firestorm raids against Hamburg and the Ruhr cities in the summer of 1943 and against Dresden in February 1945, the latter raid conducted for reasons that David Irving suggests may have been more political than military. Seldom have essentially good and brave young men died for so morally ambiguous an objective. And die they did in vast numbers. To fly unsafe, unwieldy bombers through dark, often abruptly stormy, summer and winter skies, seeking an elusive target protected by a desperate and capable foe fighting above his homeland, was an always exhausting and terrifying experience during these still-early days of flight. Death, when it came, was usually appallingly slow, certain, and bloody. Such was the fate of some fifty thousand young Englishmen. Indeed, Bomber Command suffered proportionately greater casualties in pursuing its mission through six years of war than any other Allied service branch.

As for the United States, aerial bombing was from the beginning part of a broader strategic consideration. Pearl Harbor cast America into a war of two fronts, each thousands of miles from its shores. For all its vaunted industrial might, the country found it logistically impossible to land and sustain a huge army on the Continent in a comparatively short period of time while fighting a simultaneous war in the vast Pacific that required mighty naval and air forces plus ground units of some size to seize and hold enemy island bastions. Somewhere corners had to be cut and compromises made. The solution which American planners reached was the so-called 90-division gamble. Nazi Germany, they concluded, would have to be beaten in the West by a comparatively small, but highly mobile, American army possessed of great firepower joined by the even smaller units of the British, Canadian, and French allies. Given this decision, the attractions of a massive use of air power, both strategic and tactical, proved irresistible.

Strategic bombing would bring presumably devastating power to bear on the enemy even before a single Allied soldier set foot on European soil; strategic bombing would crush the industrial base and popular morale sustaining the enemy effort. Once Allied armies came ashore in Europe, tactical bombing in front of Allied forces would disrupt the enemy's immediate rear. The cost in both men and machines would be far less, air zealots successfully argued, than a comparable investment in and total reliance upon conventional ground forces. Thus the determination to obtain as much power as cheaply as possible, what in later postwar years would be irreverently dubbed "more bangs for a buck," dictated American use of strategic air power in Europe after Pearl Harbor.

Initially, of course, the U.S. Eighth Air Force chose to follow a different—and more humane—bombing strategy than did the RAF. The Americans came to England, and later to Italy with the Fifteenth Air Force, convinced that daylight precision bombing of German industrial targets was feasible with the better armed B-17, a truly remarkable bomber aircraft. American strategy centered around mutually protective formation flying as opposed to the RAF's "bomber stream" approach. It took the Eighth Air Force over a year of fearsome casualties, culminating in the Black Thursday raid on Schweinfurt in October of 1943, to realize that even the B-17s could not stand up alone to German fighter aircraft and that precision bombing was insufficiently precise to destroy the industrial base supporting the Luftwaffe. The Luftwaffe would have to be shot from the skies over Germany before daylight precision bombing could in any way be effective. In fact, the American strategy was not infeasible. Speer has stated in a little-noted passage that the Black Thursday raid on the Schweinfurt ball-bearing plants was quite effective and that if the Eighth Air Force had been able to swallow a second day of heavy losses while maintaining a similar level of bombing precision, it might have attained its objective of crippling German industry—and thus the Luftwaffe and Wehrmacht—for some months. We are thus left to conclude that American bombing strategy in Europe down to the end of 1943 was both suicidal and effective. But neither the American high command nor the American public would tolerate 50 percent losses for 60 to 70 percent effectiveness.

After the terrible losses of autumn 1943 the Eighth Air Force retired for the winter to regroup and reflect, then returned to the Continent with the fundamental objective of obliterating the Luftwaffe. The Americans had a new weapon in their arsenal, a fighter aircraft with sufficient range to escort the bomber formations all the way to the target and back. With the coming of the P-51 fighter plane, immensely maneuverable, very fast, and long-range, the doom of the Luftwaffe, steadily depleted of skilled pilots if not of planes after five years of war, was at hand.* During several weeks in the early spring of 1944 the Eighth Air Force with its fighter escort dueled the Luftwaffe over Berlin and won. Thereafter protection of the American precision daylight-bombing program was assured. But it was never as devastating as its proponents had vociferously argued.

In general, Americans have comparatively little to be ashamed of concerning their country's air offensive against Germany. Contrary to popular belief and novelistic assertion, for example, Americans did not participate in the ghastly, initial night raid against Dresden that probably killed 130,000 people; this was a Bomber Command "show." But such comparative restraint later disappeared during the aerial offensive against Japan. Here again the fanatics were allowed full control. By the early spring of 1945, following six months of high-altitude, daylight bombing, the great new B-29 aircraft were achieving the most minimal results against Japan, and all the publicity in the Pacific war seemed to be going to the navy and marines. Curtis LeMay, angry and determined, ordered his bombers stripped of all excessive materials, loaded with incendiaries, and flown in nighttime streams at an altitude of five thousand feet literally to burn out and burn up any and all Japanese cities that could be reached. The strategy of "Bomber" Harris and Professor Lindemann was thus carried to the most inhuman extremes.

The justification for this barbaric tactic was that Japanese industry had been widely dispersed into backyard factories and that the only way it could be reached and destroyed was through completely indiscriminate assault. Again there was an available motive: the expected invasion of Japan was drawing near; every bullet, every machine, every gun built or assembled in the backyard factories could kill an American boy. But the result was the same as

* Surviving German air aces in their memoirs express profound bitterness at the chaotic state of German aircraft production prior to Speer's takeover in 1944. The indecision over what types and numbers of planes to build during the first five years of combat, these survivors complain, did much to cripple the Luftwaffe's war effort. If true, these men are complaining about a general and fatal pattern in Nazi war making.

with Bomber Command's earlier "area" nighttime bombing of Germany: thousands upon thousands upon thousands of burned acres and corpses littering the streets of smoldering enemy cities as dawn appeared. If there were no atheists in foxholes during the Second World War, there were no altruists either. The Allied bombings of Germany and Japan, unlike any other strategic decisions of the war, demonstrate that in this century no one is immune from criminal madness.

In June of 1944 Allied forces at last returned to Europe, and after a month's savage fighting at the Normandy bridgehead, they broke out to flood over all of France and southern Belgium. But Nazi Germany had already been defeated by the Red Army in the East. This was not apparent to, or at least not admitted by, the euphoric peoples of the West; it was nonetheless true. There was to be much hard fighting ahead on both the eastern and western fronts before the remnants of the once-proud Wehrmacht were at last subdued, but the European war was already winding down to its inevitable denouement by the time Eisenhower launched his crusade. What strategy did the Soviet and Western allies follow in the conquest of Germany? Was there any serious effort or thought given to thwarting Soviet achievements and aspirations at this late date? And if so, how did Anglo-American leaders believe this objective could be achieved?

To state the matter baldly, the overwhelming weight of evidence indicates that both Stalin and Roosevelt continued to wage purely military warfare once the Anglo-American armies fought their way onto the Continent, while Churchill increasingly permitted political judgments to dictate strategic decisions. But Churchill was isolated from the start. On D-Day the proportionate weight of American and British effort was nearly equal. Thereafter the preponderance of American power—and thus influence—steadily grew. Even as Overlord was being plotted, Churchill had given way on the question of supreme command; his chief of the Imperial General Staff, Alanbrooke, was passed over in favor of Eisenhower. Soon after D-Day Montgomery, initially Eisenhower's immediate subordinate, was forced to share that spot with Omar Bradley. By the time of the final drive against Germany in the West, American forces outnumbered their British and Canadian allies three to one.

This situation allowed Eisenhower virtually free rein to pursue his own strategic impulses, which were deeply rooted in the American military tradition. From the time of Ulysses S. Grant, the chief objective of military operations had always been the shattering defeat of enemy forces, not the capture of enemy territory or the subjugation of enemy political centers. This objective had been subverted by the victorious but exhausted Allied coalition in the First World War to the eternal despair of John J. Pershing, who impressed on the entire younger generation of military leaders, Eisenhower among them, the folly of allowing an enemy army to disband essentially undefeated. Ike was not about to repeat that mistake, and neither was FDR.

From the breakout at St. Lô and the successful invasion of southern France two months later, Eisenhower determinedly pursued a broad-front strategy in which the enemy was forced to engage Allied forces at every point on every day or risk being overrun. Thus was the enemy totally engaged and thus could he be totally destroyed. War would be a massive killing match in which superior Anglo-American mobility and firepower would wear down and obliterate the last disciplined columns the Wehrmacht possessed. It was a brutal strategic doctrine that Ike preached and pursued; modern war was not to be waged as an elegant minuet of maneuver either by small professional armies as in the eighteenth century or by powerful armored columns as in the twentieth. War was regarded coldly and objectively in terms of total victory. Unconditional surrender was to be achieved by so complete a destruction of enemy forces and morale as to leave no question of victory or defeat.

Ike only modified his strategy once in eleven months of steady warfare. When the sweep across France and up into southern Belgium and Luxembourg had been completed in early September, Churchill and Montgomery pressed a contradictory proposal: a "pencil-like thrust" through northern Belgium, across the Rhine, and on to the north German plain to capture Berlin before the winter of 1944. Under constant prodding and expostulation, Eisenhower finally agreed. A "carpet" of American and British paratroops was to be laid through German lines in Belgium, and Montgomery's forces were then to race across it and on into the Nazi rear, catapulting across the Rhine. But the paratroop operations failed and Montgomery's army never got untracked—the Allies had planned "a bridge too far." Market Garden, as it came to be known, failed for a number of reasons. British critics have always charged that Ike begrudged Montgomery the support and supplies necessary to insure success. American critics, joined recently by some British revisionists, such as Liddell Hart and Cornelius Ryan, reply either that the idea of a concentrated assault was conceptually faulty from the beginning or that if it had to be tried, Patton on the southern wing of the Allied armies should have been given the task, not Montgomery. (It should be noted that a number of British staff officers at Ike's headquarters viewed Market Garden with the same disquietude as their American counterparts.) Patton had for weeks swept all before him. German forces opposite his front were disrupted, disorganized, demoralized, while the Nazi forces facing Montgomery had fallen back in comparatively disciplined fashion and had lost neither their cohesion nor their morale.

Whatever the merits or demerits of the Montgomery-versus-Patton argument, the failure of Market Garden was so demonstrably injurious that Ike never again abandoned the broad-front strategy. The reverberations from Market Garden were far reaching. Market Garden was the first real defeat of Western arms on the Continent since Dunkirk. Though casualties were not as enormous as such a defeat might indicate, the blow to morale was considerable. But the transcendant effect of Market Garden was logistical and chronological. As a number of critics have observed, the chief objective of Allied forces after the Normandy breakout should have been the port of Antwerp and the Schelde Estuary which protected it, not the north German plain. As late as Market Garden, the Anglo-American armies, which had stretched out to a broad front on an arc from Belgium to eastern France, were still receiving their supplies from either Cherbourg or Marseilles, hundreds of miles behind the battle lines. Not even the famous Red Ball Express of fast truck convoys could keep the British and American forces adequately supplied. The failure of Market Garden compounded this increasingly critical logistical problem. When Montgomery turned toward Antwerp following Market Garden, he found that taking the port and its adjacent estuary in vile November weather was a formidable task. Not until the end of the year, after the near disaster in the Ardennes, were the British and American armies in northern Europe assured of sufficient supplies to mount a sustained offensive.

The surprise German offensive in the Ardennes in December 1944, the so-called Battle of the Bulge, revealed the shameful state of Allied intelligence and the comparative rawness of the Anglo-American armies still in a state of buildup. The American units facing the first great Nazi thrust, for example, had just reached Europe. But in retrospect the Nazi offensive does not appear as fearsome as it did at the time. Hitler gambled all he had in the West, yet if he had not done so, the subsequent battle for Germany proper might have been a much bloodier and more drawn-out affair for both Soviet and Western forces than it was. As it happened, the last best Nazi units were contained after a comparatively short penetration in bad winter weather, then mercilessly chewed to pieces by air and ground power when the skies cleared. The initial German bulge became an awful trap when British forces from the north and Patton's armor from the south closed around it. Those Nazi forces that managed to escape before the jaws of the trap snapped shut reeled back into Germany in a rout.

Thereafter Eisenhower had his own way, and his own way was most definitely the broad front. Regrouping his forces and building up the supplies that were now streaming in through Antwerp, Ike launched his last, great offensive into Germany at the end of January 1945.

The Soviets, meanwhile, reached the Oder River, only thirty miles from Berlin, on February 1. And here we reach one of the great mysteries of the war, whose solution reveals not only how the war was fought but how the incipient victors then felt toward each other and their own interests. Why did not the Soviets press on and take Berlin during the Yalta Conference, forcing Western acknowledgment of Soviet dominance in Germany? It is true that Nazi forces on the Oder were still formidable in terms of numbers, morale and experience. Hitler had dispatched many of his best remaining units westward to the Ardennes, but he retained forces of sufficient size and quality on the Oder to give the Russians a very rough time. It is also true that the Red Army was then hobbled by the same logistical problems that had plagued Anglo-American forces early in the year. But the Russians reached the Oder at the very beginning of February; they did not mount their final offensive toward Berlin until mid-April, ten weeks later! What on earth were they doing in this time?

What the Red Army was doing, of course, was pursuing the same broad-front strategy, with the same exterminating objective, as were Eisenhower's forces. Available evidence now indicates that Stalin enjoyed playing his generals off against one another during the eighteen months of the great Russian offensive of 1943-45 so long as they did not get out of hand. By early 1945 Marshal Zhukov was threatening to do just that on the Oder. Stalin personally reined him in, sending Zhukov to clear Nazi forces out of Pomerania, while bringing the northern and southern flanks of the Red Army into line with the central forces along the Oder throughout February and March. Not until a generally broad front was achieved in the East roughly thirty to fifty miles from the Nazi capital, did Stalin at last send Zhukov's men across the Oder and toward Berlin. Was Stalin then fighting a predominantly military, as opposed to a political, war? Perhaps. Certainly his strategy reflected that of Eisenhower. But powerful political considerations may also have been at work in his calculations. As Peter Calvocoressi has noted, had Stalin ended the war abruptly in February 1945, he would have been master of at least half of Germany and the entire German capital.

A dominant position in Germany could be more of a hazard than an asset so long as the war-weary USSR had not the strength to sustain it against a western coalition, and although Stalin banked on Roosevelt's determination to withdraw from Europe [firmly expressed on the opening day of the Yalta Conference], he must also have recalled that Churchill had in 1919 not only supported western intervention in the USSR but had advocated the use of the German army to effect it.[5]

Beyond the immediate consideration of the Soviet position in Germany lay Soviet interests in Eastern Europe. Stalin was determined to master this region as one means of forestalling future German aggression should the planned partition of the country eventually give way to reunification. How better to impress the peoples of Rumania, Czechoslovakia, and elsewhere with the power of the Red Army and the Soviet state than to obliterate surviving German units? In pursuing a broad-front strategy, Stalin could achieve both military and political objectives. He could slake his and his country's thirst for the most brutal revenge against a brutal invader by killing thousands of the invader's soldiers, while at the same time securing comparatively modest but essential political objectives.

With the arrival of the Red Army on the Oder only hours after Eisenhower had launched his last offensive in the West, any realistic hope of taking Berlin ahead of the Soviets disappeared. To have tried would have constituted an egregious insult to an ally, and Eisenhower, to his eternal credit—and the credit of the president who supported him—never tried. Indeed, by directly informing Stalin in March of his intentions to avoid Berlin in pursuit of the Nazi remnants, Eisenhower may have deferred for some months a real rupture in relations between Russia and the West. Certainly by the spring of 1945 many potential sources of disruption had emerged: Rumania, Poland, Trieste, and the clandestine surrender of Nazi forces in northern Italy to Western representatives. It was a time for discretion if the Grand Alliance was not to collapse before at least securing the cherished Western defeat of Japan. In steadfastly pursuing military victory, not impossible political objectives as Churchill so ardently wished, Eisenhower and his American superiors undoubtedly avoided a dangerous turn in contemporary history.

Comparatively little analysis has been devoted to the effects of Allied strategy in Asia and the Pacific, which is indeed unfortunate. For the strategy pursued in the Far East did as much to shape the contours of the postwar world as any comparable decisions in Europe.

From the start, of course, the Pacific and Asian theaters were primarily an American preoccupation. Except in Burma, where British forces contained a large Japanese army threatening India, the United States contributed at least 85 percent of all forces engaged against Japan. Following stabilization of military and naval balance of power at Midway, the United States seized a modest initiative. Two broad avenues to Japan were available. But the one from the Asian mainland quickly proved impossible to exploit. Japan's presence in Burma and east China effectively blocked the only readily available gateways to Chiang Kai-shek, and what comparatively meager supplies did get through to the China front during most of the war had to be flown in over the famous and always dangerous Himalayan "hump." The only serious effort to exploit China as a base came in 1944 with the buildup in Szechuan province of B-29 bomber bases, from which the initial series of assaults against Japan were launched. But these bases were terribly vulnerable to enemy attack and, indeed, were overrun soon after abandonment during the last great Japanese offensive of November 1944. By this time the B-29s had been shifted to bases in the Marianas Islands, from which they would operate for the remainder of the war. From the beginning the Pacific sea and island route proved the most feasible approach to Japan.

In early August 1942 the Americans landed at Guadalcanal in the Solomons in the first limited Allied offensive of the Pacific war. The objective was to puncture the southern flank of Japan's mid-ocean ribbon defense, which threatened to cut off the supply route between the United States and Australia. This proved a difficult task. Over a year of costly effort was needed to destroy or neutralize the enemy in the lush, fetid islands and warm, blue seas of the Solomon and Bismarck barriers that blocked the northern and northwestern routes from Australia. By late summer 1943 this task had at last been accomplished; the ribbon defense had been breached, and the next series of strategic decisions had to be made. They proved to be surprisingly modest and unimaginative.

Between August 1943 and March of the following year three groups, the Combined Staff Planners, the Joint Chiefs of Staff, and the Joint Strategic Survey Committee, advanced various plans for the ongoing Pacific offensive. Creative thought, however, was stifled by a number of factors. First, American strategists were adamantly opposed to use of either French military or British naval units, advancing logistical considerations in defense of their prejudices. It was no secret that after Pearl Harbor the United States government and people considered the Pacific theater uniquely their own. Whether employment of substantial French and British forces would have accelerated the pace of victory across Oceania must remain conjectural: it was never tried. A second crippling influence on midwar strategic planning for the Pacific lay in the earlier decision—taken by Roosevelt and Churchill at the White House conference in late December 1941—to concentrate the bulk of Anglo-American resources on defeating Hitler first. Although Admiral King was able to scrape together enough men and materiel to commence and sustain a limited offensive in the Pacific from late 1942 onward (his determination to secure and hoard precious landing craft may well have tipped the balance against the invasion of France in 1943), the "big buildup" in England and the Mediterranean areas deprived the Pacific of sufficient resources for a massive offensive. The third and final impediment centered about the person and influence of Douglas MacArthur. The ostensible hero of Bataan demanded the speediest possible reconquest of the Philippines on purely moral grounds, and public opinion supported him. MacArthur's reputation in the United States was never higher than during the Second World War, and this was a political consideration which the artful Roosevelt and the equally sensitive civil and military figures around him could never ignore.

So a number of apparently compelling factors shaped Pacific strategy along rigidly conservative lines. Having pierced the outer ring of Japanese defenses by mid-1943, American forces would launch a two-pronged attack toward the Philippines from both the southwest and central Pacific, bypassing and neutralizing some Japanese strongpoints in the inner-Pacific island rings and frontally assaulting and reducing others. It would be a bloody business, but there seemed no other way.

The question remains as to whether this strategic approach was not highly wasteful in time, men, and materiel. Did the moral commitment to reinvade the Philippines outweigh the responsibility of cold strategic calculation? Should the political influence of Douglas MacArthur have outweighed the common sense of Chester Nimitz? Could not Nimitz and King and the rest of the U.S. Navy have gone even further than they did in presenting strategic alternatives to the agonizing, island-by-island tactics that were adopted? The Pacific war was primarily a naval and air war, and it can be argued that by mid-1944 at the latest the U.S. Navy and its carrier air units were strong enough to have accelerated the offensive pace far faster than it was.

In retrospect, a central and northern Pacific offensive, bypassing the Palaus and Philippines in favor of direct strikes north from the Marianas toward Iwo Jima (desperately needed as a "way station" for crippled B-29s returning from Japan) and Okinawa, might well have been the best decision. After the first battle of the Philippine Sea in June 1944, the Japanese fleet was a helpless remnant of what it had once been. Over two years of war had substantially reduced, though by no means eliminated, its battleship and cruiser flotillas. The naval air arm was almost completely destroyed in the Marianas Turkey Shoot. Those Japanese carriers which did remain were nearly all new, run by green crews, and carried frightfully inexperienced pilots. The best airmen Japan ever had were now slowly sinking to the bottom all over the Pacific from Midway to Santa Cruz to Saipan. The U.S. Navy by contrast had grown to enormous size and complexity. As early as the spring of 1944 it covered forty square miles of ocean; indeed, as early as 1943 it had become the largest fleet the world had ever seen. And only a fraction of it was in European or Mediterranean waters.

It is interesting, if fruitless, to speculate on the might-have-beens had a "pencil-like thrust" been attempted in the Pacific in late 1944. The bulk of Japan's remaining naval forces presumably would have been at Singapore as they were before the opening of the Battle for Leyte Gulf. They could not have ignored a sudden American thrust at Iwo Jima in August or September 1944 and would have had to respond, so that the last great naval battle would have been fought in the waters in and around the Bonins, rather than in the Philippines. This would have permitted the Japanese to stage land-based aircraft from both the Philippines and the home islands through Formosa and Okinawa respectively. But these planes and their inexperienced pilots would still have been near the end of their resources when they attacked the American navy, whose own carrier forces had swollen to prodigious size and enormous competence. An abrupt, unforeseen American attack so close to Japan this soon might well have panicked Japanese strategists sufficiently to induce them to commit every plane and pilot they could, thus virtually stripping the home islands of air cover for the simultaneous mass assaults by the B-29s and the later American invasion.

What would have been the risks and costs of this bold strategy, which would undoubtedly have brought the United States to the gates of Japan by the end of 1944 rather than by the summer of 1945? Three come immediately to mind. In the first place, mass kamikaze attacks might well have been mounted against the American fleet on a scale never witnessed. For by the time the kamikazes were unleashed at Okinawa in the spring of 1945, the Japanese air force in the Philippines had been destroyed. If the Philippines had been bypassed in favor of a direct thrust at the Bonins and Ryukyus, these planes could presumably have been pressed into service. But possibly not. The kamikaze corps was admittedly a hastily conceived response to a desperate situation. Nonetheless, rather vigorous efforts were made, at least in the beginning, to provide pilots with some rudimentary training as well as a sense of total fanaticism. The kamikaze was, as he was expected to be, a unique being, and his creation took time. It may well be asked whether the Japanese could have pressed their air force in the Philippines into service as an *effective* kamikaze weapon in a short time had the Americans opted in late summer of 1944 to invade Iwo Jima rather than Peleliu and then the Philippines.

Assuming that a successful and not exorbitantly costly invasion of Iwo had been mounted in September or even August 1944, American strategists and statesmen would then have faced another deadly risk. Japanese authorities in the bypassed Philippines might well have threatened a massive blood bath against both Philippine civilians and the substantial number of American prisoners of war still in the archipelago. It cannot be forgotten that captured American fliers were executed in Japan following the emperor's announcement of surrender and that the executioners *knew* that within hours or at most days they would be called to account. Only the most reckless hatred can explain their behavior. To have permitted the enemy garrison in the Philippines to hold a huge native population and thousands of American prisoners of war under the gun for weeks if not months would have been to expect great restraint from both American strategists and Japanese soldiers. Yet in choosing the island-by-island strategy, was not the risk of a blood bath by berserk Japanese soldiers just as great? Nothing save honor, decency, and restraint kept the Japanese garrison in Manila from murdering everyone in the Santo Tomas prison compound and the surrounding streets once word came that American forces had landed at Lingayen and were nearing the city. Barbaric behavior by an enemy is a constant threat in every war and has seldom dominated strategic considerations.

A possible third risk in choosing to race toward Japan proper in mid-1944 revolved, interestingly enough, around Soviet-American relations. Although Allied planning teams did not assume a Soviet entry into the war against Japan in 1942 or 1943, American officials sought such a Russian commitment from mid-1942 onward, and at last, at the Moscow Foreign Ministers Conference of October 1943, Stalin gave it. Over a year later Roosevelt went to Yalta burdened with the warning of his planners that an invasion of Japan would be necessary and that it might cost upward of a million casualties. The president sought and obtained Stalin's renewed pledge to enter the Pacific conflict within three months after victory in Europe. Thereafter Roosevelt, Truman, and finally Harry Hopkins in May-June 1945 continued vigorously and successfully to hold Stalin to this commitment. At Potsdam, just two weeks before Hiroshima, Soviet and American military officials held a most fruitful meeting at which respective zones of military operations against Japan were defined and the limits and levels of mutual cooperation were worked out to general satisfaction. Truman considered the conference a success if for no other reason than this.

But what would have been the impact on Soviet-American relations at Yalta in February 1945 had American forces appeared on Japan's doorstep at the same moment that the Red Army reached the Oder? Might not Stalin have believed that something was rotten in the state of the Grand Alliance? Would he have sent what forces he had in the Far East rushing precipitately into the Asian war before the Americans could conclude it? And would not the presence of American forces in the Bonins and Ryukyus this early have been self-defeating politically if not militarily? Surely the Pacific offensive could not have been sustained to the point of invading Japan in the spring of 1945, and the atomic bombs did not constitute at that time a ready and certain weapons system. Surely an American rush to Japan's doorstep in late 1944 and early 1945 might well have induced further strain in the Grand Alliance just at the moment when it seemed to have been revived in all its comradely vigor at Yalta.

Yet with all the risks, possible costs, and might-have-beens inherent in such a contrary strategy, was not the decision to expend vast amounts of men and blood and material in the long-drawn-out reconquest of the Philippines equally questionable? Had a thrust toward the Bonins and Ryukyus been made in late summer or early autumn 1944, might it not have been possible to hasten that crippling air and naval blockade of Japan which came only in the summer of 1945? The U.S. Strategic Bombing Survey concluded after the war that Japan would have been starved into submission no later than November or December 1945—in other words, after six months of steady blockade. Had that blockade commenced in December 1944 or even February 1945 (always presuming that the Japanese fleet would have sailed in defense of the Bonins as it did in defense of the Philippines—and with the same fatal result) would not Japan have surrendered by late spring or very early summer? The Japanese and their enemies would then have been spared the horror, however brief, of atomic warfare. What then would have been the contours of the postwar world?

Here speculation must finally end, for the fact is that from the beginning, early reconquest of the Philippines was the cornerstone of American strategic planning in the Pacific, and this decision, given the geographic position of the archipelago, dictated the waging of that same kind of broad-front war which Eisenhower was conducting in northwestern Europe. Douglas MacArthur had pledged an American return to the Philippines, and his commander-in-chief refused to contradict him. The Philippines, no less than China, had been a long-time charge on the American conscience; the reconquest of the archipelago and all that it meant in terms of redeemed commitments as well as just retribution for the humiliations of Bataan and Corregidor could not be avoided. Thus no thought was seriously given to the kind of "pencil-like thrust" in the Pacific that Montgomery had tried at Arnhem. Rather, pressure was applied unremittingly, on island after island, with only the strongest Japanese bastions bypassed and neutralized. Such a grinding, broad-front war in Asia as in Europe demanded the kind of coalition diplomacy, the kind of Grand Alliance, that was forged, however briefly, between East and West. Self-interest rather than temperamental affinity or even common aspiration thus at last defined the great Allied coalition of 1941-45. And when common victory removed mutual self-interest, both the dictatorships and democracies felt themselves free, in Churchill's memorable words, to resume those follies which had so nearly and so recently cost them their lives.

The Victims

5

STANDING FOR a moment in a frozen, shell-shattered street in Stalingrad near Christmastime 1942, a German staff doctor who must have been a great man—or a small man suddenly seized by a great vision—remarked, "In this war, the victims are more important than the victory." Thirty-five years later his comment remains a fitting benediction to the agony of 1939-45.

For a third of a century the global landscape has remained strewn with the victims of the great holocaust. Who were and are they? Well, to begin with there were the dead. So many millions perished so unspeakably that the term "obscene" can scarcely encompass their ordeal. Consider for a moment what it must have been like to end one's life at nineteen or twenty-four or twelve or younger in the death camps of Nazi Europe, tortured, terrified, starved, exhausted, before being driven at last into the gas chambers. One had little or no time to rationalize fright, to taste the fullness and fragility of love, to hate or to oppose with that passion which all too often passes for intelligence, to sense the full wonder of one's mortality and possibilities. How stunted, wretched, and bewildering the brief flicker of existence. For so many souls, life was defined by horror and doom before full self-consciousness could take hold. Here lay the real theory and practice of the Nazi hell: innocence was not only slaughtered; it was first deformed. In the very denial of life itself lay the real barbarism of the Nazi age.

But the dead, however poignantly they perished, however deeply they have been missed, can tell us nothing more beyond their ordeal.

What of the survivors, so many of whom are with us still? The list of victims here is very long, indeed. Where should we begin? With the physically and mentally maimed, locked away in countless soldiers' homes or carrying on as best they can in the daily life of great cities and remote villages across Europe and Asia and America? With the wretched victims "of pure blood" who were either directly bred or as small children torn forever from homes and parents to satisfy the perverted Nazi *Lebensborn* program of "racial superiority"? With the nisei, whose memories of half a dozen western American concentration camps will never dim? With the pitiful remains of Europe's few monarchies—the Yugoslav and Rumanian to name two—who managed to survive the collapse of kingdoms in the Great War of 1914-18 only to be ground to pieces twenty-five years later between the brutal Nazi onslaught and the ruthless demands of a powerful collective movement? With the utterly defeated political idealists such as Eastern Europe's socialists or agrarian democrats who were brushed aside by the Communist juggernaut in 1944 and 1945 and again in 1948? With those comparative few marked for doom of one sort or another who somehow managed to evade their fate, like the handful of survivors of Auschwitz or Hiroshima, only to suffer the horrors of a perpetually living death until their bodies at last expired? We have scarcely begun.

What of the victims of imperial pretension who not only refused to heed the palpable lessons of the war but fruitlessly sought to stem that tide of political awakening among the peoples of Asia and Africa which the war brought to climax? We may not grieve for their anguish but we must grieve for their actions. So many of the old men of Europe refused to surrender their ancient pretensions without a fight, and so once again they sent the young men out to die in defense of them. Suez and Algeria, Malaya and Indochina, Palestine and Indonesia are a few of the names that mark the failures of the old and the graves of the young, sacrificed to a fallacious imperial cause.

What of the Poles, whose ultimate folly was simply to lie between the two greatest powers on the European continent? A bastard people geopolitically, the Poles were no wiser or more foolish in their behavior during the interwar years than anyone else, yet their struggle for firm and enduring national self-identity and self-sufficiency was crushed by the Nazi and Soviet invaders in 1939, largely ignored by the leaders of the West in pursuit of a grander cause thereafter, and obliterated for all practical purposes by the Soviets once more in 1944-45. One can argue a terrible necessity in all this, given the frightful facts of international life one-third of a century ago. But the tragedy remains.

What of the Kuomintang Chinese, another group ground to powder by the fearsome forces of mid-twentieth-century history? For a time they had striven to bring order and a measure of modern reform to a land fallen into chaos and bloodshed. But they never really had a chance. Increasingly challenged by a Communist opposition which waxed in power and support on every failure and folly of the national government, gravely threatened after 1937 by a Japanese invader who soon controlled the richest coastal and urban areas of the country, driven back a thousand agonizing miles up the Yangtze to Chungking, whose citizens were hounded by pitiless bombardment from the air day after day, the Kuomintang regime by 1944 had begun a fatal descent into corruption, incompetence, apathy. It was at this moment that the well-meaning but grossly ignorant American ally insisted on foisting upon the exhausted regime the prestige and expectations of great-power status. Little wonder that relations between American and Kuomintang officials became charged with venom as the Chinese sought to extract every advantage and evade every responsibility while the Americans increasingly refused to confer advantage without evidence of responsibility. The United States moved into Nationalist China, tried to re-create its government and peoples in an American image, and then wondered why the Communist opposition and millions of articulate Asians believed that the Kuomintang was nothing but a client state of the last Western power with imperial ambitions. Whatever the respective merits and demerits of the Kuomintang and Communist positions in early postwar China, America used China during and immediately following the Second World War as a symbol of moral imperialism, and subsequent American disillusionment is dwarfed by the awful tragedy which American policy helped set in motion.

What of France? In 1940 she was seemingly the greatest and most efficient military power in the world, possessing a vast and seemingly placid global empire and a multimillion-man army crouched within and behind the magnificent Maginot Line. By 1959 the country had been totally defeated in war, physically and emotionally ruined by occupation, and ravaged by the slow, agonizing losses of Indochina and Algeria, the richest jewels in the imperial crown. For nearly thirty years a vestige of national pride was maintained by glorious tales of citizen resistance to the Nazi invader, but ultimately that illusion too was destroyed. A younger generation made—and flocked to see—films such as *The Sorrow and the Pity* and *Lacombe, Lucien*, which pitilessly exposed the depth of national collaboration. Long-suppressed memories of active help in the Nazi search for and elimination of France's Jewish population were revived with all the inherent sense of shame and hypocrisy. For countless Frenchmen the war has not yet ended— and possibly never will end short of the grave.

And what of the Jews, those born after 1945 and outside Europe, as well as those who survived the holocaust? Theirs has been a strange odyssey. Unshakably determined to carve a religious state in the ancient biblical homeland in order to obliterate the specter of the pogrom, fitfully aided for the first time by a world stunned by the knowledge of Treblinka, Dachau, and Auschwitz, thousands of Jews crept into Palestine only to find themselves in the midst of a native Arab population whose traditional anti-Jewish prejudices and cultural pride were roused to fury by an unprecendented threat to long-cherished homes, lands, and religious sites. The forcible creation of the state of Israel finally set the somnolent Middle East ablaze, and that blaze has not yet been quenched. Forced from the beginning to fight zealous Arabs and confused and angry Britons for the right to create a homeland, the remnants of European Jewry often revealed how deeply the holocaust had corrupted their own souls. Terrorist Jewish bands of long standing in Palestine received an influx of eager recruits, and before long the *Stern* and the *Irgun* and other groups were bombing British hotels and clubs and exterminating Arab villages with as eager and stealthy an abandon as ever had been used against the Jews of Europe.

When we speak of the Jews and of the pathetic survivors of Hiroshima and Nagasaki, we come to those whose "relationship to the contemporary technology of murder" (to use Robert Jay Lifton's phrase) has been most intimate. These are the people who have been most fully exposed to the "death dominated history" of our times. But have not all of us imbibed to a greater or lesser degree "the psychology of massive death immersion"? Lifton speaks of "the systematic murder of millions of Jews—*and the extent of psychic numbing this project required of both victim and victimizers*" (italics his).[1] But systematic murder has not been a Nazi—or a Communist—monopoly in the mid- and late-twentieth-century world. For whatever reasons, however compelling they may have been or seemed, few peoples alive today can escape identification with some project of mass death. Therefore few can claim to have escaped exposure to the "psychic numbing" such projects require of the victimizer. The words of the German staff doctor at Stalingrad steal into the mind in inverted form. The victors of the Second World War were as victimized by the bloodshed as the vanquished.

The history of the postwar world—in poignant and gruesome contrast to the aspirations of millions a generation ago—has been the history of death on a massive scale and of the increasing acceptance of death as a way of life. In China, in Czechoslovakia, in Korea, in Palestine, in Indochina, in Algeria, in Hungary, in Berlin and Greece and a score of other places around the postwar world, violence has become the accepted means of resolving all problems, all tensions, all confrontations, all frustrations. To this day power remains a harlot to be picked up in the street by the man with the machine gun. Not even the oldest or ostensibly most secure and stable of societies has escaped the lure of violent confrontation, as the wave of assassinations, bombings, gassings, and shootings in the United States in the 1960s indicates.

It is this very lack of stability anywhere, this very susceptibility to violent confrontation everywhere, that so distinguishes our wartime and postwar era from any other in modern times. Formerly entire classes and regions and, for long periods, certain countries as well were exempt from the threat of violence and terror. If, for example, violence has been "as American as apple pie," it is nevertheless true that violence in the United States was confined to certain times and places, classes and processes. No more. Now the meanest citizen and the most exalted statesman, here as elsewhere, share a sense of threat and menace in their daily lives. No one feels safe from assault and abuse. Comparative wealth is everywhere; true security and comfort are nowhere to be found.

Some will argue that this trend is at once universal and beneficial, that the "comfortable" classes of the earth, whether imperialist, capitalist, racist, sexually chauvinist, parental, or otherwise, are being forced to surrender ill-gotten or assumed privileges of exploitation. But the very meanness of contemporary dialogue and behavior at last argues against such an easy generality. The several generations of human beings now inhabiting this earth have been victimized more than they dare admit by the systematic murders of our time, to which all have either been participants or witnesses, and by that psychic numbing which exposure to mass murder invariably creates.

The United States provides a perfect social laboratory within which these contemporary trends can be assessed and analyzed. America has *not* acted with unique brutality in the postwar world. Indeed, when one examines the options open to the government and people of the United States, one is forced to conclude that in comparison with other world powers of earlier and modern times America has generally behaved with some restraint, a striking degree of generosity, and occasional wisdom. In a consistently imperfect world, that is all that probably can ever be expected of any society and polity. Yet the American nation has been widely accused of perpetrating atrocious crimes even as American society has been increasingly wracked by the rhetoric and actuality of mass social violence. Between 1968 and 1970 America drifted perilously close to civil war, in which the educated young and a significant body of equally ardent followers "over thirty" faced the rest of the country in militant, "nonnegotiable" confrontation. Lives were lost, and innocents as well as participants on both sides perished before the squall of social protest blew itself out. How did it come about? One answer can surely be found in the experiences, values, perspectives, and actions of that veteran generation of Americans who came home from Europe and the Pacific at the end of the Second World War determined to fashion lives of security and meaning for themselves and their children's children.

Generalization is inherently dangerous and deceptive. The influence of collective experience must always be weighed against the uniqueness of private lives. Nonetheless, it can be said that those Americans born between, say, 1910 and 1925 did share an experience of depression and war which cast a pattern of tragedy and triumph over their lives. Throughout the postwar era that pattern was worked out in millions of variations until at last a social order was fashioned of such affluence and rigidity as to insure an explosive counterreaction.

If you were born in the United States between 1910 and 1925 and were poor or nearly so as many were then, you imbibed certain beliefs and standards and assumptions, and certain things happened to you or you saw certain things happening which forever after shaped your outlook and behavior and instincts. There were norms, standards, and traditions that had been handed down from generation to generation, and you did not question them. You were taught to revere the country and flag even if your parents could not speak the language. The sanctity of the family structure, with its pattern of male careerism and female homemaking, did not need to be preached; it was assumed:

> You learned about cleanliness by walking on the newspapers spread over your mother's freshly washed floor. When you got a present of any kind, even a spool without thread, you played with it for two weeks, kept it in your box of valuable possessions along with bottle tops and baseball cards and, if your father consented, put it under your pillow before dreams about the Gas House Gang filled your thoughts. Loyalty to wife and family, appreciation for what you had, kindness, respect, cheerfulness, hard work, often beyond the requirements of the job— these were what counted.[2]

Maybe you came to adolescence in the mid-twenties and your family was making it well for the first time, and life was good and seemed secure. But then, suddenly, there was the Depression, and you had to give up your room and move away from the comfortable new neighborhood and maybe live in with relatives and share a room with strangers. Your father was home a lot and wasn't working when he was away, and then he was home all the time, the breadwinner, sitting in a chair all day with a vacant, distracted look, and you were shooed away from him, but you could tell that all the things that had made him the adored, respected idol were

oozing away, leaving a frighteningly empty yet bitter husk. Your
mother, who used to pride herself on her clean floors and her
ample table, went out and got work and cleaned the house and
cooked the meals when she got back, while the quiet figure in the
chair said less and less. It wasn't much of a job that your mother
had; it was menial, it was degrading, but it put some kind of food
in your belly and an occasional new pair of shoes on your feet.
Perhaps one day your father just wasn't there anymore, and your
mother cried for a time, and things kept going somehow the same
way, day after day, month after month, year after year. You worked
when you could, where you could, and were damned grateful, all
right, and you didn't question too closely whether you were being
exploited; you were working and earning and that was enough.

More likely you came to adolescence in the middle of the Depression. You saw the same pattern of blighted hopes and rotted
self-esteem, but it was nothing new, simply a familiar pattern. Life
was hard, life was tough; you were grateful for what you had. And
maybe you had nothing, like the Okie kids picking fruit day after
day in the hot fields of California's Central Valley and wondering
what would happen when the work ran out. Maybe you were one
of the thousands of boys and girls with no families to speak of, no
hopes, no settled jobs, hoboing around the country on the rails.

Probably you were one of the lucky ones—one of the two-thirds
of the nation which, even in the depths of the Depression, was comparatively speaking not ill-clothed, not ill-housed, not ill-fed. Still,
you saw things that frightened and toughened you. If you lived in
the city or in a medium-sized town, you saw the men in their remnants of formerly good clothes selling apples on the street corner;
possibly you saw the strikers fighting with the cops in San Francisco
or Akron or Flint or Minneapolis—you certainly heard about it.
At least some of your friends had parents who had lost jobs, and
maybe they moved away or just didn't come to school very often
and dropped out as soon as they could to go to work, and when
you saw them behind the counter at Kresge's or Woolworth's or
their parents' delicatessen or grocery store fronting a noisy, dirty,
city street, maybe they didn't want to look at you directly anymore
and were distant in a lonely but fiercely proud way. And even if
your father worked, he often took a cut or two in pay, and that

dream of going to college quietly died, and probably something of you died with it too.

Wherever you were, whatever you did or did not do in those long, terrible years between 1929 and 1940, you learned some things. You learned determination; somehow, some way, you would not be destroyed. You would get what you could and not expect much and be grateful for what you had. But if you were like most, you would not take a back seat to anyone; you would get ahead, you would make it, come what may. One thing above all you were aware of: society was cut in slices. Nearly everybody had it rough, but some had it a lot rougher than others. If you lived in that broad area of the country that included the states of the old Confederacy and that swath of midlands stretching westward from Pittsburgh across Ohio, Indiana, and Illinois to the treeless plains beyond Omaha and Kansas City and the Central Valley of California, then your town was sharply divided into classes and subclasses. You didn't need the Lynds to tell you that the country-club set of old, interlocking families ran the town—the bank, the newspaper(s), the radio station, and all the fashionable charities. Beneath these half-dozen or so families, town social life divided into the nearly upper crust, the truly middle classes, the top professional and business people, the lower middle class that included people like your schoolteachers and barbers and corner grocery-store owner, and the mass of the working population whose sons came to school even in the best of times in neatly patched pants and whose daughters wore cheap paper dresses that crinkled when they walked and could not be exposed to the rain.

You probably would have needed a sociologist to inform you in elegant prose that poverty reinforces rather than destroys existing social patterns, but there were behavioral codes and social taboos that you were expected to follow, and if these codes were often as not honored in the breach, they nonetheless defined a rigid and rigidly prescribed respectability. "Nice" girls didn't swear and didn't drink very much and were as feminine and pretty as possible. They were supposed to "save" themselves for the "right" boy. They were not to be "fast," and they should set their hearts on marriage in hopefully better times. They worked if they had to and accepted menial jobs, because with father out of work every pay-check counted.

Boys from the upper classes were generally expected to follow their father's footsteps into business or the professions. It was all right for a banker's son to aspire to a professorship, but not to a life as a plumber or a riveter on an assembly line. Boys from what was characterized as "the working class" were expected to go into the mill or the mine as soon as high school was over and maybe earlier. With existence marginal—even if the father was working—it was essential that every able hand in the family that could find work do so as soon as possible. There had been dreams earlier that a man worked and slaved so his son—maybe even his daughter—could improve themselves. The boy could get at least some college schooling, the girl could get through "business college," and neither would have to live a life of grinding toil, if not outright poverty. But the Depression killed all that except for those boys in the coal-mining country of Pennsylvania and a few other places who got to college on athletic scholarships.

After 1930 you stopped dreaming for yourself or your kid. You just stuck with what you were doing and what you had and what you were and hoped for the best. And, of course, there were few jobs opening up for anyone. Whether you came out into the job market at seventeen with a high-school diploma or at thirty-two with a Ph.D., there was little to be had. The New Deal, for all the attention paid to it by historians of later years, meant practically little to most people. Washington was still very far away and poverty was right at hand. As late as 1938 at least 20 percent of the American work force was unemployed.

Then came the war, perhaps the most powerful and stirring expression in both human and physical terms of the might and potential of modern America. And the foundations were laid for a wholly new social order, stupefyingly rich. A young generation that had shared the ordeal of want now assumed the burden of sacrifice amid increasing plenty.

It is nearly impossible now—thirty-five years later—to recapture the sense of national unity and dedication that defined America's effort in the Second World War. This is not to say that the tensions and animosities of the Depression decade had earlier disappeared. Racial conflict was intensified by the war as the great boom towns like Detroit and Mobile attracted poor white and black labor in an explosive mix. Lonely, frightened servicemen far from home set upon Los Angeles's Pachuko (Mexican) teenage population with barbaric fury. Black soldiers in the South were humiliated, demeaned, and beaten with frightening regularity. John L. Lewis and his United Mine Workers threatened the war effort with a walkout in 1943. And, of course, there was the shocking treatment accorded thousands upon thousands of decent, sober, hard-working, law-abiding Japanese-Americans who soon after Pearl Harbor were herded from their homes and businesses on the West Coast and dragged off to cold, miserable "relocation" camps in the wilds of eastern California and other remote corners of the West and Southwest. For people such as these, America remained a land of frustration and misery.

But for the great majority of Americans the years 1942-45 were a time of mounting prosperity and of what Randolph Bourne once accurately described as "the wonderful peace of being at war." Of course, there were shortages of every kind; of course, there was the terrible anxiety for the fate of loved ones in nearly every home; of course, there was unassuageable grief for the parents and wives, brothers and sisters of the third of a million men who never came back; and there was sorrow and hardship for the relatives and lovers of those who came back maimed in body or spirit. But the years of national triumph transcended the days of personal sadness. Pearl Harbor marshaled the country's emotions and seemingly illimitable power behind the national leadership. Sacrifice was universally accepted as being in an unquestionably noble cause. And for those men—and women—who donned a uniform, life took on a tone of peculiar moral intensity.

All the young warriors were dedicated in those brief years, and they would always carry with them memories of their dedication, their earnestness, their frequently prodigious feats of heroism or organization, competence or sacrifice. For the rest of their lives the members of the veteran generation, particularly those who had fought, would view their wartime experiences as an integral part of their character and careers. They had been blooded and had triumphed. They were set apart and above their fellow men:

> We few, we happy few, we band of brothers;
> For he to-day that sheds his blood with me
> Shall be my brother; be he ne'er so vile,
> This day shall gentle his condition;
> And gentlemen in England now a-bed
> Shall think themselves accurs'd they were not here,
> And hold their manhoods cheap whiles any speaks
> That fought with us upon Saint Crispin's day.

Seldom in American history had the hearts of an entire generation of young men and women been so touched with fire. The Second World War was a crusade against unmitigated tyranny, a sharply etched struggle between good and evil, right and wrong, throughout the world. A host of strange names and of simple associations—Nanking, Rotterdam, Coventry, Pearl Harbor, Bataan, Treblinka, Auschwitz—testified to the bestiality of the foe. There was no time for the luxury of critical thought and evaluation; the very idea of moral ambiguity which truly refined peoples have to confront at many points in their lives was denied the veteran generation. The youthful ordeal of separation, alienation, and violence precluded sophistication in the minds of all but a very few. Reality seemed to conform to the most egregious and simplistic stereotypes. And so, when one looks back on the forties from the perspective of a full generation, one sees an incredible innocence at once touching and frightening.

The veteran generation very quickly developed its own style and perspective. Its members were sufficient unto themselves. There were bonds between crewmen and infantrymen that no one else could ever quite break or understand. Once home, one never dwelt upon the frequently terrifying experiences and hardships of the battlefield save in quiet moments over beers in a bar, at the Legion Hall, or over drinks at the country club—and then only with fellow "vets." And when you did talk about it, you tended to speak mockingly of the experience of war and death and effort, for the Depression, the war, and the hard and bitter peace that followed forced the young men of the veteran generation—and the women who had waited for them in fear and loneliness—to assume a veneer of toughness.

Life was hard and demanding and exacting and always would be. One was compassionate, but did not wear one's heart on the sleeve; one knew of misery and hardship, but did not dwell upon it and worked to relieve it when and where possible, quietly, diligently, competently, as one had fought the war. Personal and collective bonds were not spoken of; they were quietly demonstrated in countless ways over the years. Excellence had been a quality demanded and demonstrated countless times as the country struggled toward victory. One strove ceaselessly to demonstrate and apply it to the problems of peace. If life was equated with endurance, there was yet no reason not to snatch a measure of gaiety from it, not to seek pleasures both simple and complex and, above all, material. Illusions were not to be cherished; impossible dreams were to be recognized for their impossibility. Progress, material and spiritual (and here the veteran generation became increasingly careless in its differentiation), was known to be slow but attainable. Conflict, hostility, and disillusion were given truths in a less-than-perfect world. Vigilance, even a measure of cynicism about one's opponents, was mandatory. Hard work was an unquestioned virtue; the need to be harsh and unyielding with an enemy was often a regrettable necessity. Competition proved the measure of the man. Success was the sole legitimate instrument of personal and social advancement.

Of course, the veteran generation did not develop these perspectives and values all at once. They emerged with ever-increasing clarity as the younger Americans of the forties and fifties endlessly struggled with the problems of power and affluence.

The veteran generation did not come back to a land basking in opulence, despite the assertions of latter-day critics immersed in the heartbreaking struggles of the Vietnam-era veterans to resume some sort of normal and productive life. The veterans of 1945 returned to a country whose enormous economic potential seemed hobbled by the incompetencies of government bureaucrats trying to guide and shape the material and social reconversion from war to peace, a country where very real poverty remained close at hand

and easily observable (for example, one out of every four American homes in 1946 lacked indoor plumbing). Moreover, within months after their discharge, all for which the veteran generation had fought, bled, and sacrificed seemed utterly lost. The threat of a third world war with the near certainty of massive, indiscriminate use of atomic weapons was actively spoken of as early as 1947. It was initially met with a wave of revulsion that ebbed in direct proportion to mounting popular disillusion with the wartime Russian ally. Czechoslovakia, Korea, and Soviet discovery of the atomic secret—with critical aid provided by Western spies, it was widely assumed—proved the turning points. All that had been said and written about sleepless Communist aggression and subversion seemed true, and after 1949 the prospect of an atomic Armageddon hung over the earth. Thereafter anxiety for one's future and the future of everything that one held dear became a staple of American life. Stupid and unscrupulous demagogues soon discovered that a traumatic national mood provided fertile ground for the development of a divisive politics of paranoia in which the amplification of discontent and resentment seemed the surest avenues to influence, if not power.

Wearied yet exalted by the taste of war, initially frightened by the prospect of further economic hardship, and then rendered disillusioned and neurotic by the specter of an "international Communist conspiracy" of enormous power and competence, the veteran generation returned to America and doggedly pursued its inchoate and uncertain dreams. The key that unlocked the door to ultimate prosperity for hundreds and thousands was, of course, access to higher education. Across America during the late forties college campuses were inundated by members of the veteran generation, anxious to exploit fully the gift of the GI Bill. Young men —and women—who five or ten years before had looked forward to a life in the mill or behind the counter now found the door to upper-middle-class, white-collar life magically opening before them, and they embraced the opportunity with grim determination. In later years those who had taught them would recall that the students of the veteran generation were the best single group of scholars American higher education had ever had. These same professors, if pressed a bit, would also admit that the veterans were unusually competitive, highly "professional" in orientation, in a very great hurry, and most of them uninterested in those abstract courses and curricula not immediately germane to the "real world" of business or the professions.

Life in the late forties, both on and off campus, was hard for the veteran generation. Years of depression and war had created a massive housing shortage, and young veterans and their wives, the majority already in their mid- or late-twenties and anxious to settle down and start families, often had to begin—both on and off campus—in grim circumstances. Cold, drafty garages and basements were turned into crude apartments; thousands of flimsy "temporary" units were built; leaky old house trailers were sold or rented; and on one midwestern campus, at least, the university skating rink was turned into a single men's dormitory with triple-tiered bunks and lockers resembling nothing so much as the enlisted men's barracks at Fort Dix. And nearly everywhere landlords and "supers" and nice little old people, who just wanted to rent out a room or two, gouged their helpless lodgers unmercifully. In these harsh circumstances families were begun and raised, books were studied, papers were written, jobs were pursued. And the bleak perspectives of the veteran generation were confirmed once again.

But as they came out of college and put on their white collars or as they struggled up the harsher, blue-collar ladder toward the status of modest security, as they bought their first homes in city or suburb and, after many a month's wait, got their first new car or refrigerator, the veterans first sensed and then knew that the terrible specter of depression and want was slowly being dispelled. Soon the first of them began falling into affluence with an exhausted sigh. Millions more would follow.

Prosperity resulted largely, it appeared, from the accommodating behavior of the Russian enemy and of that "international Communist conspiracy" which Senator McCarthy and his ilk, and many others who should have known better, claimed ran half the world. After the outbreak of the Korean War, America rearmed massively, and as the war reached its frustrating, inconclusive end, the decision was made that this time there would be no foolish demobilization as in 1946. Thus the country became a garrison state, in increasingly firm bondage to the weapons culture and to the self-fulfilling prophecies and neuroses of the high cold war era. Affluence thus came to be purchased at the price of anxiety and the diplomacy of ceaseless confrontation. But the weary survivors of depression and hot war never seemed disposed to seriously count, assess, or question the cost.

The veteran generation readily settled into the affluence-anxiety pattern after 1950. Wartime memories and an often willful ignorance of the world at large blended easily with the instinctive realization that a militarily strong, diplomatically assertive America had created an affluent America, and vice versa. To a generation and country that prior to 1941 had aggressively resisted tutoring in the subtleties, complexities, and inevitable reverses inherent in international life and was now busily engaged in the often exhausting effort at making an ever-richer living, the apparent truths of the cold war seemed beyond question.

By 1960 the veteran generation had created its own distinctive culture, its own distinctive style, and had largely imposed this culture and style upon American life. It was fitting that in that year, two of its most ambitious and assertive young representatives would battle for the presidency. John Aldridge has summed up perfectly the often barren achievements of this remarkable generation and the extent to which the Second World War continued to define its monuments, its products, its values.

Coming out of the war with long-deferred ambitions to live our lives, we settled down, began at once to breed, as if to prove we were still alive, and then proceeded to let our children do our living for us. It was a strange process, gradual, almost imperceptible, as natural as dying. Without quite intending it, we stopped—if we ever really began— making demands on life perhaps because we thought there was no longer enough time for such frivolity, that our youth had been used up in the war, and that nothing must interfere now with the grimly earnest business of becoming middle aged. Or it may be that the Depression and the war together accustomed us to asking nothing for ourselves, to seeing ourselves with a certain bleak pride as the sacrificial generation, to being grateful simply to have the necessities and utilities of existence.

With this paltry perspective before it the veteran generation began to create a culture which was the perfect physical reflection of our impoverished expectations of life. And not at all surprisingly, it resembled nothing so much as the military world we had just escaped.

From coast to coast we bulldozed the land into rubble, tore out the grass, uprooted the trees, and laid out thousands and thousands of miles of company streets all lined with family-sized barracks. We turned forests and farmlands into mucky service areas and converted the rural outskirts of every major city and town into slurb-belt jungles of used car lots, gas stations, hot-dog stands, motels, Army surplus stores, garbage dumps and junkyards—our civilian equivalents of the honky-tonk and trinket-shop strips outside the Army camps of Alabama and Texas. It was all ugly beyond belief and beyond bearing except to men who had become so environmentally desensitized by military life that they were no longer aware of their surroundings or could see no difference between the military environment and this one, simply because essentially there was no difference.

The little square boxes of houses set in precise orderly rows "could easily have been the married enlisted men's quarters at Fort Benning. The processed, powdered, concentrated and frozen foods, the TV dinners, were the barest transition from emergency field rations, K, C, and Ten-In-One. The shopping centers and supermarkets were simply enlarged PX's."

Perhaps the greatest irony of all lay in the fact that for this

most domesticated of generations, a permanent condition of wartime impermanence was the central fact of life. Families were constantly moving from one housing development to another like infantry replacements being endlessly transferred from camp to camp. And the atmosphere of military drabness and uniformity lay over everything. The houses, income levels, clothing, behavior patterns all seemed to be government issue. Even the children appeared to be interchangeable, as if their parents had drawn them at some supply depot.

For children, of course we had, were *all* we had. . . .[3]

If the countless children bred by the veteran generation's "baby boom" seemed interchangeable, it was largely because they were determinedly regimented by their parents to be that way. To read some of the numerous critical studies about coming of age in post-war America is to realize how thoroughly children came to be indoctrinated in military habits. Schools and parents have always striven to teach children obligation, obedience, and, at the very best, a sense of responsibility. The veteran generation, whose members increasingly staffed and ran the country's secondary schools after 1946, added another crucial factor—regimentation. Anyone who has gone through basic training in the military and who then turns to accounts of America's high schools in the fifties will instantly recognize that high school had become the boot camp of life. Here the male and female recruit was taught reverence for conformity to rigid social and behavioral patterns through the twin agencies of pressure and punishment. A caste system was defined by football heroes and cheerleaders, "student government" leaders and prom queens, who formed the apex, the elite, while a vast mass of adolescent proles were made to understand at an early age through countless cruelties, both calculated and gratuitous, conscious and unconscious, their eternal, predestined, societal role. And, too, all recruits were fully exposed to the psychically and intellectually impoverished notion of the veteran generation that life was essentially bleak and disillusioning and that pleasure was essentially definable in material terms.

While the children of the veteran generation seemed interchangeable, the role of the sexes was most emphatically not. Sometime around 1920 men and women had begun talking to each other in a recognizably modern vernacular. The Western world seemed poised on the brink of a major—and peaceful—social revolution. But the Great Depression wiped out the burgeoning movement of the late twenties toward greater and greater sexual freedom and equality. And while relations between the sexes remained unprecedentedly free and frank, not for forty years would this seemingly irresistible urge to total equality erupt once again. The veteran generation craved the certainties of daily life and fixed societal patterns; its members were uninterested in, indeed actively hostile to, experimentations in social change that would inevitably question and disrupt the orderly flow of things. The veteran generation harbored too many painful memories of fathers unable to work and of mothers and daughters pressed into often menial labor for family survival during the terrible thirties to entertain any notions of a change in the traditional pattern and habits of sexual roles, which routinely assigned the breadwinning and power seeking to the male and the homemaking and the decorative roles to the female.

It is important to emphasize how deeply and completely nearly all of the women of the veteran generation accepted sexual stereotyping. Anyone who walked a high-school corridor or a college campus during the 1950s will recall how fervently almost all young women embraced the ideal of a life of adolescent popularity, marriage, and family raising as the supreme expression of personal worth. Mothers and older sisters could relate tales of the routine humiliations which anyone who earns his or her bread must endure, particularly in the drab environment of depression. And memories of homes and families disrupted by the wartime separations were never far from mind or expression. To be sufficiently secure, to be financially and emotionally "free" to indulge in homemaking was, it was maintained, a rare privilege. And so the role of the woman in postwar America came to be portrayed in public discourse in the most rigid terms; she was pictured in a thousand advertisements and in a hundred popular stories as the keeper of hearth and home and the gay, plucky, and pretty little helpmate of the stalwart, competent husband whose several flaws she understood and neutralized or helped to overcome. It is perhaps not stretching analogy too far to say that the ideal wife of the 1950s was supposed to possess all the talents, charms, energy, and competence of a senior WAC corporal attached to Supreme Allied Headquarters at London in 1944.

It is this very militarization of American life, thought, and rhetoric (in the fifties and early sixties presidents and politicians ceaselessly spoke of "waging" peace and of "wars" on poverty) generated by the national experience in the Second World War that has so completely escaped the current generation of revisionist scholars seeking the clue or set of clues to America's responsibility for the origins and development of the cold war. Their utter fixation upon economic factors and causation has served them ill. As Aldridge has noted, the veteran generation used the existing economic structure for *its* purposes, not vice versa. Economic motives do not explain American absorption with the plight of the "captive" peoples of Eastern Europe; the lure of fresh markets does not define the tragedy of Indochina. Capitalist interest in these areas never was intense nor ever could be. Rather, it was the lure of one last moral crusade, the felt necessity of defending one more remote outpost of "freedom" against "godless international communism" that fixed American attention upon the unhappy peoples of Eastern Europe on the one hand and projected American interests, power, and lives into Indochina on the other.

But it is unfair and inaccurate to stress the ultimate presumption of much postwar American thought and action without emphasizing as well the outright fear and sense of intimidation from which much of that thought and many of those actions originally issued. Nothing is more reflective of the poverty of historical understanding and imagination in the country today than the clear implication in nearly every piece of revisionist writing on the cold war era that the United States was everywhere and at all times far stronger than the Soviet Union. This was simply not the case in military terms between 1945 and 1949 except in the area of nuclear weaponry, and there the Truman administration was sufficiently burdened by the moral stigma already attached to Hiroshima and Nagasaki to hesitate ever to practice atomic blackmail or aggressive atomic diplomacy.

The image of the Soviet Union held in the United States after 1947 was of a malevolent leader of a cohesive and coherent worldwide conspiracy backed by the greatest *conventional* military might the world had ever known in peacetime. And after 1949 public anxiety was immensely heightened by the trip-hammer blows of abrupt Soviet possession of atomic weaponry and the apparent "fall" of China to the Kremlin's trusted agent, the Chinese Communist party. Those of us who lived through those years and recall them, however faintly, remember a private sense of dread and of dismay and rancor in public discourse which even the most careless perusal of the press of that time quickly confirms. There seemed no way to stop the march of international Communist conspiracy except through the suicidal medium of a nuclear exchange. After 1946 all that America had to oppose the massive forces of "international communism" was the doomsday weapon; after 1949 even that weapon could not be employed without fear of retaliation. Truman and his colleagues had thus placed the country in an impossible situation, it was widely charged. Soon Senator McCarthy would color such charges in a far more sinister hue.

Whether such horror stories of American weakness were in fact planted in the media by the government itself to generate public support for rearmament is a moot question. The stories were widely believed, they were discussed, and they became part of the conventional wisdom. Yet later scholars, most of whom did not live consciously through that period, persist in assuming real or implicit American global domination. Thus, to take but one example, they tend to interpret National Security Council Report 68 of April 1950 as a document confidently setting forth a grand strategy of global containment. In fact, a careful reading of NSC 68, in conjunction with what else was being said and written in and out of government on the eve of the Korean War, reveals a pervasive dread of further Communist expansion and a very real fear as to whether America and her handful of formal allies in Western Europe possessed the requisite will and means to contain the latest manifestation of man's baser appetites.

It can be legitimately argued that the American people—or an articulate and politically active majority of them—from President Truman and Dean Acheson on down, simply spooked themselves in those drab and unhappy years between Hiroshima and Korea, that the Soviet threat, military and moral, was grossly overblown, that there never really was nor ever really could be an international Communist conspiracy of the omnipresent, omnicompetent dimensions imagined. Yet history is the record not only of what happened, but of what men and women think happened or was happening. Those who grew to maturity amid the stridently self-confident, moral and military rhetoric of the Johnson years understandably find it difficult to imagine a time in the recent past when the country and its leadership were largely motivated by anxiety. But that was the case throughout the formative years of the cold war era. To miss or ignore this is to distort history.

Younger readers may plausibly ask why there was not a revulsion against the programs, premises, and perspectives of the veteran generation long before 1963-65. Granted an initial and understandable anxiety on the part of the American public, why did the garrison state and mentality which that anxiety produced become so pervasive and last so long? The answer lies in the awful hold that the

Second World War continued to exert upon public and private life in the United States long after its close.

Joan Didion has eloquently observed that those of us who grew up in the 1950s were "a generation not for barricades." And for good reason. The Second World War and the veteran generation it spawned fashioned a terrifyingly austere atmosphere in which social and political criticism had all but disappeared. In the cold war environment of the fifties and early sixties criticism could be, and all too often was, equated with treason of a greater or lesser intensity. It was not so much that there were no barricades to be stormed or manned; quite the contrary. But the barricades were seen to lie not at home but overseas, along that "iron curtain" that divided the "free world" from the "Communist camp." The duty of every American citizen was to see that those barricades were vigilantly manned every moment. Tyranny, like hell, had proved to be hydra-headed and not easily conquered. The crusade against Hitler had not brought forth the millenium but merely another dictatorship of equally horrifying proportions and appetites. It had proved a grand disillusion, and those who came of age in the fifties docilely accepted that disillusion which ironically underlay and informed much of the veteran generation's cold war world view and crusades.

"We were all very personal then," Didion has said, "sometimes relentlessly so, and, at that point where we either act or do not act, most of us are still."

I suppose I am talking about precisely that: the ambiguity of belonging to a generation distrustful of political highs, the historical irrelevancy of growing up convinced that the heart of darkness lay not in some error of social organization but in man's own blood. If man was bound to err, then any social organization was bound to be in error. It was a premise which still seems to me accurate enough, but one which robbed us early of a certain capacity for surprise. . . . We were that generation called "silent," but we were silent neither, as some thought, because we shared the period's official optimism nor, as others thought, because we feared its official repression. We were silent because the exhilaration of social action seemed to many of us just one more way of escaping the personal, of masking for awhile that dread of the meaningless which was man's fate.[4]

Some of the sensitive and despairing—perhaps the best among the youth of the fifties—found solution in suicide. For others a little house on some still (but not for long) remote beach was the answer until society appeared with its remorseless summons.

Those who dwelt upon their condition as seriously and deeply as did Didion—and there were not too many in those days of austerity-turning-to-affluence—were, I think, as touched by the war, by war in general, and by the garrison state that was emerging in America as were their parents and older brothers and sisters. Everywhere we turned in the fifties it seemed that memories of the Second World War and the trappings of a cold war garrison state were all about us. Motion pictures and television programs constantly invoked the themes and recalled the events of 1939-45. In a thousand implicit and explicit ways fathers and brothers imparted to us their own weary disillusion with a world gone mad on violence from which there could be no escape, only ceaseless containment with the predicted need of an occasional armed reaction. And so with greater or lesser apathy we entered and waged wars of our own, given to us as our heritage. There was the eternal cold war with international communism on every front and for a long time the apparently eternal hot war with several of its agents in Korea. Some kind of war with all its sense of stress and sacrifice and implicit doom became the very essence of our lives. Amid rising plenty, generated in large measure by the needs of the garrison state, we were too cowed to question.

But no country and no generation can long maintain a general mood of unquestioning social discipline or impose it upon a people habituated to a limited measure of intellectual freedom. And the American environment itself provided a peculiar tradition of restlessness and skepticism in the face of success that guaranteed the early emergence of a vibrant opposition to the status quo.

A persistent, often tragic theme runs through American history from Massachusetts Bay to the presidency of Lyndon Baines Johnson. A self-conscious, highly motivated generation sets itself a seemingly impossible task, the establishment of a perfect theocracy or the winning of a comparatively liberal independence, the total abolition of black slavery or the near-total eradication of national poverty. The goal is strenuously pursued. The result is never failure but repeated, stunning success. The essence of the recurrent American tragedy lies in achievement. For "the end" does not then appear on the screen of national life; a final sense of tranquillity and victory is never attained. Quite the reverse. Life goes on beyond the triumphal moment. Success is found to breed not only fresh problems, but a whole host of them. The richer or more successful the life-style, the less secure, less well defined, and less morally justifiable it seems.

This fact becomes poignantly clear with the arrival of the next generation, which invariably views its parents' considerable achievements with either apathy or outright hostility. The triumph of the colony at Massachusetts Bay seems to the founders' children a triumph of gross restriction, if not outright despotism; the achievement of the Founding Fathers is followed by bitter and divisive debate in the next generation over the precise political character and moral dimension of the new republic; the abolition of slavery precedes a callous, if not barbarous, descent into racism within the perimeters of an ostensibly free society; the achievement of mass affluence and comparative security in the post-1945 era ultimately results in a cruelly abrasive questioning by a new generation of the material and moral dimensions of a cold war culture defined by a nuclear balance of terror. And always, as the children tear at the achievements and pretensions of the older generation, that generation finds it increasingly difficult to measure its successes and retain its pretensions in the face of inevitable change. This was as true of the twentieth-century veteran generation as it was of the seventeenth-century elders of Massachusetts Bay.

By the end of the 1950s a perilous mood of virtual nihilism gripped the country, and there was a sense of growing frustration with things as they were. If this particular public mood had been promoted by a boredom with national achievements perhaps less lofty and ethereal than those of the past, it was no less profound or pervasive.

The frustration was first sensed and exploited by a remarkable young entertainer named Elvis Presley. It was then understood and expressed by a stylish group of comedians led initially by Mort Sahl, to be followed soon after by the more complex, influential, and nastier Lenny Bruce. Albert Goldman has written of Bruce's intuitive, unrehearsed ability to "hit the late fifties' mainline—the sense of smothered rage."

Everybody was pissed off in those days, but there were no socially acceptable outlets for hostility. "Hostile" was a word you heard constantly—but it was a scolding word, like "bad," "naughty," or "no-no!" All over this heavily psychoanalyzed country, people were saying to other people, "Why are you being so hostile? . . . That's a hostile remark! . . . There's a lot of hostility behind something like that!" It was an incredible age, the fifties! An age of stifled violence obsessing about The BOMB!

The Bomb was right inside the guts and brains of every American man, woman and child. People were burning with repressed sexuality, anger, fear. They were making incredible sacrifices to pay their mortgages, educate their children and keep everything cool at the office. Eating crow every day for lunch. Lying low, trying to "adjust," trying to "conform," being "mature." Being taught by the analysts—whose wisdom and authority extended far beyond the tiny number of patients they treated—that the first rule of life was: "you have only yourself to blame!" No matter what happened to you—whether you were fired from your job, cheated on by your husband, fucked over by your kids, afflicted with disease or riddled with anxiety—*all your own fault*! If you hadn't taken that job, married that man, given birth to that kid, inhaled those germs, built up those worries, *none of this would have happened*! You could have had a wonderful job; a doting husband; beautiful, darling children; perfect health; the nerves of a brain surgeon—if you had just acted *normal*! That was the wisdom, the comfort, the faith, hope and charity of the "mature" fifties! Now, wouldn't you be angry, schmuck?![5]

William Whyte's best seller of 1956-57 said much the same thing in more elegant, less frenetic prose.[6] The Organization Man was a man trapped in boredom and frustration. The very sense of integrity and purpose whereby the individual eventually comes to know and define himself was being ground to pieces in the regimented atmosphere of corporate America, which controlled the scope and pace of that mass affluence so feverishly sought after by the veteran generation. The only recourse for the Organization Man, Whyte maintained, was deliberate falsification of one's character and aspirations when the time invariably came to submit to the numerous "personality tests" that both expressed and reflected the rush to conformity.

It is tempting to conclude that the sense of smothered rage which pervaded the late fifties was in and of itself completely responsible for the youth revolts of the early and mid-sixties. But such a conclusion is too facile. Although a sense of rage certainly suffused not only the confrontation politics of the radical young but of the reactionary politics of the elders, the roots of American social protest, 1960s style, are far too complex to be so easily explained.

The so-called counterculture of the sixties is extraordinarily difficut to dissect and analyze this soon. It was at once dynamic and passive, hedonistic and Calvinistic, alternating between sporadic waves of disciplined opposition and apathetic acquiescence to a repugnant status quo, between communal orientation and insistence on the transcendant rights, demands, and interests of the individual. Indeed, there have been few self-conscious movements in American history so quickly and deeply beset by internal contradictions and stress. Consistently simplified and sensationalized by media overexposure and underanalysis, the counterculture of the sixties will require attentive study over many years to be fully understood.

Nonetheless, few would deny that basically the counterculture represented a generalized revolt against the values, perspectives, and, above all, the *social discipline* so firmly imposed by the veteran generation upon all areas and aspects of private and public life in postwar America. One element of this revolt was a romantic dissociation from societal concerns and a concurrent effort to create some kind of hedonistic, new life-style. "The ancient manners were giving way," it was truly written of this new style.

There grew a certain tenderness on the people, not before remarked. Children had been repressed and kept in the background; now they were considered, cosseted and pampered. I recall the remark of a witty physician who remembered the hardships of his own youth; he said, "It was a misfortune to have been born when children were nothing, and to live till men were nothing."

There are always two parties, the party of the Past and the party of the Future; the Establishment and the Movement. At times the resistance is reanimated, the schism runs under the world and appears in Literature, Philosophy, Church, State and social customs. It is not easy to date these eras of activity with any precision. . . . The key to the period appeared to be that the mind had become aware of itself. Men grew reflective and intellectual. There was a new consciousness. The former generations acted under the belief that a shining social prosperity was the beautitude of man, and sacrificed uniformly the citizen to the State. The modern mind believed that the nation existed for the individual, for the guardianship and education of every man. This idea, roughly written in revolutions and national movements, in the mind of the philosopher had far more precision; the individual is the world. . . . It is the age of severance, of dissociation, of freedom, of analysis, of detachment. Every man for himself. The public speaker disclaims speaking for any other; he answers only for himself. The social sentiments are weak; the sentiment of patriotism is weak; veneration is low; the natural affections feebler than they were. People grow philosophical about native land and parents and relations. There is an universal resistance to ties and ligaments once supposed essential to civil society. The new race is stiff, heady and rebellious; they are fanatics in freedom; . . . They have a neck of unspeakable tenderness; it winces at a hair.[7]

The writer, of course, was not of our time. He was Ralph Waldo Emerson describing that remarkable period of social reform and transcendental revolt against materialism which immediately preceded the American Civil War. Yet his description is wonderfully evocative of the temper and times of the contemporary counterculture. To read Emerson's description of the New England atmosphere over a century ago is to bring to mind the mood of "stiff, heady and rebellious" dissociation and alienation created by and reflected in the words and behavior of such apparently disparate youth spokesmen as Mario Savio, Joyce Maynard, Charles Reich, Janis Joplin, James Kunen, John Lennon, Bob Dylan, and a score of more or less equally ephemeral champions of a newer, tenderer, and tougher life-style. For all its violence (and there was much violence in antebellum America also) the 1960s was a time of individual and collective severance, of weakened patriotism of the traditional and unreflective variety, of fanaticism in freedom. *Plus ça change* . . .

But, of course, there were vast differences between Emerson's America and the land of Dylan and Lennon. The sense of suicidal desperation and nihilism that was almost, though not wholly absent from antebellum New England was full-blown in the America of the 1960s, culminating in the emergence of the acid-rock segment of the counterculture after about 1967. Eventually the romantic, dissociational wing of the counterculture found itself atomized, the victim of its own hedonistic, narcissistic preferences and perspectives, at dead end, mired in drugs and despair and a blank-faced, gaping vacuity.

There was another, by-and-large earlier aspect to the youthful revolt of the sixties, however, which reflected an opposite strain of thought and conduct: Calvinistic, socially committed, purposeful, and, above all, conformist and disciplined. This aspect of the sixties counterculture led to an intellectual and procedural regimentation among the young every bit as great in degree, if certainly not in kind, as could be found within the "silent generation" of the fifties. The Calvinistic wing of the counterculture took increasingly emotional issue with the premises and perspectives of the veteran generation. Sporadically, but with ever-increasing vehemence, the Calvinists undertook principled, disciplined opposition to what they perceived to be the technological dehumanization and vast social injustices deliberately perpetrated by an exhausted old order. Where the romantic withdrew, the Calvinist enlisted. He or she swelled the ranks of mass protest, subsuming personal identity in the behavior and perspectives of the mob. Whatever the merits or demerits of their cause, the Calvinists sought salvation through immersion.

The two aspects of the counterculture were never mutually exclusive. From the beginning there was frequent mix and blend of persons and styles. The use of drugs, particularly of such "soft" drugs as marijuana, was nearly total among the young by the close of the sixties at the latest. The acid-rock culture at one time or another demonstrably attracted hundreds of thousands of young people. And the confrontation at Kent State, to take but one example among several such incidents, seems to have been as much or more the product of romantics as of Calvinists. Similarly, many self-professed radicals of the early and mid-sixties professed disenchantment and/or heartbreak with the ultimate impermeability of "the system" and drifted off into the drug culture. Other radicals, particularly at the close of the sixties and deep into the seventies, assumed a frighteningly twisted romantic stance and became, like Diana Oughton, Bernardine Dohrn, and the Weatherpeople, out-

and-out terrorists, spawning, in an even more horrifying spinoff, such groups as the SLA and the Manson "family."

Yet it was the political Calvinists, not the dissociated romantics, who mounted the most sustained and significant opposition to the assumptions and life-style of the veteran generation after about 1964. In the behavior and values of this group, the veteran generation correctly saw its mirror image and the greatest threat to its predominance.

"I have prayed just one prayer in my life: Use me." These are the words of Spegel, the actor, in Ingmar Bergman's film "The Magician."

For my generation that is no strange prayer, no unknown request; it has been on our lips, silently, for a long time.

The writer was David Horowitz, who would soon become prominent in the radical causes of the sixties; the year was 1962. The subject of his book, *Student*, from which these lines are taken, was the initial outburst of revolt by the children of the veteran generation, the effort by a group of highly politicized, well-organized students at the University of California's Berkeley campus first to destroy the stranglehold of the Greek system on student affairs, then to save Caryl Chessman and other ostensible victims of a brutish system from death, and finally to drive the House Committee on Un-American Affairs out of San Francisco. All this took place in 1959-60, more than a year before the first Greensboro sit-ins and the subsequent freedom rides across the South brought profound social and political protest to public attention.

Horowitz and a steadily growing number of youthful critics told the country between 1960 and 1964 that it had lost its humanity. Abroad, the nation had on countless occasions since 1945 betrayed its own expressed values and standards; at home, the price of expanding, frequently gross affluence was institutional rigidity and tyranny. The privilege of attaining abundance and an unprecedentedly high degree of education in the America of the 1960s was irretrievably compromised by the bending, folding, spindling, and mutilating of the individual. The school, in particular—and this soon came to include any American school—was run *by* management *for* management; institutional imperatives held dictatorial sway over personal need.

This analysis quickly came to be accepted by a significant proportion of the country's educated, articulate, affluent young. The boots began to agitate against the rule of the chiefs. One generation's truth became the next generation's satire—and vice versa. And when black Americans, pursuing their own imperatives to be free, at last rejected quietism and gradualism in favor of militancy (and for a time accepted the aid of privileged but disaffected young whites), a social crisis of real dimensions began to brew. All too soon the carefully contrived and defended life-style of the veteran generation began to unravel. Dozens, then scores, of groups and critics abruptly emerged to challenge the bedrock premises and perspectives of an entire dominant culture. So vibrant was the revolt, so sweeping and unrestrained the reaction against astringency, that eventually everybody seemed to define himself by his own grievances. This proved to be a sorry spectacle in itself and raised the question as to whether the critics of the veteran generation could in their turn develop an alternative life-style and value system of any greater worth and acceptability.

In a very real sense the veteran generation had provided its offspring and its critics with the tools and perspectives for successful challenge. For years the highly regimented children of the veteran generation had placed before them the examples of their parents' moral and material success through sacrifice and crusade, during hot war and cold, in hard times and good. But where were the fresh ordeals and trials through which the younger generation could triumphantly test itself and thus find a measure of that individual and collective self-esteem upon which all social stability and order must be based? This came to be a crucial question. Ultimately the veteran generation provided no compelling answer except the waging of further wars of increasing dubiety. Kennedy's Peace Corps represented but a feeble alternative. The veteran generation was fatally hobbled in responding to its children's idealistic aspirations by the tendency to view its offspring in a most human but paradoxical fashion: having struggled and sacrificed to give its children all the things it had never had, it then viewed the children with contempt because they had never had to struggle for anything. Having striven to perpetuate the competitive and stressful environment in which its own members had flourished, the veteran generation found itself utterly incapable of comprehending the mounting, ultimately hysterical determination of its children to break out of such an atmosphere.

And so many of the children, distressed, then disgusted, then enraged by what they perceived as a constantly widening gap between their parents' principled promises and hypocritical practices, groped unsteadily toward a position of militant, disciplined, and, above all, regimented alienation. They were helped at every step of the way by the older generation, which all too often proved to be as stupidly rigid, as unimaginatively tyrannical, as dehumanized, as the children maintained. The more outrageous, the more fallacious the demands of the young and the more outrageously they were framed, the more unyielding the response of the establishment until at last the series of explosive confrontations began, first at Berkeley, then San Francisco State, Ann Arbor, Madison, Columbia, and Chicago and on and on until at last, at Kent and Jackson State, the old defined the young's limit of dissent in terms of death. Shortly thereafter youth's maddest fringe, personified by Charles Manson and his band of harpies, responded in kind, and the accumulating horror finally reached a climax that exhausted both sides.[8]

The veteran generation had never resolved the two great challenges facing twentieth-century society: racism and war. Of the first, it seemed to care but little (although significant advances were made in the eradication of the most egregious forms of public anti-Semitism and anti-Catholicism). Most people in the late forties and fifties were content to mouth the platitude that "Negroes" (no one twenty or more years ago thought much about Indians, Puerto Ricans, or Mexican-Americans) were moving slowly but majestically toward eventual equality. And, except for a courageous and farsighted few, the consensus seemed to be that the slower the pace the more majestic it was to behold. Of the challenge of war it need only be repeated that the entire thrust of postwar American life which the veteran generation had shaped was defined by a garrison-state mentality, a quasi-war environment, in which the possibility of a suicidal nuclear exchange with the "enemy" seemed to grow rather than diminish with time.

The scope and duration of the youthful rebellion of the early and mid-sixties might well have been far less had its targets been confined to institutional rigidities and injustices or immoral racial practices. Despite their gross impersonality, American high-school and college campuses in the early sixties—Berkeley included—were not unpleasant places to be; there proved to be a great deal of youthful passivity to overcome. Moreover, black activists discovered no later than 1965 that their white cohorts could not be trusted to follow black aspirations to the point where they impinged upon or conflicted with traditional or implicit racial privileges. It was one thing for white youth to go to Mississippi in the summer of 1964 to be cursed at, spat upon, even violently threatened by the local white constabulary. There was something deliciously adventurous, morally clean, in such an act. It proved quite another thing for white youth in later years to relinquish power gracefully to their black brethren in the civil-rights movement or to give way to their black competitors in law or medical schools in the name of equal opportunity or, on an even more basic level, to acquiesce in the courtship of white girls by black men.

But to the educated, articulate, overwhelmingly white young who managed to avoid fighting it in droves, the Vietnam War appeared to sum up all that seemed corrupt, inhuman, hypocritical, racist, and threatening to the general peace in a contemporary America run by and for the veteran generation. In reaction against the moral and military quagmire of national involvement in Indochina, the youth of the sixties at last discovered and exploited in a variety of ways a cause which it felt to be as noble, as imperative, above all, as sacrificial, as any engaged in by its parents. Disaffected youth of radical bent had already developed during the brief and abortive flirtation with civil rights between 1963 and 1965 the techniques of mass protest that demanded strict regimentation and conformity to the cause. Between 1965 and 1968 the radical gadflies wou'd use those techniques with greater determination in an attempt to force the end of an "unjust war."

So without in any way intending it, the veteran generation through folly and default handed its children that morally imperative crusade for which they had long yearned but which their parents had been unable to fashion for them. The veteran generation's own rigid commitment to a somber foreign and domestic status quo, which had yielded such affluence and peculiar comfort, insured that the parents would eventually come in violent, ultimately bloody conflict with the young upon whom they had lavished such riches and such eccentric concern. Thus did the greatest victors of the Second World War at last become their own worst victims.

The Two Cold Wars

6

A DISTURBING paradox informs much of contemporary writing on the recent past. The military, moral, and conceptual failure of America in Vietnam is, at least within liberal intellectual circles, a matter of record and of general consensus. That United States involvement in Southeast Asia stemmed directly from and was a natural part of the ongoing cold war with "international communism" is equally beyond dispute. Yet the now sizable school of historians who have deduced American responsibility for the cold war as a logical preliminary to American responsibility for My Lai and a host of related Indochina tragedies has in recent years come under increasing attack for indulging in superficial analysis and shoddy scholarship. Its premises have been assaulted as thoroughly as its research.

As with all other past and current scholarly conflicts, vituperation becomes fatal when it obliterates edification. Revisionist critics writing after 1965 performed a valuable service by reflecting, clarifying, and codifying the rapidly changing mood of the post-veteran-generation young in America. If revisionist scholarship in the end has proved as simplistic, unsatisfactory, and self-serving as the scholarly defenses of American cold war behavior and policies which preceded it, this should elicit neither surprise nor undue alarm. Moreover, revisionists have from the beginning been divided over a number of issues and assumptions; there is no monolithic revisionist thesis.

And yet a revisionist consensus can be discerned. If differences exist over specific points and emphases, many young scholars assume that the basic responsibility for the early postwar breakdown of the Grand Alliance and the subsequent outbreak of cold war lies with the United States and with a series of aggressive American policymakers who were determined to coerce a war-weakened but equally adamant Soviet Union to relax its grip upon Eastern Europe and to renounce legitimate demands for security there and elsewhere. Most—not all—revisionists would accept a further proposition: that American aggression in the cold war era stemmed from an ungovernable capitalistic impulse to shape and dominate a war-ravaged and servile economic order of global dimensions for the sake of the Open Door. In the assumption of an aggressive postwar United States and an essentially weak and defensive Soviet Union lies the core of revisionist thought.

It is well to recall that throughout American history one generation's truth becomes the next generation's satire. From this perspective it is clear that the revisionists have assumed the role of second-generation critics. Their scholarship is rooted in almost total rejection of the supposedly sacred truths of their elders. Revisionists have expressed their generation's revulsion against the crass materialism of the veteran generation by insisting that such materialism, in the form of an inexcusably aggressive foreign economic policy, was largely responsible for the coming and continuation of the cold war. Revisionists have condemned the growing militarization of postwar national life by denying that the Soviet opponent ever constituted a viable threat either to important national interests or basic national security. Revisionists have denounced their elders' preachment and practice of democratic universalism by invoking a standard of double judgment. Plans, policies, and actions which in the American case are invariably—often bitterly—condemned as aggressive, abusive, and disruptive, are explained in the Soviet or Chinese cases as legitimate defensive reactions to predatory American power.

Given the state of uncertainty and self-doubt which prevailed in this country throughout the late sixties and early seventies, revisionist assumptions were as attractive as they were facile. They were attractive largely because they seemed to explain the intervention in Indochina as the ultimate adventure in reckless cold war imperialism. Having instinctively added Communist China to the list of enemies after 1949, American policymakers felt free to coerce and kill hundreds of thousands of Asians in order to fulfill cold war universalist imperatives to power.

Revisionist assumptions are in fact facile: first, because they do not adequately account for the realities of early postwar power politics within whose context the cold war emerged; and, second, because they fail to explain satisfactorily the nature and scope of the Indochina catastrophe. If the origins of the cold war are to be found in something other than predatory American economic appetites and defensive Soviet responses, then most, if not all, of the revisionist conceptual structure collapses. If the *ultimate* expression of America's aggressive cold war behavior is other than economic, then a key assumption in much revisionist literature is destroyed.

Early postwar international life was defined by two realities: first, the apparent predominance of the Red Army and its increasing employment from late 1945 on as an instrument of intimidation and repression throughout Eastern Europe and portions of the Near and Far East; and, second, the economic prostration of Europe as a whole. Although vast areas of Russia had been repeatedly laid waste during the unprecedented land battle of 1941-45 and although the Soviet economy was undoubtedly depleted for a time, the Russians possessed a military machine of enormous size and experience. Indeed, in conventional military terms the Red Army and Air Force together constituted in 1945 the largest, most battle-tested military unit in the world.

Recently a number of scholars, most notably Adam B. Ulam, have suggested that Western fears of conventional Soviet military strength in the early postwar world were greatly exaggerated. Ulam invites his reader to accept Stalin's statement of October 1946 that Russian military contingents "in Germany and some East European countries amounted to barely sixty divisions and would be soon reduced to forty." But this was no negligible figure, as Ulam himself implicitly accepts when he states in a footnote that the size of a Red Army division at this time was 10,000 men. Thus, the Red Army had some 600,000 men garrisoned in portions of Eastern Europe alone.[1] When one added to that figure—as prudent Western policymakers had to do by this time—an even larger number of men under arms in the Soviet Union itself, plus a like number, maybe more, in the Far East, then Western fears that the Soviet military machine still contained some millions of men were not exaggerated.

But what of American monopoly of the bomb? Although this undoubtedly disturbed, even frightened the Kremlin for a time, it is also true that the bomb was something of an albatross. Hiroshima and Nagasaki had demonstrably sickened and alienated much of world public opinion. Could the United States ever again employ nuclear weapons except in the ultimate moment of national survival or extinction? Specifically, could or should the United States use the bomb to save war-battered Western Europe from a conventional Soviet military thrust if the result would be to make of the Continent one vast, atomic funeral pyre? As early as the autumn of 1945, Truman sensed the deadly ambiguity of nuclear power. When he complained to his budget director, Harold D. Smith, of Soviet intransigence at the London Conference, Smith countered with the observation that, after all, the president had an atomic bomb up his sleeve. "Yes," Truman replied, "but I'm not sure it can ever be used."

Thus Americans and Europeans living through those grim, early postwar years between 1945 and 1949 were fully cognizant that their destinies were largely shaped by the Red Army. While the American military establishment dwindled from a peak of 12 million to a low of little more than 1 million in the first year of the peace, the Red Army remained nearly intact. There was little demobilization east of Turgau. And when those scores of Red Army divisions were employed as the chief agents of Soviet political pressure upon all of Eastern Europe, with the consequent suppression of all civil and political liberties throughout the region, when scores of other divisions lay poised on the borders of northern Iran and north China, when the Kremlin demanded unprecedented concessions from Turkey and the entry of the Red Army into postwar Japan as part of the occupation force, Western leaders not unnaturally reacted in fear and opposition.

American leaders cannot be held blameless for the coming of the cold war. Inheritors of an isolationist tradition centuries old, they looked upon *all* foreign powers and leaders as intrinsically corrupt and dangerous. Adhering from the start to the inevitable Soviet domination of postwar Eastern Europe, they could not resist criticizing a Soviet policy of suppression and tyranny which they did not care—indeed did not dare—to challenge formally. The rising tide of American scolding in late 1945 and throughout 1946 constantly fueled Soviet suspicions without in the least deflecting or modifying Soviet policies. Moreover, crude efforts to chastise and punish the Soviets through the withholding of postwar economic aid and above all the sharing of nuclear weapons technology (which the Soviets were bound to discover for themselves sooner or later) could only intensify, not ameliorate, emerging cold war tensions.

Nonetheless, it is difficult to condemn early postwar American policymakers too harshly for their reactions to Soviet behavior unless one is willing to see the Soviet state and policies of the late 1940s for something other than what they were. The fact that many scholars, viewing events from the context of the 1960s, are willing to do this in no way absolves them from the charge of distorting history. The inexcusability of American foreign policy after 1965 in no way excuses Soviet policy after 1945. Stalin's Russia, postwar as well as prewar, was a tyranny of immense and terrifying proportions. No later than the Iranian crisis of 1946, it appeared to alarmed Washington policymakers (most of whom had not enjoyed long and intimate exposure to the subtleties and complexities of international life) that the Soviets were determined to thrust beyond their immense Eastern and Central European heartland in a bid to seize the balance of global power if not the substance of world domination.

But Soviet military preponderance was only half of the early cold war equation. Economic power was the other half, and here the United States was unquestionably predominant. Having reminded ourselves of the reality of Soviet power in the early postwar world, is it not just to view American foreign economic policy with a suspicion and hostility equal to that accorded the Kremlin for its employment of conventional military strength for political objectives? Many revisionists would argue yes. The record suggests a more guarded response.

To state the matter baldly, the record indicates that the United States used its economic predominance in the early postwar world for defensive rather than aggressive purposes. Congress and the country were deeply fearful of a renewed economic depression in the early postwar period, and while a number of revisionist scholars writing twenty-five to thirty years later have seen a strong connection between this fear and an ostensible national economic policy aimed at securing a firm global market area, it must be said that contemporary policymakers never made such a connection. America was still deeply tinged with the prewar isolationist tradition which had defined national foreign policy for most of three centuries. The vociferous, if not prevalent mood in Congress (which, of course, originated all national spending programs) was to bring home as many American boys and dollars as possible from the distant battlefields and coffers of the Second World War and to isolate the national economy and polity from the dislocations and violence of a shattered and angry world. Americans were far too concerned about their domestic markets in the immediate postwar era to worry very much about foreign market areas, much less about establishing a single global market. As for the assertion that they saw the two as one and the same thing, it can only be said that the available record simply does not bear out such a contention.

How then did America become involved in the Eastern European market region? The answer is through the initiative of Eastern European governments themselves. It was the governments of Poland and Czechoslovakia (and the Soviet Union) who came to Washington for aid in 1945 and 1946; Washington did not seek out Warsaw, Prague, or Moscow in an effort to force American capitalist interests into Eastern Europe through various advantageous loan arrangements. At the time that Polish and Czech officials appeared with their requests, American officials and the American public felt, rightly or wrongly, that they were being hard-pressed by numerous other such demands: by the need to grant large sums to the United Nations Relief and Rehabilitation Agency;* by the need to ensure that both the International Monetary Fund and the World

---

* According to the Colmer Committee of the House of Representatives, the United States was underwriting nearly 80 percent of the UNRRA budget in late 1945. Gabriel Kolko claims the sum subscribed at any one time was only 71 percent at the most.

Bank would get off to effective beginnings; and, finally, by the need to prop up the British pound sterling through a massive loan which in turn could be used as a lever to combat imperial preference and thus weaken a British Empire which American isolationists had long assumed was callously exploitative and inexcusably exclusivist.

Nonetheless, despite such pressures American officials in 1945 and 1946 agreed to grant reconstruction credits to both Poland and Czechoslovakia if two modest conditions were met: first, that both governments provide sufficient data so that the reconstruction needs of the respective countries could be adequately assessed and a sufficiently strong case made to a parsimonious Congress and country concerned about foreign aid "giveaways"; and, second, that adequate compensation be arranged for United States citizens whose Polish and Czechoslovak properties had been recently nationalized.

Polish and Czech reactions to these comparatively modest demands were strident and, American officials soon came to believe, slanderous. In an atmosphere of mounting political and civil repression in both countries, the controlled press led a strong attack on overall American foreign-policy objectives. Polish and Czech —and eventually Soviet—insistence that *any* American loan conditions in Eastern Europe constituted an outrageous invasion of sovereignty by an inveterate imperialistic power finally caused American officials from Secretary of State James F. Byrnes on down to retract the aid offers. In doing so, Washington condemned to exile or death two of its staunchest friends behind what was rapidly becoming the iron curtain. Soon after negotiations for the Polish loan fell through, Stanislaw Mikolajczyk fled Poland; within a year Jan Masaryk was dead in Prague. If American economic policies such as those pursued with regard to Poland and Czechoslovakia can be characterized as "aggressive," "imperialistic," or even as constituting a fatal adherence to the Open Door, then it is obvious that a great deal of linguistic refinement and clarification is necessary in our scholarly discourse. Far from seeking to contest Soviet control over the Eastern European area or to force American business interests into that "market area," Washington policymakers withdrew just as soon as it was evident that minimal American requests and demands were going to be rebuffed.

But, of course, there remains the problem of Western Europe and of the Marshall Plan. Did not the United States in this instance use economic aid as a weapon to suppress legitimate European impulses to radical social and economic reform? Here the answer may well be yes, but once again significant qualifications and reservations exist.

The Marshall Plan was couched in the loftiest, indeed the most smug terms. Europe would not necessarily love us for what we were about to do for her, Marshall told his Harvard audience on June 5, 1947. But we must do what we could in the area of massive reconstruction for the sake of basic humanity. But, of course, as revisionists have quite correctly observed, Marshall, for all his protestations that aid was open to all of decent mind and heart, equated humanity with capitalism and reconstruction with restoration of an economic *ancien regime* which seemed to many morally bankrupt and intellectually exhausted. The conditions laid down by American officials for Marshall Plan aid in the late forties practically precluded the triumph of any form of social, political, or economic radicalism in Western Europe.

Perhaps Washington's insistence that European governments "open their books" to American aid officials was not specifically designed to force the Soviets away from the program or to discourage indigenous radicals from even applying. But several revisionist scholars have made a strong case that such was certainly the result. Moreover, American policymakers literally prayed that Stalin and Molotov would find such terms unacceptable as they eventually did after Molotov attended a number of early European Recovery Plan meetings. The revisionist thesis can be faulted in only a single area: American officials had no prior assurance in the summer of 1947 that the Kremlin could politically or economically afford to reject Marshall's gesture. No senior official in Washington thirty years ago would have denied the terrible destruction which war had visited on the Soviet Union no matter how strong the Red Army was or appeared to be. That a rapidly emerging adversary might accept Marshall Plan aid seemed to many a very real possibility. Nonetheless, the invitation was extended. Thus, while it may be too much to argue that there was a wisp of genuine humanitarianism behind Marshall's assertion that his Plan was not meant to discriminate against any state or ideology which genuinely sought the welfare of Europe as a whole, the proposition cannot be entirely dismissed.

Once the Soviets did pull out of the European Recovery Program, Marshall Plan aid was used as a weapon to bind Western European governments and peoples as tightly as possible to the United States. The published record in the *Foreign Relations* series clearly indicates that in Italy, at least, economic assistance was directly channeled only to those persons and parties best able to hold the political line for American interests against the increasingly popular leftist groups and coalitions. Moreover, on several occasions Washington made it clear to Italian political leaders that they had better follow the American road or risk loss of precious economic aid for their country and people. The "chaos" and "extremism" to which Marshall and others continually alluded in speaking of early postwar Western Europe were ever more readily equated with Communist or extreme left-wing groups. By 1948 neither Marshall nor anyone else in Washington could conceive of any other form of political economy for the nations on this side of the Elbe but a form of "democratic capitalism."

And yet, having given critics of America's foreign policy in the late forties their due, we may still ask if that foreign policy was either excessive or brutal in the contemporary context. Since late 1945 American foreign economic analysts and policymakers had become disturbed by the fact that while the Russians were demanding immense postwar aid from this country and the United Nations, they were also looting and stripping Eastern Europe and Germany in the name of war booty and reparations, while refusing to undertake a reduction in arms in any way commensurate with that of the United States. The American military establishment of the Second World War was dismantled during the first twelve months of the peace except for the strategic air arm. The Soviet military machine remained largely intact to be used as an instrument of Soviet foreign policy around the Eurasian land mass from Turkey to Manchuria. Yet the Soviets persisted in expecting a large postwar credit and from the first exhibited great irritation at being asked to account for the expenditure of relief and aid funds. Given the record of ruthless Soviet behavior in Eastern Europe by late 1947 and the menacing presence of the Red Army there and elsewhere—to say nothing of prior Soviet probes in Iran, Turkey, and Japan—can it not be argued that it would have been the height of folly for American officials not to have asked the Soviets for a decent accounting of funds received either through a bilateral loan or through participation in Marshall's European Recovery Program?

For it is this very ruthlessness in Soviet behavior after about mid-1946 that had so understandably alarmed Washington officialdom. The Central Committee resolution of August 1946 had touched off a new round of government purges and suppression of all "alien influences" in Russian cultural and scientific life. With this resolution Stalin and his henchman Zhdanov determined to isolate Russia once more from *all* "foreign influences," Western or otherwise. Indeed, as Ulam observes, many of these "influences" "were identified, in line with Stalin's growing prejudice, as Jews."[2] As for the Marshall Plan itself, Stalin obviously—and understandably—perceived it as an immediate threat once he had discarded it in his own mind as a possible benefit. This threat

. . . had to be warded off by taking speedy measures in the most vulnerable area, the East European satellites. Hitherto the pace of subjugating those countries had not been hurried [after August 1946 Stalin was too busy at home disciplining his own people!]. Czechoslovakia was ruled by a coalition which, though headed by the Communist Party, left considerable scope for free political life. Elsewhere—except in Yugoslavia . . . shreds of democratic freedoms persisted, and the more strenuous Soviet policies, such as forced collectivization, had been avoided. Now all this had to be changed, politically and socially. . . . Were the local Communist parties there entirely reliable? During the war all sorts of unreliable elements had been let in and the usual vigilance against ex-Trotskyites had slackened. . . . All in those countries and parties had to learn some of the lessons Stalin had taught his own country and his own Communists in the 1930s [during the so-called Great Terror]. . . . The major Communist parties of Europe had to go back to school. This school, organized in September 1947, was called the Communist Information Bureau. If the title had reflected its true purpose the Cominform would have been known as the anti-Marshall Plan Bureau.[3]

No Communists were to be immune from the teachings, demands, and discipline of the Cominform. When the Italian and French

Communists did not immediately bend into line, Stalin passed the word that during the war these ostensible comrades had in fact allowed themselves to become the tools of the bourgeois Western powers. The only way to live down such charges, the appalled Palmiro Togliatti and Jacques Duclos were told, was to lead their nation's working classes in resolute opposition to the Marshall Plan.

Thus did the rapidly aging and senile old tyrant let loose a new reign of terror upon his people—particularly the Jews. Temperamentally suspicious of and often murderously spiteful toward all elements and individuals he could not control, Stalin naturally came to regard not only the United States and Western Europe but even significant elements east of the Elbe with fear and loathing. Russian and Eastern European life once more fell into a pattern of apparently random and aimless terror from late 1947 through the Doctors' Plot of 1952. Eventually, it seems, Stalin got so bad, Stalinism so terrible, that the generalissimo's own underlings decided he had to be gotten rid of.

That such a comparatively benign initiative as the Marshall Plan, no matter how calculated and self-serving, no matter how much or how little it may have aided American business expansion, should have so intensified an already emerging reign of terror and suppression in those areas under Stalinist control tells us far more about the malevolent and unstable nature of Stalinism than of the aggressiveness—real or ostensible—of early postwar American foreign policy. If Marshall Plan aid was used as a political weapon to unite Western Europe in a general democratic and capitalist alignment against Stalinism in 1948 and beyond, does not the Soviet record at this time make American behavior understandable if not entirely creditable?

American foreign policy between 1945 and 1950 was essentially limited and defensive. It was grounded on a weak military base (indeed, on no real military base at all short of a hypothetical atomic bombardment of Soviet cities in an apocalyptic Third World War) and on an economy that was often hobbled in its efficiency and productivity by divisive labor-management disputes and an administration uncertain as to the extent and depth of its domestic social reform commitments.

The basis of American foreign policy between Hiroshima and

the Korean War was summed up cogently by an influential, mid-career Foreign Service officer named George Kennan. As he tirelessly reiterated in later years, Kennan conceived his containment doctrine in very limited terms. From the perspective of 1947 or 1949, Communist expansion was *not* to be confronted everywhere, at every point, on or beyond the confines of the Eurasian land mass. The United States and its allies simply did not possess the resources or the will for such protracted confrontations. The containment doctrine of 1947 presupposed a prudent husbanding of resources and commitments to stop the Communist tide from engulfing those areas considered essential to the security and prosperity of the democratic-industrialized West, namely Western Europe and Japan. Kennan never conceived a United States projection of power on the mainland of Asia beyond the borders of South Korea. He and Bohlen have told us that they opposed the United Nations effort to unify Korea by force in late 1950 and were unsurprised, although deeply concerned, by the result.

And yet, if one leaps ahead a decade from Korea to the early and mid-1960s, it is indisputable that a change had come over the leaders and peoples of the West and particularly of the United States. As the Pentagon papers clearly demonstrate, an atmosphere of crusading zeal and an attitude of arrogant presumption were present and deeply informed policymaking. By this time the model of aggressive American cold war policymaking projected by the revisionists was an obvious, evident reality. The ultimate expression of American cold war behavior was nearly at hand in the chilling truth of My Lai. But My Lai, like Lidice and a host of other atrocities, was not susceptible to an economic interpretation; it could not be viewed as the inevitable climax of a thirty-year search for a secure, global market area or even as part of an instinctive reaction to a long-departed Stalinism. Somewhere in time between, say, 1947-48 and 1965, the cold war mentality of the United States had drastically changed. The sense of limited power expressed by Harry Truman to Harold Smith had vanished.

One of the great failings of much historical writing and imagination is the tendency to view epochs in terms of rigid totality. There is this era and that age, and within the given chronological framework all is rigid and unchanging. The cold war has been peculiarly susceptible to this kind of thinking. But the cold war meta-morphosed at several points and at no time more so than during the Korean War of 1950-53. Korea represented the grand water-shed of the cold war and justifies a thesis of "two cold wars," the first lasting roughly from the spring of 1946 to June of 1950, the second lasting from 1950 to at least 1970.

While it is impossible to assess with any precision what Stalin's motives were in either unleashing or supporting the North Korean invasion of June 1950, it is intriguing to look back and view the world as it then was and seemed.

From the perspective of more than a quarter of a century, it is evident that by the spring of 1950 Washington and its European allies had almost put a stop to any possible Kremlin hopes to sub-vert the West. American economic aid to Southern and Western Europe under the Truman Doctrine and the Marshall Plan had begun to lay the foundations for an ultimately vigorous political and economic recovery. The Berlin Airlift, that desperate response by a militarily weak West to Soviet military pressure on a key cold war point, had resulted in a Kremlin backdown. In April 1949 NATO had come into being, always (and particularly at the outset) more of a promise than a reality, yet a promise of resistance to the Soviet threat nonetheless, and one which the Soviets always took seriously as clearly demonstrated by their persistent efforts either to destroy or eviscerate the organization.

Thus by the early 1950s whatever designs the Soviets might have had upon a rapidly recovering Western Europe were checkmated. There is a temptation then, and this is sheer speculation, to argue that a frustrated Stalin turned eastward and, perceiving that the Americans had clearly excluded South Korea from their defense perimeter, allowed an eager Pyongyang to unleash its forces upon its neighbor. This temptation is reinforced by the fact that the Com-munist camp had only recently received its newest and most glam-orous recruit, Maoist China, which could be expected to support any North Korean venture.

Whatever the worth of this argument, it is undeniably true that Western statesmen and peoples did not view their situation nearly so favorably at the end of the forties as we can nearly thirty years later. The rather decisive checkmating of Soviet power in Europe went unheeded; statesmen chose to dwell upon NATO's current weakness rather than its future potential or even contemporary promise. Moreover, the West had been stunned in 1949 by two events of enormously evil implication: the "fall" of China to communism and the Soviet explosion of a nuclear device, which ensured early Russian possession of the atomic bomb. The entire world balance of power, held precariously and uncertainly at best by United States air power since 1945, had apparently swung abruptly and decisively to the Communist world.

While Stalin thus *might* have struck in Korea out of a sense of frustration, America and the West *surely* responded there out of a sense of fearful weakness, an emotion, incidentally, that was simultaneously generating the sinister campaign of Senator McCarthy against "domestic traitors." Korea seemed to confirm every anxiety, every assumption, every belief, about the insatiability of "international communism." Thereafter the mood in America and throughout much of the West changed. Resigned and often apathetic resistance to Soviet pressures in Central and Western Europe was transformed into a vibrant, global strategy against an international enemy who must be confronted at every turn and "rolled back" wherever possible by great crusades for freedom. In the Korea-McCarthy years, American paranoia at last approached Stalinist proportions, to be expressed on more than one occasion in Hitlerian terms. The age of Acheson and Truman was ending; the age of the Dulles brothers was about to begin.

The change in public mood and national policy during the Korean years can be demonstrated in a number of ways. In the first place, during and following the Korean War Kennan's containment doctrine was expanded and warped in a fashion with which its author repeatedly disagreed. Now, to Kennan's expressed horror, "containment" was to be practiced universally; any and all movements that either defined themselves or were defined by increasingly suspicious Washington bureaucrats as "Communist inspired" were to be opposed with greater or lesser intensity—overt and covert—depending upon the national will, resources, and interest. The inevitable concomitant of this new commitment was the garrison state, the weapons culture, and a runaway international arms race all too often defined domestically by defense profiteering, foreign payoffs, and all the other corruptions attendant upon an unsupervised military-industrial complex. Most tragic of all, perhaps, was the almost immediate transformation of the European Recovery Program into the Mutual Security Program with all that implied in terms of a switch from butter to guns.

Along with the expansion of the containment doctrine, the garrison state, and the weapons culture to global proportions came, of course, the equally enormous and chilling expansion of the Central Intelligence Agency. It is interesting to note that, as with the containment doctrine, the universalist *implications* of the CIA were present from the beginning, that is from 1947, when "the Agency" was established, but that such implications did not become reality until the Korean War. From what we now know of CIA activities, covert operations of the murder-and-mayhem variety—including the LSD-laced cordials, the alleged assassination attempts upon certain foreign leaders, the shellfish toxins and the cobra venoms, the exotic-weapons systems, and all the rest—did not really begin until after 1950. Most began in 1952 or 1953, the years when the Korean stalemate was breeding the new and fetid second cold war environment of total opposition to "international Communist expansion" everywhere on the earth.*

When the cold war era is thus broken down into two intimately linked yet discrete periods, much of the confusion and disputation that currently wracks the American historical profession over United States responsibility for the cold war and its more prominent horrors evaporates. The first cold war era, 1946-50, can be seen as a time when Stalin's tyrannical and expansive appetites bred an understandable sense of Soviet threat in the minds of Western— and particularly American—statesmen, who responded with a policy of *implied but consciously restrained* universalism. The second cold war era, which began in June 1950 with the Communist assault on South Korea, transformed the universalist implications of the first period into full-grown, often frightening realities. From the Amer-

---

* CIA involvement in Iran and Guatemala fell naturally into the instinctive anti-Communist pattern of this period.

ican perspective, the first cold war was limited, comparatively clean, and defensive. The second cold war was global, dirty, and frequently aggressive.

As we move out from beneath the shadow of generational dispute and beyond the attractions of simplistic explanation and condemnation, based on our experiences and impressions derived from the second cold war era, as we learn more of our recent past and assess and refine its lessons, the formerly monolithic "cold war era" will surely fragment even more, and scholars will be able to discern perhaps three or four or even more cold war eras. Hopefully, this will also permit future scholars to view our past follies and our past achievements not only with greater precision and balance but, it can be assumed, with greater equanimity as well.

World War, Cold War, and the Communist Myth in America

7

BETWEEN 1946 and 1950, as the veteran generation began its journey up the ladder of time and the country found itself confronting the former Soviet ally along a multitude of political, territorial, and ideological frontiers, America permitted itself to fall into an ancient, easy, and fatal pattern of public thought. The veteran generation burdened itself still further with a fresh manifestation of the old American myth of internal subversion.

The fear of political or social subversion by secret factions dedicated to some alien ideology has long been a staple, not only of American, but of Western thought. Dread of the Sans-Culotte, the Sinn Feinist, the Jacobin, the Carbonaro, the Bolshevik, is a product of the modern age of revolution that first swept over the West two centuries ago. The United States, with its excitable, populistic order, has been peculiarly vulnerable to the many dangers inherent in frequent and jarring change. The terrifying notion of political termites steadily eating away at the foundations of republican order has always found a ready audience. Anti-intellectualism, xenophobia, isolationism, all have contributed immeasurably, if unevenly, to the successive waves of public panic over the imminent subversion of national institutions that have swept the country during times of real or imagined crises.

The myth of imminent subversion is as old as the republic; indeed, from the perspective of legitimacy the republic owed its very birth to prior years of assiduous subversion eventuating in outright treason against duly constituted authority. Perhaps the Founding

Fathers recognized or sensed this somber fact when they realized with growing horror that they who had made a revolution could not agree on what to do with it. Not only did Republicans and Federalists accuse each other throughout the late 1790s of seeking to destroy the fruits of Constitutionalism, if not independence, but many in and out of public life came to believe that the new nation was threatened by sinister conspiracies directed by the political opposition. Freemasons, "illuminati" (a group as shadowy in configuration and ultimate purpose as it was believed to be menacing in intent), Democratic-Republican clubs, the Society of the Cincinnati, Tammany Hall: each group, real or fancied, was believed by one side or the other at one time or another to constitute a measurable and immediate threat to the legitimate sociopolitical order spawned by independence and nationhood.

Half a century later the strains and animosities generated by the flood of immigration from Catholic Ireland and rising sectional tensions over slavery and abolition produced a "Protestant crusade" as absurd in its assumptions as it was violent in its manifestations. Thousands believed in the existence of a Popish plot to subvert republican America and pored over salacious stories of sexual skulduggery in convents and parish houses. The Protestant crusade culminated in the Know-Nothing movement of the mid-1850s, which enjoyed a powerful if brief impact upon local and national politics.

With the coming of mass industrialization and the shift in geographic patterns of immigration following the Civil War, there developed a fitful but discernible public concern with "radicals" and "anarchists," who preached and practiced alien philosophies spawned in the hate-filled, class-ridden, tyrannical environments of the Old World. Public anxiety over the morals, behavior, and ostensibly sinister objectives of the "new immigrants" from southern and eastern Europe simmered for years and boiled over just after the First World War. The Great Red Scare of 1919, in which nearly five thousand Russian aliens were rounded up in a single night and subsequently charged as Communist agents on the flimsiest evidence,* was only the first and most sensational product of a long-festering xenophobia. Soon thereafter ostentatious congres-

---

* Of those arrested, 250 were later deported.

sional investigations into Bolshevik propaganda in the United States were made the forum for a public identification of bolshevism with domestic radicalism. A country already disillusioned by the unhappy outcome of the First World War, frightened by the triumph of communism in Russia, angered by the unprecedented demands of organized labor for a significant share of the national wealth, and suffering from long-standing hostility to the millions of Europe's poor who had come to the New World looking for a new and better life, accepted, where and when it did not applaud, this shocking display of government contempt for civil liberties. When Nicola Sacco and Bartolomeo Vanzetti were subsequently arrested for a payroll robbery and accompanying murder in South Braintree, their immigrant background and outspoken defense of anarchism almost certainly doomed them.

But as in so many other areas of American life, it was the Second World War which to an almost unprecedented degree intensified and amplified existing trends to produce a nearly unique situation. By 1950 panic over subversion of national institutions and the social order had become widespread; it could be found nearly everywhere and within almost all groups. Moreover, now the focus of hostility and suspicion was not on the religiously, politically, and ethnically alien so much as on those who had achieved a comfortable niche within the mainstream of national life. It is true that many victims of the hysterical witch hunts that swept the country after 1946 were Jews or came from other ethnic backgrounds that had traditionally been a source of contempt to white, Anglo-Saxon, Protestant America. But many were not; there were numerous good-old-fashioned Anglo-Saxon names sprinkled among those called before the numerous House and Senate committees investigating "un-Americanism," "conspiracy," and "twenty years of treason" within the American government. While "McCarthyism"—to define a period, a perspective, and a process by its indisputable symbol—thus owed much of its force and popularity to a long-standing national propensity, it possessed unique ingredients that were added as a direct result not only of the cold war with its immediate stress upon anticommunism, but as a result of the world war which had preceded it.

The Communist myth as it emerged in America between roughly

1946 and 1954 projected a frightening scenario of widespread sub-version. The most important (although not necessarily the most sensitive) agencies of the federal government—not excluding, it was often hinted, the presidency itself—were honeycombed with secret agents of the international Communist conspiracy; the very fabric of the republic, and of the free world it increasingly came to define and defend, was gravely threatened. Hysteria soon gave way in some quarters to paranoia and sheer lunacy so that for a time in the late fifties and early sixties those on the far fringes of political primitivism seriously argued that a 100,000-man Chinese Communist army had been infiltrated into Baja California and was waiting to strike across the border at San Diego and Los Angeles.

The source of this peculiar cast of demonological thinking can be traced to that strange prologue to the holocaust of 1939-45, the Spanish Civil War. For it was in Iberia in the late thirties that some-one—it is not clear now who—first used the term "fifth column." According to the most popular legend, a Nationalist general about to attack a Republican town boasted that not only did he have four columns approaching the besieged city, but a "fifth column" of sub-versives inside the unhappy town who would arise at the right moment and fatally sabotage the defense. The Second World War had found its image of subversion; it now needed only a personal symbol, and this was obligingly provided by a hitherto obscure Norwegian army officer, one Vidkun Quisling, who openly sub-verted his unprepared nation's feeble efforts to resist Nazi invasion in April 1940 and was handsomely rewarded by his German allies. After 1940 the terms "Quisling" and "fifth columnist" became virtually synonymous.

Wartime America proved particularly susceptible to the Quisling and Fifth Column demonologies. While Britain, in the front lines of war, achieved a comparatively humane record in the treatment of "enemy aliens" between 1939 and 1945, the United States from the beginning was fatally prone to waves of hysteria. The first wave, of course, struck thousands of hapless Japanese-Americans on the West Coast. While virulent and long-standing racial prejudices surely account for much of this scandal, terror of an early Japanese invasion of California that would trigger widespread sabotage from within the issei and nisei community was a factor in policymaking that cannot be ignored. Indeed, the myth of internal subversion increased throughout the war, and when it blended in many unstable minds with the myth of a wartime crusade that would produce a postwar millenium of peace and prosperity American-style, a volatile mood crystallized, which made the coming of McCarthyism predictable.

Wartime books and films kept the apparition of the saboteur, the fifth columnist, vibrantly alive in the public imagination. One of the most popular writers of the war and immediate postwar years was John Roy Carlson, whose books *Under Cover* and *The Plotters* sought to expose the extent of alien underground networks across the country that were working sleeplessly to undermine or destroy the national will and effort. Carlson claimed to have obtained his material firsthand, to have gone fearlessly underground at great personal risk, posing time after time in city after city under alias after alias as a willing convert to enemy or alien ideologies. The ostensible Fascist agents whose cover was blown by Carlson proved to be rather pathetic and quite petty people—much like the Elizabeth Bentleys, Judith Coplons, and Julius and Ethel Rosenbergs of a later time. But as was pointed out by a flood of laudatory reviewers in the pages of such leading publications as the *New York Times*, the *New York Herald Tribune,* and the *Book of the Month Club News* (to say nothing of Clifton Fadiman and Walter Winchell, who volunteered encomiums on their own), Hitler, "that crazy paper hanger," had come to power in Germany, Austria, the Sudetenland, and elsewhere over the backs of such moles as Carlson had unearthed. At Armageddon one could not afford to be merciful or compassionate toward those who were seeking to undermine the right way of life.

Carlson does not appear to have been a complete fool. He was a shrewd manipulator and exploiter of the wartime mood of fervent, unquestioning patriotism, and he was adept at pandering to the public's gamier anxieties. Moreover, he was careful to state on numerous occasions that his investigatory forays into the "un-American" underground were taken in defense of that generous democratic order which Franklin Roosevelt and the New Deal had brought to the country. He was particularly insistent on this point throughout *The Plotters*, his second book, which dwelt on the threat posed to immediate postwar American life and organizations by not only proto-Fascist groups but also the Ku Klux Klan and the Communist party. He deplored the implicitly Fascist response of many conservative Republicans and businessmen (mostly unnamed) to the postwar threat to liberal America while congratulating such farseeing liberal Republicans as Wendell Willkie who had the wit to realize that only through pursuit of the goals and aspirations announced by Franklin Roosevelt could the internal threat to the country be at last neutralized.

The saboteur proved to be a staple of wartime films. Indeed, a motion picture with precisely that title was quite a popular hit, as was one of Humphrey Bogart's less memorable efforts entitled *All through the Night*. In both films, particularly in *The Saboteur*, the chief theme was the foolishness of everyday Americans who laughingly or haughtily dismissed the very notion that they or their country were in danger from within. No one would believe the increasingly frantic hero and heroine who had unwittingly uncovered a nationwide Nazi spy ring. Interestingly enough, the Nazi agent in charge in both motion pictures was that suave veteran of the screen, Otto Krueger. Krueger's specialty was the villain of taste, refinement, and urbanity, supposedly so respectable as to be utterly above suspicion. Only the hero realized with a sense of growing horror that this inhumanly competent mole had placed his agents at the very heart of national life. A disturbing twist in the plot of *All through the Night* had Bogart playing a raffish but unmistakable gangland leader with a heart, finally, of pure golden patriotism. The not so subtle message of the film was that when the chips were down most American gangsters would support their country—a dubious proposition at best—and, most disturbing of all, that only gangsters from their position outside and beyond the law could effectively penetrate and destroy subversive organizations.

This idea was somewhat countered by the spate of FBI movies between 1941 and 1945, which stressed both the omnicompetence of the nation's chief law-enforcement agency and the diabolical cleverness (and moral sickness) of the subversives. The most notable of these films, *The House on 92nd Street*, had as its villain a woman —ostensibly a respectable businesswoman—who confounded her pursuers through periodic escapes into transvestitism. Thus were stereotypes of rot, corruption, and perverse righteousness in high places and low driven deeply into the minds of thousands of political unsophisticates through the medium of supposedly frivolous entertainment.

While wartime Americans were being continuously exposed and habituated to the sinister notion of widespread internal subversion, they were also, of course, being bombarded by official and unofficial propaganda on the theme of a postwar millenium that justified the wartime crusade against Nazi Germany and samurai Japan. The nature and dimensions of that crusade have already been suggested. But it is necessary to emphasize here how decidedly leftist in tone and assumption the crusade was. It presumed a continuation not only of the Grand Alliance with the traditionally mistrusted Soviet ally, but also of those highly controversial domestic measures and strategies which the New Deal had imposed upon the country during the grim years of the Depression. So totally did those measures and strategies win general, if often grudging, acceptance in later years that now it is necessary to stress how bitterly contested they were by so many Americans throughout the war and early postwar era.

Roosevelt—and Truman—might have done far more to preserve a modicum of fundamental and enduring consensus had they not made both the New Deal and the Grand Alliance the cornerstones of their wartime and early postwar policies. But the imperatives of warmaking on a global scale really offered Roosevelt no alternative. He—and his immediate successor—had to place the popularity of his programs, his person, and his foreign policies at the very core of the American crusade in order to bring force, coherence, and legitimacy to the enterprise. But the cost was high, perhaps prohibitive. Millions of Americans who had never been reconciled to the New Deal viewed the Grand Alliance and the wartime crusade with the gravest suspicion. The alienation of many simple and susceptible minds within the anti-Roosevelt ranks could only have been reinforced by popular wartime preoccupation with fantasies of internal subversion and treason often emanating from the most polite quarters. Who is to say that widespread belief in Alger Hiss's guilt by association with wealth was not the product of wartime preoccupations and assumptions.

Thus it was that the wartime experience and the inevitable postwar disillusions that followed provided direct and forceful antecedents to McCarthyism. The feverish atmosphere of commitment and concern, the fixation upon threats to domestic institutions and tranquillity, and the fear that internal subversion could be found in the most comfortable circles prepared the way, once the Grand Alliance collapsed into mutual hostility and recrimination, for that hysterical preoccupation in America with "pinkoes," "Comsymps," "dupes," and "conscious tools of the international Communist conspiracy" which so marked the tragic years of the late forties and early fifties. There was just enough truth in what McCarthy and Jenner, Nixon and Styles Bridges charged as to give a superficial plausibility to public alarm. There had been, after all, a handful of Communists in the administrations of Franklin Roosevelt and Harry Truman as well as throughout some areas of the American labor movement; not until 1947 did the positions of most such individuals become untenable. The historic and heroic effort at mutual East-West cooperation during the war possibly did lead to greater territorial and ideological gains for "international communism" than might otherwise have been the case had Roosevelt and Churchill undertaken the immense gamble of waging a separate war against Hitler and Japan, leaving Stalin to work things out in his part of the world as best he could. And, finally, there was the apparently disastrous series of miscalculations about China—beginning with the Roosevelt administration's assessment of Chiang's strength and popularity—which led to an utter defeat of American policy and hopes.

But the hysterical response of many millions to these mistakes and setbacks—and the shameful silence of many millions more in the face of this hysteria—demeaned and weakened the country. The loss of competence in the formulation of postwar Far Eastern policy due to the purge of many Foreign Service officers was but one among many retributions which history exacts for folly. McCarthyism laid another heavy burden upon postwar America, soured even more the already grim perspective of the veteran generation concerning the nature of public and private life, and brought forth, in conjunction with the Korean War, that second, sinister stage of the cold war era, and lengthened still further the baleful shadows of the wartime mentality of 1939-45.

America and the Postwar Far East: Perceptions and Realities

8

NO MORE tragic legacy of American isolationism can be found than in United States policy toward revolutionary East and Southeast Asia after 1945. For decades before Pearl Harbor, American citizens and policymakers alike had been conditioned by the isolationist tradition to believe that Asia was a strange, wondrous, and far-off place. It was filled with "teeming masses" who were, like all "colored" peoples, inherently inferior. Yet, for that very reason, Asia's millions were seen as charges upon the American Christian conscience and political system. While strategic prestige and expanded trade—the latter expressed in terms of the Open Door—lay behind American seizure of the Philippines in 1898 and the expanded American presence in China after 1900, the missionary impulse was a vital component of public thought and government policy toward Asia. And when, during the first few decades of this century, the Great Powers, already firmly ensconced in China and Southeast Asia, made it clear to Secretaries of State Philander Knox and William Jennings Bryan and to the house of Morgan that American economic penetration of this potentially vast market area would be minimal, the evangelical perceptions of the missionary took precedence in America's Asian policy and thought.

The missionary perceived East Asia and particularly China as a vast vineyard of the Lord waiting to be fruitfully exploited in his name. China was seen as the great challenge to Anglo-Saxon Christian morality and standards. If China could be evangelized, educated, and even democratized, then the traditional American mission of moral uplift and regeneration would be measurably advanced.

The missionary perception was never static. Originating in mid-nineteenth-century Protestant evangelism, which, among many other things, led to the sending of Christ's agents throughout the "heathen" non-Western world, the missionary impulse soon focused on China. From the first, Christian missionary life in the often remote, rural enclaves of China was hard, and the crust of ancient Chinese tradition, practice, and perspective proved heartbreakingly difficult to crack. Those Chinese who seemed most susceptible to missionary teachings all too often used what they had learned to frustrate Western interests. Almost completely impervious to the splendid culture which stubbornly continued to exist amid the physical squalor and social and political chaos that was late Manchu and early revolutionary China, Western missionaries could not grasp the depth of shame and bitterness which many proud young Chinese felt in the defilement of their ancient and honorable life-style. And so the missionary could never see that what he taught would inevitably be used against him, that what he was and what he represented was at once attractive and anathema to those he tried to save. However fervent his promises of success to skeptical church audiences during home leave, however fascinating and intriguing the slide shows of quaint mission houses and strange peoples flashed on wooden, midwestern church walls, it was obvious to nearly all Americans by 1920 or so that no great religious convulsion would occur in China. China would remain largely beyond the pale of Christianity.

But even as one illusion faded, another was born. The triumphant sweep of the Kuomintang north from Canton in the late 1920s seemed to promise that the culmination of the Chinese revolution of 1911 might well be some form of recognizable democracy, Western-style. An ignorant, idealistic America persisted in seeing China in its own image.

In its determination to rule China, the Kuomintang was never above contriving to be all things to all men. During the mid-twenties its leader, Chiang Kai-shek, even convinced Josef Stalin that the Kuomintang was quasi-Communist, and the ruthless Soviet leader was induced to send a mission to Canton under Mikhail Borodin to teach Chiang and his men the intricacies of firm and effective revolutionary leadership. Having learned all he could from the Borodin mission—having sucked it dry—Chiang threw it out of China and turned against the Communist wing in his own party. At the same time the Chinese generalissimo began an equally effective selling job in the West, especially in the United States. The spiritual leader of the Kuomintang, Sun Yat-sen, had spoken during the first years of this century of China's need to adopt democratic practices, and naive Americans both in and out of government believed that Sun wanted China to become just like the United States. They completely missed the thrust of Sun's message, that the best way for China to rid herself of the foreign devil—Americans included—was to adopt some of the devil's practices, but not necessarily his ways, much as Japan had already begun to do. A quarter century later, with national power very precariously won and the Japanese menace looming, Chiang and his lieutenants began to embellish the theme of political similarity with the liberal West. A number of leading figures in the Kuomintang, including Wellington Koo, T. V. Soong, and Chiang's own wife Mei-ling Soong, had been at least partially educated in American missionary schools in China and then had come to the United States for college work. Madame Chiang, for example, had gone to Wellesley. Thus the American public and government, long habituated to looking at China from the missionary perspective of uplift and moral regeneration of an inferior people, quickly saw in Kuomintang China tangible promise of an early realization of their messianic hopes, not in the religious sphere, but in the political realm.

Japan proved the catalyst that turned vague, still largely disinterested assumption and goodwill into firm commitment. After 1937, when Japan's excitable militarists abandoned their country's highly successful policy of piecemeal digestion of Chinese political and territorial integrity for outright war, liberal opinion in the United States quickly viewed China as one more embattled outpost of democratic freedom along with Ethiopia, republican Spain, and Czechoslovakia. The Open Door doctrine, which in the past had often been either interpreted largely in economic terms or completely abandoned in order to appease Japanese pretensions, was now reinterpreted. In 1940-41 the Open Door was invoked in terms of democratic idealism. The defense and promotion of Chinese sovereignty under the aegis of the Kuomintang suddenly became an essential component of American foreign policy. Eventually Roosevelt and Hull made the impossible demand on Japan to terminate her "China incident," and a desperate Tokyo responded at Pearl Harbor.

America's Asian policy at the time of Pearl Harbor was and always had been limited, grounded in ignorant idealism, and based upon a condescending racism. The Second World War, while expanding American interest and commitments in the Far East, failed to alter measurably basic American perceptions about the area. European imperialism was not liked, but given the terrible weakness of our European allies, which perceptive American policymakers grasped even before the Pacific war ended, there was no real desire to force our friends across the Atlantic to disgorge immediately their rich and long-held colonial possessions in Asia. Despite Roosevelt's expressed desires to supplant French rule in Indochina with a United Nations trusteeship, a desire which the dying president did not press in the face of State Department opposition, America's Asian policy in 1945 remained largely what it had been. There was an instinctive willingness to defer to the prewar status quo, which imparted a distinctly conservative cast to American diplomacy.

But total victory brought undeniable changes to America's Far Eastern policies and perceptions. Deference to the prewar status quo was now modified by a somewhat crude but clearly emerging strategic concept of how postwar East Asia should look, should develop, and should be run. This concept was first summarized in the Yalta Far Eastern Accords of February 1945. Russia was promised the return of southern Sakhalin and Port Arthur, which had been lost to Japan in 1904-1905. In return the Kremlin pledged to make a bilateral treaty of friendship and territorial demarcation with Kuomintang China. This Sino-Soviet treaty, signed in Moscow on the day the Second World War ended, after weeks of hard Soviet bargaining, laid the foundation for America's postwar Far Eastern policy. It apparently guaranteed postwar East Asian stability through universal recognition of the Kuomintang as the legitimate Chinese government while forcing upon the two great Asian powers a clear demarcation of their respective territorial and economic spheres of influence.

A second cornerstone of America's early postwar Asian policy was laid in Japan. From the beginning American policymakers were uncharacteristically blunt in insisting that the Japanese occupation and the guidance of Japan toward Western-style democracy was to be a strictly American interest. The angry protests of the Australians, New Zealanders, British, and Russians that Japan had in the past posed as clear and present a danger to their interests as to those of the United States were simply dismissed as were the corresponding claims to an equal interest in shaping Japanese destiny through a share in the occupation. American policymakers from Secretary of State James F. Byrnes on down would only permit the limited participation of foreign "observers" and "advisers" in Japan. But in practice Douglas MacArthur, with unwavering support from Washington, ran the occupation as he wished. After 1945 Japan became, in American eyes, the new Asian vineyard, the new arena within which democratic hopes and pretensions could be realized. The United States had no desire to share such hopes and pretensions with others.

The third cornerstone of American postwar Far Eastern policy was laid in the ribbon of islands stretching south from Japan to the Philippines. American strategists at the close of the Second World War were determined to hold island bases in the western Pacific as outposts against largely unspecified, future aggressors.* Okinawa was kept; old Japanese bases in the home islands were taken over and refurbished; base rights in the Philippines were reconfirmed; and, of course, Formosa was returned by Japan to our "stout" allies, the Kuomintang Chinese. Moreover, the United States, in conjunction with the Russians, occupied the strategically important Korean peninsula, and in the American zone south of the thirty-eighth parallel, ignorant and untrained proconsuls began their first

---

* Records of numerous conversations among American military and civilian strategists at this time indicate that, when specified, the future enemy most often mentioned and feared was a somehow resurgent Japan. The Soviet Union was spoken of but not in such terms of grave concern.

painful and never successful efforts to guide native political development along democratic lines.

From the perspective of traditional great-power politics, America's early postwar strategic perceptions and policies were sound and cogent. And it must be emphasized that the great-power perspective was all that Americans possessed. Neither the government nor the public, with a few honorable exceptions, had ever taken the time or effort to try to know Asia, its peoples, or its many cultures. Like the British, the French, the Dutch, and the others, Americans preferred to dominate and exploit Asia rather than comprehend it. Even in the Philippines, where United States policies were most direct and benign, the population was perceived through the medium of a handful of powerful native families and bureaucratic structures in Manila and the few outlying cities. From 1898 to 1946 most Americans persisted in seeing the Filipinos as "our little brown brothers" with all the condescension that phrase implied.

Thus reliance upon the great-power perspective in Asia came naturally and instinctively to early postwar American policymakers. Chiang Kai-shek's China had been sufficiently aided and encouraged during the war, diplomatically if not militarily, so that it had apparently achieved in nearly all eyes the status of a great world power and, in conjunction with its treaty ally, the Soviet Union, a dominant regional power. In Japan the Americans would resume in the fresh setting of occupation their long-term program of uplift and regeneration in the hopes of creating yet another democratic and friendly oriental partner. Just to make sure that the national presence would always be felt and heeded in the area, a ribbon of island bases would be maintained off the Asian mainland to support and, if necessary, project America's chief agents of force, air and naval power. And presumably, as the years passed and European nations recovered their indigenous economic vigor and sociopolitical self-confidence, they would be induced to surrender their imperial holdings in Asia to carefully tutored and properly grateful native nationalists.

The only thing wrong with such a naive and benign set of perceptions was their truly staggering lack of appreciation of current Asian realities. For in the Far East, as in Europe and even Africa, the holocaust of 1939-45 had not only been a world war, it had constituted a world revolution as well. Japan—an Asian power— had swept the ancient imperial regimes of the West out of the Far East in 1942, and her subsequent defeat by those resurgent regimes three years later had not dimmed the immensity of her initial triumph in countless Asian minds. What Japan had almost done throughout the Orient during the war a host of native nationalist leaders were convinced they could do in a score of more restricted locales after the war. In Java, in Annam and Cochin-China, in Burma, in Korea, in India, the Philippines and China, the Sukarnos, the Mao Tse-tungs, the Ho Chi Minhs and their countless brethren were more than ever convinced that their corner of postwar Asia should be for the Asians, free from any Western influence and interest whether overtly imperial or merely supervisory or tutorial. Asia was in revolt in the autumn of 1945, but since that revolt simply had not been taken into account by strategic planners in Washington, it was not acknowledged or accepted for many months and years.

In the face of mounting cold war in Europe, American policymakers instinctively deferred to their pitifully weak allies there who had no intention of relinquishing ancient colonial power and prerogatives east of Suez without some sort of struggle. And the Americans themselves were loath to abandon traditional assumptions and perspectives about Asia. Throughout the late forties and fifties and into the mid-sixties, policymakers refused to surrender greatpower strategic perceptions of Asia in order to comprehend new Asian realities. The great revolt of most of Asia's millions against either Western bondage or influence was never fully acknowledged in Washington. Instead it was swiftly compressed into the cold war mold, instinctively incorporated into the predominant cold war atmosphere of the later forties and after. Compression and incorporation were made easier by Mao Tse-tung's willingness to subordinate himself and his revolution to the Soviet leadership until Kremlin demands and pretensions became, in their turn, unendurable to Asian sensibilities.

The Korean War, and especially its Sino-American portion that began in November 1950, at once intensified and rigidified traditional American strategic perceptions of Asia while banishing once and for all the greatest portion of Asia's peoples from American consideration. The People's Republic of China officially ceased to exist. Japan was encouraged not only to democratize but to rearm modestly. Economic strategists in Washington began to count on a resurgent Japanese industrial and corporate system to provide a flow of cheap goods to the rest of Asia, thus successfully frustrating Chinese Communist or even Soviet economic penetration. The island bases off the Asian mainland were strengthened, and renewed efforts were taken to support anti-Communist liberal leaders such as Ramon Magsaysay in the Philippines in their successful struggles against indigenous Communist movements.

Above all, containment of communism in Asia became a supreme consideration in American diplomatic and strategic thought. Following the Korean settlement in the summer of 1953, leading American policymakers such as Secretary of State Dulles and President Eisenhower as well as influential congressional figures, including Senator William Knowland and Congressman Walter Judd, proclaimed that communism could not be allowed to invest or invade one more Asian land without some sort of American response. In 1956, in justification for not permitting free elections in South Vietnam under the 1954 Geneva accords—free elections which he admitted would give all of Vietnam over to Ho Chi Minh —Dwight Eisenhower invoked the "domino theory" of Communist aggression: if one "free" nation in Southeast Asia fell, others would go too, until the whole Asian arc from Saigon to Delhi and perhaps beyond would "go Communist."

The simplistic perceptions and assumptions behind such thinking were nowhere more evident than in the policy of support for Chiang Kai-shek and his exhausted Kuomintang regime on Formosa. In 1949 and early 1950 Secretary of State Dean Acheson had given some careful indications of the Truman administration's utter exasperation with the Kuomintang, and the secretary of state had cautiously held out the possibility that Mao might someday become an Asian Tito at the very least and therefore someone with whom we could do business against the Russians. By 1955, under the impact of the Korean War and nearly a decade of cold war thinking and planning, Chiang, for all his admitted weaknesses, had become America's last cornerstone of power and prestige in

Asia. Chiang would presumably be supported without question or reservation; not even Quemoy and Matsu, those militarily indefensible and strategically unimportant spits of land only scores of yards from mainland China itself, would be surrendered. Twice, in 1955 and again in 1958, Communist bombardment of these islands brought forth dangerously provocative American responses in the form of naval convoys up to the limits of the coastal territorial waters properly claimed by the People's Republic. What was understandably viewed in Peking—and possibly in Taipeh as well in quieter moments—as a Chinese civil war had long been interpreted in Washington by this time as one more aspect of the global struggle between "communism" and "freedom."

In that struggle Washington was always looking for the Winston Churchill or George Washington of Asia. Chiang seemed to qualify for a time, but as the years passed and memories of Kuomintang ineptitude and tyranny on the mainland were refreshed by similar examples on Formosa, Chiang's image as a doughty fighter for freedom faded along with the dream that he would somehow return to the mainland as the conqueror for freedom. The next candidate seemed to be Syngman Rhee of South Korea. But he too eventually proved tyrannically intransigent, and his overthrow in 1960 obliterated yet one more American pretension. Finally, at the close of the 1950s, another hero appeared. Ngo Dinh Diem had obtained precarious rule in Saigon with initial liberal backing in this country and had somehow held on and prospered. If he was no Asian Washington or Churchill, he nonetheless seemed to represent the linchpin of "free world" hopes on the mainland south and west of China. Neither Eisenhower nor Kennedy, until the last, ever felt that they had any other choice but to support Diem with all he could use—and more. Articulate, even vociferous opinion in the United States would permit no other course.

The gulf between perception and reality in America's postwar Asian policy, however consistent it was, never reached tragic proportions prior to 1965 (Communist China excepted) because of the long-standing existence of one intelligently conceived, cogently argued restraint. America never would, if she could help it, fight a major land war in Asia. American diplomacy during the Second World War had been directed largely toward obtaining a Soviet declaration of war against Japan so that the Red Army, not United States forces, would subdue the fanatical Kwantung Army in Manchuria and north China. The American intervention in Korea in 1950, eventually supported by the armed contribution of sixteen member nations of the United Nations, had led to such a traumatic stalemate that a "never again" school swiftly emerged in the Pentagon and State Department whenever future land war in Asia was discussed.

But at last even this single deference to Asian reality was swept away by the apparent strategic imperatives of universal cold war containment policy. Diem, no matter how increasingly unpopular, inept, isolated, and brutal his regime, could not be abandoned. Kennedy agonized over possible intervention for two years. It would be like an alcoholic taking a drink, he told one listener. One drink would lead to another and another and another until sobriety was totally destroyed. Kennedy's assassination saved him from the decision of complete withdrawal or total commitment. Lyndon Johnson enjoyed no such luxury but rather sought to resolve the growing impasse through acceptance of the last and most fatal Asian illusion of them all: that the United States could still impose its will on the stubborn peoples of the Orient cheaply through the use of air and naval power alone. The president and his men discovered too late that modern air power is more vulnerable than useful in a guerrilla war. Strategic bombing is of little use, even against urban bases, because the guerrilla demands comparatively little in way of support. Conversely, tactical bombing, which may yield some immediate results, is highly vulnerable to guerrilla attack since tactical assault aircraft must be based close to the guerrilla's known areas of operations to be successful. Thus the Johnson administration quickly discovered in 1965 that if North Vietnam and the Viet Cong were to be dissuaded from further assaults in the south through the application of air power, the air bases would have to be protected by ground forces. And given the nature of guerrilla warfare in Vietnam, defense by ground forces could not be static, but must be aggressive and mobile. This, in turn, demanded much larger ground forces than had originally been thought or planned. In Kennedy's metaphor, the drinks were taken one after another in 1965 and after.

The best and the brightest of the veteran generation walked into the Indochina quagmire with their eyes wide open but their jaws set in determination. And the result was one of the two greatest tragedies in American history (the other, of course, was slavery). America's postwar experience in the Far East thus constitutes a sober lesson to any statesman who would substitute unsubstantiated perception, however hopeful or generous, for reality, however painful or harsh. For all of us the world remains as it is, not as we would wish it to be or to become, and in this simple proposition so amply borne out by recent history lies both the limitation of and challenge to grand policymaking.

The Last Warrior

9

FEW YOUNG men have ever achieved the status of legend so quickly as John Fitzgerald Kennedy. Even before his tragic death much of the world, Communist as well as "free," sensed that an unusually vigorous, bold, purposeful, and immensely captivating personality had risen on the international scene. Assassination transformed promise and prominence to myth; the unfinished presidency, to use Henry Fairlie's phrase, became Camelot at the hands and in the typewriters of scores of grieving followers, journalists, and scholars.

Legends irresistibly invite revision. Less than a decade after Kennedy's death revisionism was fashionable. A mere glance at the public record, the swiftest run-through of the major events of the "Kennedy years" was enough, it was claimed, to shatter the ideal of Camelot. The young president had been nothing more or less than an inflexible cold warrior and counterrevolutionary whose "doctrine" was vigorous defense of an inherently unjust status quo, often through the employment of lofty rhetoric combined with military force, economic pressure, and internal subversion. By far the best critical study of the Kennedy presidency condemns the young man from Massachusetts for employing a "politics of expectation" so flagrant as certainly to mislead and ultimately to disillusion his millions of idolators both at home and abroad.[1] If Kennedy was a man whose like, taken measure for measure, the world might not look upon again for some time, he was nonetheless a man, warts and all. The fatal flaw in his public character, demeanor, and language (to say nothing of his apparently shocking private conduct on occasion) was that he promised an impossible salvation and that he set himself up, wittingly or not, as a deliverer. His death might indeed have been the salvation of his reputation, much the same way as it has been argued that, however tragic, Lincoln's assassination saved his country and himself from probable folly and subsequent despair.

Revisionist and journalistic revelations of Kennedy as a mortal man possessed of great, possibly fatal flaws will constitute a salutory balance of assessment and perspective only if they lead to a new and mature synthesis of the man and his works. If Kennedy's defenders all too often portray him as a demigod, his detractors all too often misread what he said and what he wished to do. As is frequently the case, the man has been obscured by the myths of others and by the rush and drama of the events that crowded his thousand days of power.

We might begin with the simple observation that, contrary to some revisionist implications, Kennedy never promised to end the cold war. Rather, he promised to transform it to America's advantage after what he and his followers claimed were eight years of drift and setback under the benign and incompetent stewardship of Dwight Eisenhower and the Republican party. A second observation that can legitimately be made from the record is that Kennedy was very much a member of the veteran generation and thus he shared its frequently flawed and harsh perspectives. Benjamin Bradlee, his good friend and journalistic Boswell, wrote immediately after the assassination of how firmly and gracefully Kennedy fit into his time and place and how well he understood it.[2] Such understanding, we have regrettably learned, included subscription to the impersonally malevolent notion that one did not "get mad" at one's opponents or enemies, one "got even." And if this meant the waging of steady, covert warfare against certain foreign countries (possibly including tacit presidential acceptance of assassination attempts against certain foreign leaders), then so be it.

Kennedy's very identity had been forged in the crucibles of the world crisis of the late thirties and the world war of the early forties. His was, above all else, the mentality of the warrior. As a youth Jack Kennedy was remarkable only for his very ordinariness and ready willingness to absorb the hard-driving, aspiring, intensely competitive virtues of his family atmosphere. Only in his apathy toward academic achievement could one sense any degree of latent rebellion in the youngster. As late as his junior year at Harvard, Kennedy was an unremarkable, second-generation, Boston-Irish rich boy, no more. Then he journeyed to a Europe on the brink of catastrophe and transmitted to his father at the embassy in London some interesting and mature, if not astoundingly revelatory, observations.

He was still in England when hostilities actually began and was soon dispatched by his father to Scotland with responsibility for caring for a shipload of torpedoed American tourists. Thereafter he resumed a wandering existence—a stint at Stanford, a six-month tour through Latin America—until Pearl Harbor suddenly rescued him and millions like him from a life of essential aimlessness. Military command, however minor, the terror and ecstacy of war, however brief and sporadic amid the general tedium of life in the South Pacific, and eventual heroism, however perplexing its origin (accounts of the destruction of PT-109 leave any reader with a nautical background somewhat skeptical), gave Kennedy an identity and eventual purpose he had hitherto lacked.

At the heart of the Kennedy presidency—and, indeed, a crucial component of the Camelot legend—was a real gaiety of power that in the grim postwar context of American life proved most affecting and wonderfully refreshing. As Kennedy brought his young generation to power, it seemed for a long moment that the veteran experience had produced neither cynicism nor despair nor even profound disillusion, but rather had kindled nobler impulses toward preservation, reform, and overall concern. After years of battleship gray, postwar leadership under both Truman and Eisenhower, power had been seized, in Kennedy's own words, by a new generation of Americans, born in this century, tempered by war, disciplined by a hard and bitter peace, proud of the ancient national heritage, and unwilling to witness or permit the slow undoing of those human rights to which the nation had always been committed and to which it remained committed at home and abroad. "Let every nation know, whether it wishes us well or ill," he cried on that bright, cold, snowy Washington day in January 1961, "that we shall pay any price, bear any burden, meet any hardship, support any friend, oppose any foe to assure the survival and success of liberty. This much we pledge—and more.' "

Here was the credo, at once smug and sacrificial, of the veteran generation of which Kennedy had been so conspicuous a leader and so frequent a spokesman ever since that seventeenth day of July 1944, when John Hersey's brief, eloquent article on the adventures of PT-109 and its youthful skipper had first appeared in the pages of the *New Yorker*. Now a new young administration, whose members had first tasted combat and leadership on the battlefields of Europe and the vast expanses of the Pacific, was coming to power easily and gracefully. The New Frontier seemed to possess above all a very real, occasionally downright boisterous sense of humor, and its members were convinced that enough competent application, enough dedication, enough firmness of manner and policy, would ameliorate many, if not all, of the world's and the nation's ills. That, at least, was the promise.

Kennedy himself contributed a crucially important ingredient to the emerging self-image of the veteran generation: family background. If he himself was rich, urbane, and highly educated, his predecessors had not always been so. It had taken at least three generations of Kennedys to lift the family out of the slop and muck of mid-nineteenth-century, Boston-Irish poverty into which the first Kennedy had come, a miserably poor immigrant from Ireland, that land of tragedy, tears, and laughter. John Kennedy and his young siblings played the game the American way. With his money and security and undeniable talent, the young president could have been a prominent journalist, perhaps an eminent historian. He chose the rigors and uncertainty of public life instead—with, to be sure, a little push and strong support from an overbearing parent— and he excelled in it from the first, often rejecting the aid and counsel of the founding father where and when necessary. Yet, as he observed to Dave Powers in 1961, there remained fashionable Protestant clubs in Boston where no Irish Catholic, no matter who he was, could find welcome. In his sense of grievance, uncertainty, and anger, coupled with deference to the status quo, he was at one with millions of fellow veterans.

So much for the promise, the perspective, the affiliation. What of the performance? Did a supremely confident young man seize (some would say buy) power in part through lofty, liberal rhetoric and demeanor only to become an instinctive conservative, a consistent proponent and supporter of the status quo? The public record suggests otherwise.

Throughout American history political men have sought the presidency for a variety of reasons. John F. Kennedy, that most political of men, seems to have sought it when he did because of a very real and legitimate concern that he might not live long enough to obtain it through the normal course of party promotion. Available evidence indicates quite strongly that Kennedy's brush with death as the result of his spinal operation in 1955 induced his rush to the White House. Defeated by the narrowest of margins for the vice-presidential candidacy at the Democratic convention in 1956, the junior senator from Massachusetts thereafter set his eyes, his formidable energies, and the enormous resources of his family firmly on 1600 Pennsylvania Avenue. The fabled Kennedy luck held fast: removed from any association with Adlai Stevenson's crushing second defeat at the hands of Eisenhower, Kennedy could and did present himself as a fresh, vigorous, young yet experienced alternative to the established national leadership of both parties. As early as 1957 *Time* magazine was quoting enthusiastic political leaders in a number of states as saying that Kennedy was the front runner. The young senator spoke tirelessly and piled up political IOUs. When in 1960 older members of the Democratic establishment in and out of the Senate, both conservative and liberal, realized that the nomination was rapidly going to Kennedy by default and mobilized for what they claimed would be an "open convention," Kennedy and his large and formidable band played as rough as any of the bosses opposing them.

Kennedy thus sought and won his party's presidential nomination in 1960 largely for personal reasons, not because of any burning ideological or emotional commitment to change such as motivated Goldwater four years later and McGovern eight years after that. Moreover, the prevailing atmosphere conspired to channel Kennedy's program and appeal along traditional lines. Nineteen sixty appeared, at the outset, to be another Republican year. Eisenhower's phenomenal personal popularity held to the end, and if

Richard Nixon blundered in not calling for Ike's personal help earlier, he surely ran on a platform which Eisenhower found quite congenial. Moreover, the country seemed self-satisfied and relatively prosperous. Thus the underdog Democratic challenger was forced into a position that is quite familiar to anyone who has lived in one of our fundamentally one-party states.

In such a state, the nearly permanent minority party seldom presents a radically differing alternative. Rather it bases its appeal, not unnaturally, on the promise that it can carry out the existing policies of the entrenched party better, more expeditiously, and often more economically. Kennedy did the same thing in the national arena in 1960. He avoided condemnation of the contents or assumptions of Republican policy and concentrated upon real and ostensible Republican shortcomings. Were the Republicans committed to the defense and extension of "freedom" in Asia? Then why were they so niggardly in supporting Chiang's position on Quemoy and Matsu? Were the Republicans committed to a democratic Western Hemisphere? Then how had they permitted the implantation of a Communist state "ninety miles from home"? Were the Republicans committed to a firm posture of national defense that would cloak broadly assumed commitments with adequate power? Then why had they allowed a "missile gap" to come into being vis-à-vis the Soviet antagonist?

Such critical jabs and alarming pronouncements were not the products of hypocrisy. They were the natural expressions of Kennedy's own, long-ripened cold war perspective. As early as 1947, he had condemned his party's president for doing too little to save democracy in Italy. As early as 1949 he had joined the rising outcry against State Department officials who wittingly or not (Kennedy was conveniently vague on this point) had helped to ensure the triumph of communism in China. Throughout the 1950s Kennedy's perspective never appreciably changed—as his firm support for Ngo Dinh Diem in 1954-55 attested—and he never sought to disguise it. Along with 95 percent of his countrymen, this rising spokesman of the veteran generation was a dedicated and practicing cold warrior.

He was also an egregious nationalist. Throughout his career the labels "liberal" and "conservative" discomfited him, and rightly so, for he was neither. His political philosophy revolved around the conception of a republic of Platonic dimensions presided over by a philosopher king whose lieutenants would be the best and the brightest of their generation. The New Frontier for which he campaigned in 1960 could be, Kennedy maintained, a new frontier for the arts as well as for politics, an intellectual and artistic Camelot, if you will, in which the products of the human mind, spirit, and imagination would be venerated fully as much as the works of statesmen. Properly conceived and managed, America's New Frontier might in time rival Periclean Athens and Elizabethan England. Years later the young candidate's more lofty pronouncements would be literally carved in stone in the front of that vast, surprisingly cold marble palace of the arts which bore his name and lay alongside the Potomac River cheek-by-jowl with Watergate. But when he spoke thus of the arts, Kennedy was thinking primarily in terms of the elevation of the state rather than the promotion of human creativity. Artistic revival was perceived primarily as a further adornment to the political system, not as anything desirable in its own right. Indeed, available evidence indicates that for all his ostentatious courting of the great minds of science and the arts, Kennedy was not much interested in what might be termed "high culture."

In fact, as Christopher Lasch has noted, what was distinctive about Kennedy's ephemeral New Frontier was the final co-optation of veteran-generation intellectuals by the state coupled with a very real degradation in the definition of an intellectual.

The cultural tone of the New Frontier was the tone of Broadway sophistication with an admixture of Hollywood. The nerves of the administration reached in one direction through the President's brother-in-law to Frank Sinatra's Hollywood "clan" and to Hollywood liberalism in general, and in the other, via the first lady, to the world of fashion . . . and of the fashionable arts. On the political side the influence of the Cambridge academic and technological community—that other center, not so much of the intellectual life, as of the new educational bureaucracy—was everywhere to be seen.[3]

As a leading symbol and spokesman of the veteran generation, Kennedy had come out of the Second World War filled with a taste for "excellence" in many forms. But, of course, his family's own background had been in precisely those worlds of Broadway and Hollywood in which Joseph P. Kennedy had achieved so much financial success. Jack Kennedy's very ability to project himself as a cultural as well as political spokesman lay in the fact that his definition and experience of culture was closely tied to that of the general public. Kennedy claimed from the first that his New Frontier must be a showcase of excellence, and many took him at his word and mistook breadth for depth. Thus, in Richard Rovere's revealing eulogy, Kennedy was "interested in and amused by and critical of everything in American life" and was "the first modern President who gave one a sense of caring—and of believing that a President ought to care—about the whole quality and tone of American life." Genuinely concerned with the vulgarity of the veteran generation's affluence and with the ugliness and intellectual impoverishment of much of urban life, Kennedy "proposed to have, in time, an impact on American taste. He proposed to impress upon the country—to make it, if he could, share—his own respect for excellence of various kinds."

Yet it was a measure of the impoverishment of the veteran generation's own perspectives and aesthetics that Kennedy projected no appreciable taste of his own—style, yes; taste, no. Rovere admitted that the youthful leader of the New Frontier "did not respond much to painting or music, or even to literature" but rather "looked at painting he didn't enjoy, and listened to music he didn't much care for, because people who he thought were excellent people had told him they were excellent things."[4]

Kennedy thus entered the presidency as a rather callow and pretentious young man, instinctively committed to existing cold war and domestic verities and bold only in his determination to make things better, not different, to "get the country moving *again* [italics mine]" with all that that implied in terms of an unreflective deference to the underlying status quo. If he had led a new, young, distinctive generation into political power, if his youth, charm, charisma, drive, and determination had undeniably challenged, then broken, the stranglehold of the older, entrenched generation upon state and national political power, he had never infused, never sought to infuse, his crusade with strikingly new ideological ingredients. Nor did the young president give any indication either im-

mediately or for a long time just *what* he wanted to do or *how* he
wanted to do it. For many months the New Frontier remained a
hollow campaign phrase, not a grand political design. One suspects
that perhaps deep down inside Kennedy had not expected to win
in 1960, had not expected to become a world leader so early in
life with so little preparation, and that the job at once mystified
and often even frightened him.

Certainly he was unsure at the start just whom to enlist in the
New Frontier. There were a number of people, of course, whom he
knew and trusted and wanted. But in general he had to go to Washington's old Democratic political establishment—to people like
Clark Clifford and Robert Lovett—for suggestions. He had never
met the man who became his secretary of state prior to his election. His cabinet came together on the day following the inaugu-
ration as perfect strangers. At one point during the interregnum,
he confessed to Galbraith at Palm Beach that he was having trouble
forming an administration and was accepting people whose character and qualifications he did not know well, if at all. "Within a
year I'll know who I want," he added. All that the president did
demand from his people was membership in good standing in the
veteran generation (a glamorous war record was highly preferable,
though not quite essential), a demonstrated capacity for "excellence"
(which was usually defined as possession of some measure of public
prominence), and, of course, youth. With a few exceptions* people
over the age of forty-five did not achieve high position in the New
Frontier.

The administration which Kennedy thus patched together from
elements new and old soon found itself lurching from one crisis to
another. While the country was sporadically captivated by the
glittering parade of artistic, intellectual, and show-business celeb-
rities who trooped to the White House, while millions were bemused
by Mrs. Kennedy's determination to bring a new sense of taste and
elegance to the executive mansion, while the press dutifully stressed
the exuberant partying and serious work undertaken by the youth-

* Both J. Edgar Hoover and Allan Dulles, for instance, were swiftly
reappointed to their posts; Kennedy had no wish to interfere with the
existing national police and intelligence establishments.

ful New Frontiersmen and reported such fads and novelties as the fifty-mile hikes, the Hickory Hill "seminars," and the scores of noisy and precocious children that surrounded the New Frontier at play and occasionally at work, the Kennedy administration suffered one setback after another. The new president allowed himself to be talked into continuation of the disastrous Bay of Pigs adventure devised and developed by his Republican predecessor. In so doing he unwittingly set in motion a long train of disasters. An increasingly radicalized section of the younger generation, already smitten with the more romantic implications of the Cuban revolution, was further alienated. Countless Cuban exiles were estranged; the more unstable among them would ultimately contribute in no small measure to the Watergate "horrors." Kennedy then allowed himself to be bullied by Khrushchev at Vienna and returned to Washington greatly sobered, if not frightened, by Soviet intransigence. As a result he possibly overreacted to the Berlin crisis of the summer of 1961. Finally, amid mounting gloom, he permitted the first significant military expansion of the existing but vague American commitment to South Vietnam.

Domestically, too, the New Frontier could boast of few achievements during the first two years. The Kennedy administration so badly botched its first legislative offensive in Congress, the aid to education bill, that it was never again able to dominate the Hill or even find a comfortable working arrangement despite a Democratic majority in both houses. A few pieces of promising legislation did get through in these early years—the Peace Corps and the Alliance for Progress, to name two. But even here revisionist critics have pointed to the ultimately limited effect of the former program and the outright failure of the latter, geared as it was to a feckless effort to raise mass living standards in Latin America by the all-too-frequent dispensation of aid through precisely those entrenched elements who profited most from the continuation of general poverty. Beyond his failure in Congress, critics have pointed to Kennedy's fight with Roger Blough and "big steel" in the spring of 1962, which seriously, perhaps permanently, damaged Kennedy's standing with the business community. And it is certainly true that the "Negro revolt," to use Louis Lomax's phrase, which exploded across much of America in 1962-63, caught the Kennedy brothers badly off guard and revealed them to be as interested in enforcing existing laws as in supporting the impulse of black Americans to full civil rights.

Moreover, Kennedy from the first displayed a driving interest in expanding American military power to unprecedented dimensions, and here, as usual, the president found little opposition from a Congress by now steeped in the mystique and influence of the weapons culture. No matter that the missile gap proved chimerical; Kennedy expanded America's missile superiority over Russia to a ratio of five to one. No matter that Korea had proved that the people of the United States were restless under the cloud of a long, inconclusive, distant war, however limited; Kennedy developed the concept of an American counterinsurgency force whose very raison d'être would be to enter and wage protracted limited war upon distant frontiers.

True enough, there were moments when Kennedy and the New Frontier acted with restraint and even some wisdom. Intervention in Laos (which the departing Eisenhower told Kennedy might prove to be his greatest crisis) was rejected, and a peace of sorts between the warring parties, one of whom might or might not have been overtly Communist, was patched together in 1962. The nuclear test-ban treaty of early 1963 was a clear-cut triumph of statesmanship, moderation, and decency for all concerned.

Yet even in these instances the record is ambiguous. Sorenson has told us that a major factor in Kennedy's rejection of intervention in the Laotian civil war was simply that Laos was a landlocked country, and thus the problems of logistics and supply might well prove insurmountable. The test-ban treaty immediately followed and was largely a direct outgrowth of the Cuban missile crisis, created, many have claimed, by Kennedy's overreaction to Khrushchev's foolhardy but understandable effort at abrupt neutralization of American nuclear supremacy.

Even the justly lauded American University speech in the spring of 1963, it is claimed, has been misinterpreted. It did not represent a significant departure from prior policy, but in fact an aberration; within weeks Kennedy was berating the Soviets again at Berlin while the New Frontier was actively, if clandestinely, intervening in Latin America.

Surely recent evidence that the Kennedy brothers actively, indeed enthusiastically, "bugged" their "enemies" in the steel industry during 1962 (knowledge of FBI harassment of the steel magnates has long been known) and that it was they who instituted agency "watch lists" on "suspicious" figures in and out of government will further tarnish the Kennedy legend.[5] So, too, will the shocking exposures of CIA excesses, which apparently climaxed during the earliest stages of the Cuban missile crisis when members of the intelligence agency actively discussed and overtly planned the assassination of Fidel Castro. Such discussions, along with plans to enlist the Mafia as a tool of cold war policy, apparently began in the late Eisenhower years, but both John and Robert Kennedy apparently continued to promote and support such activities to the point of tragedy. In a very real sense, it may be argued that the road to Watergate began at Camelot.

All this is true, and yet it is a half-truth, as anyone knows who lived through the Kennedy years. For all his pretensions, all his faults, all his follies—and they were many and profound—John F. Kennedy seemed to be moving slowly during the last year of his life to a more realistic, more generous view of the world about him. To be sure, he remained to the end a tough, even ruthless politician. If the tales of his defenders are to be believed, he proposed to stay in South Vietnam until he decisively beat Goldwater in 1964. Then, and only then, would he seriously consider pulling out. It has been widely alleged that he stalked Castro to the end and may well have been "gotten" by Castro before Castro was "gotten" by him. Yet impressive evidence is at hand that a good mind and an increasingly understanding character were beginning to reassess old but unexamined assumptions. If we are to measure Kennedy with fairness and balance, then we must do him the courtesy, indeed extend him the right, to be understood in the context of his own time and place and not in ours. This involves looking again at the world of 1961, not as we perceive it from our own day, but as it was perceived at the time. And despite a rising if seldom discernible tide of alienation among the young, that world remained in bondage to the perspectives, programs, and rhetoric of the cold war.

It was a time when what was then known as the radical right was riding high, when such political hucksters as Billy James Hargis and Dr. Fred Schwartz with his Christian Anti-Communist Crusade had reached the peak of their considerable influence. Outrageous claims that it was "five minutes to midnight," that more and more of the world was being "colored red," that Dwight Eisenhower might have been "a conscientious tool of the international Communist conspiracy," were rampant. Thousands, if not millions, who should have known better were not even immune to the hysterical claim—widely spread by rightist hate groups at the time—that a 100,000-man Chinese Communist army was lurking in Baja California. A paranoid concern with the apparently deteriorating status and power of America vis-à-vis the Soviet antagonist dominated public discussion. If the hysteria of the radical right of 1961 seems scarcely creditable in 1977, it was all too real and vigorous at the time.

Kennedy had sensed and exploited a profound paradox in the American voting public in 1960. While Eisenhower was venerated personally and credited professionally with providing the country with peace abroad and a measure of rising prosperity at home (though the lingering effects of the 1958 recession could be discerned in the over 7 percent unemployment rate), Americans were fearful that under his cheerful, easygoing leadership the cold war initiative had passed to the Kremlin. Nikita Khrushchev had seized sole power in the Soviet state after 1956 and had launched, it was automatically assumed, a whole set of initiatives in Laos, in Vietnam, in Berlin, in Africa, and in the Middle East, that had thrown America on the defensive. These initiatives had been followed by the spectacular success of Sputnik and by the Kremlin's subsequent "rocket-rattling." *Time* magazine gloomily conceded that 1957 had belonged to Khrushchev, and the plump, bald little Soviet premier was pronounced "Man of the Year." Three years later Eisenhower's presidency closed with the embarrassing U-2 incident (which, among other things, seemed to demonstrate the terrifying effectiveness of Soviet rocketry) and the spectacular breakup of the Paris summit conference during which Ike was forced to sit in stony silence and listen to a dressing down by his Soviet opposite.

The notion that America was losing the cold war had thus become a staple of scholarly, journalistic, and popular belief by 1961. A cautiously favorable and generally balanced assessment of the first six months of the Kennedy administration concluded that America was the "underdog in the balance of power" between East and West and implied that all disarmament proposals not only would fail but should fail until the United States regained the upper hand.

As the Soviets see themselves pulling ahead in the balance of power, they push ever harder armed subversion abroad, which they term wars of liberation, and insist upon "troika" systems in international relations which would put them "one-up" on the West in the United Nations and in disarmament inspection.

The Soviet Union still is apparently where the United States and the Soviet Union were at San Francisco in 1945, which is where the world was in the sixteenth century, that is, in a position of insisting that any major power may do whatever it wishes to do in its national interest as it sees it. This giant Soviet country which has deified planning, seems thus far entirely incapable of inventing a plan which can prevent the rapid drift toward war. It is one of the ironies of the time that not only in economic ideas but in political ideas as well the Soviet finds itself so deeply imbedded in earlier centuries that it cannot even consider what the mid-twentieth century requires.[6]

Liberal critics of the Kennedy administration in the aftermath of the Bay of Pigs, Vienna, and Berlin crises were more blunt in their assertions that the world was a tough and cold place and that the arrogance of the New Frontiersmen in assuming that they could change it was not only misplaced but constituted a positive disservice to the nation. "If the early months of the Kennedy Administration demonstrate anything, they demonstrate there are no new problems and no essentially new ways of meeting them," William V. Shannon wrote in the *American Scholar* in the autumn of 1961.

Elections occur, Presidents come and go, but the three fundamental problems confronting American statesmen remain stubbornly what they were sixteen years ago when the United States emerged from World War II into the cold war: how to contain the outward thrust of Soviet imperialism, how to bring the underdeveloped countries out of the past without subjecting them to the rigors of totalitarian tyranny, and how to manage our industrial economy, the foundation of the nation's greatness, without inflation or depression.

Kennedy, Shannon asserted, had yet to prove that he could manage any one or a combination of these problems.[7]

The liberal-intellectual community—or much of it, anyway—had been traumatized by the Bay of Pigs fiasco, and while Shannon bespoke a broad conventional wisdom in taxing Kennedy for committing a military blunder, some other liberals, most notably Alfred Kazin, probed deeper to expose the hypocrisy, the deceit, and, above all, the unmitigated and terrifying arrogance of the act itself. Yet as the British writer and ostentatious friend-of-America David Butler observed, in the White House as elsewhere nice guys finished last, and

> The fact is, of course, that no successful President could satisfy the intellectual's longing for logical, uncompromising purity. The ruthless Bobby Kennedy side of the President's nature is potentially one of his greatest assets, although misplaced ruthlessness, as in Cuba, is far worse than woolly do-goodism. Toughness in defining problems and carrying out decisions without too much regard for people is essential to a successful President. The Kennedy toughness, when tempered in the fire of administrative experience, promises to be one of the great assets of the next four years.[8]

But it was perhaps Henry May who most successfully caught and reflected the mood of those veteran generation intellectuals who either gravitated to Kennedy or who, in May's case, wished him well in a spirit of gentle skepticism. May's mood was one of fashionable exhaustion. The status quo was fundamentally unsusceptible to dramatic reform. The title of his essay, "In a Time of Unmanifest Destiny," said it all. The Kennedys had promised too much, had said too much about changing a world stubbornly resistant to change. There were things—four of them, in fact—which could be done and were in the national power to do, but not too much should be expected when and if such goals were achieved. There had to be a rebirth of freedom at home that would transform "our choked and ugly cities, our blatant and foolish mass media, our obsolete racial customs and qualified civil liberties"; there had to be renewed efforts to achieve "relative—since there is no absolute—military security"; there had to be a truly global New Deal along the lines of an "alianza para progreso, in all languages"; and, lastly, there had to be a return to the national habit "of telling the truth, not only to our friends and enemies, but still more to ourselves." This program of do-goodism, at once vague and universalist in nature, was characteristic of veteran-generation thinking throughout the brief Kennedy era, and within a very short time it was to be condemned as hypocritical and then dispatched with murderous ease by the very students whom May taught at Berkeley and elsewhere. And even such a vaguely defined program was laden with timid qualifications. "Merely to abandon the illusions of manifest destiny will not, I repeat, give us the answers to any problems," May concluded. "We would find the same alternatives that confront us now still before us, and we would doubtless follow much the same policies. But perhaps we might, for a change, follow them with dignity. We might get out of the habit of panicking at every setback [the allusion here was, in part at least, to the Bay of Pigs debacle]. That would make a very big difference."9

If during the early Kennedy years popular, scholarly, and journalistic criticisms of the cold war status quo were comparatively few in number and usually tentative and muted in nature, a strikingly broad consensus developed about America's role in a corner of the earth which would soon be associated with the most tragic of national adventures—Vietnam. Henry Fairlie has recently compiled a list of journalistic pronouncements between 1961 and 1963[10] concerning the national mission in Vietnam that is, in the light of what followed and what was to be said later, truly astounding. "The war in Vietnam has caused enough mischief," Fairlie writes. "It can only cause more if the legend is allowed to persist that an innocent people and an innocent press (think of that!) were trapped into supporting the American involvement in the war by politicians who kept them ignorant." Far from restraining policymaking or antagonizing the policymakers, public opinion in the United States in 1961-63 was far ahead of White House decision making regarding Southeast Asia. The press faithfully reported the administration's developing program of counterinsurgency warfare and accurately prophesied that that kind of warfare would first be applied to the "Communists" in Laos and South Vietnam. As early as April 1961 the *Washington Post* declared:

> There is reason to think that South Vietnam is the real target of the southward push by the Communists. . . . The United States has a major

interest in the defense of Vietnam not only because of the vast amounts of economic and military aid (which only recently has been turned to the all-important guerrilla training) but also because American prestige is very much involved in the effort to protect the Vietnamese people from communist absorption.

Neither Walt Rostow nor McGeorge Bundy could have put the case for eventual intervention any better.

That same day the *New York Times*, in response to a State Department statement that the United States government would not let the people of South Vietnam down, editorialized: "Free world forces . . . still have a chance in South Vietnam, and every effort should be made to save the situation." As Fairlie notes: "The authors of the narrative summary in the Pentagon Papers criticize the Kennedy Administration for consistently thinking in terms of a communist bloc; but this was also the thinking, with few exceptions, of the spokesmen of informed opinion." As the situation in Vietnam deteriorated in 1961 and 1962 and Kennedy sent more and more advisers, "informed opinion" in the press and elsewhere kept those citizens who wished to know abreast of the developing commitment in terms that clearly reflected a we-have-no-choice perspective. As Fairlie shows, not even David Halberstam was immune to such reporting. In March of 1963 Halberstam wrote from Saigon of the increasing "de-Vietnamization" and growing "Americanization" of the civil conflict, adding: "The stakes are sizable. Americans have given their solemn word that they will stay to win here: if they fail, the word will be out throughout this region that Americans are paper tigers, and no little country will want to be on the wrong side of China." Not even Dwight Eisenhower or John Foster Dulles could have stated the domino theory case with greater clarity.

A month later the *New York Times* described the use of napalm and defoliants in South Vietnam in terms that were far from condemnatory: "Napalm has been used by the South Vietnamese air force against real or imagined havens of Vietcong guerrillas. Its use has certainly killed innocent people—as other weapons have done. . . . Defoliation chemicals (common weed killers) have been employed largely in attempts to strip leaves from heavy jungle growth near lines of communication." *Newsweek* magazine's Francois Tully had bluntly warned an entire year before that the small but quietly growing American casualty lists "underlined for every American the reality of United States involvement in the Vietnam war. . . . The United States, in short, has passed the point of no return—short of victory—in South Vietnam." And on September 6, 1963, less than two months before the assassination of Diem, the *New York Times* editorialized: "The lessons of the present crisis are plain. One is that the anti-communist war in South Vietnam, which has produced the best fighting force in Indochina, is not only, as President Kennedy declared, 'their war' but our war—a war from which we cannot retreat and which we dare not lose." Barry Goldwater would not achieve such eloquence in speaking of the American commitment to Vietnam barely a year later.

Benjamin Bradlee's words immediately following the assassination—that John F. Kennedy was uniquely a man of his time and place—assume portentous meaning when the atmosphere in which he moved and worked and decided is taken into account. To say that he was a cold warrior and counterrevolutionary is to say, eventually, nothing at all. By instinct and training we were, with a few honorable exceptions, all cold warriors—and, yes, counterrevolutionaries too—in 1961 and 1962 and 1963. Kennedy did not lead the country into Vietnam; the country pushed him in a direction which, as Halberstam shows in *The Best and the Brightest*, the president instinctively rejected and fought against.

Does the secret of the Kennedy legend lie precisely at this point, then? Was he no more than a captivating man of his time and place elevated to heroic stature by tragic death? Or was there a genuine element of greatness to the man which death cut short and myth has obscured?

The available record indicates that prior to the Cuban missile crisis Kennedy was very much the American warrior, the outstanding symbol of the veteran generation, which in 1960 was eager to seize and use the reins of national leadership in order to prove its mettle once again in a series of global showdowns with the forces of darkness. But the missile crisis, whoever was responsible for its inception, seems to have both sobered and steadied the man. Memoirs and journalistic accounts of those fearful October days agree that the president was as sensibly frightened (as opposed to being scared, which implies a paralysis he never displayed) as at any time during his life. He was quite aware that he might well be responsible for the literal end of civilization, if not the outright extinction of the human race as we know it. Yet within the crisis context itself he acted with superb coolness and above all with a very real sense that the incident should never be used to humiliate Khrushchev in particular (who also showed remarkable restraint—so much so that it ultimately may have cost him his job) or the Kremlin and the Soviet system in general. The missile crisis at once presented Kennedy with the opportunity to reopen a meaningful "dialogue" (to use the bureaucratic jargon that came into being at that time) with Khrushchev and to justify that dialogue in terms of a personal and national power and influence that had been lacking prior to the installation of Soviet rockets in America's backyard.

Characteristically, Kennedy moved slowly and carefully, refusing to throw over old policies and orthodoxies while exploring new ones. Thus the transformation of American foreign policy after the Cuban missile crisis was not dramatic but slow and cautious. As late as the summer of 1963 the president spoke at Berlin with possibly gratuitous harshness about Communist domination of East Germany, culminating in his famous *ich bin ein Berliner* flourish.

Yet the record of his final year is one of a slowly growing number of actions and utterances, of which the test-ban treaty, the American University speech, and the approved wheat sale to the Soviet Union stand out, reflective of a dim but growing awareness that the cold war had gone on long enough and that some way had to be found to defuse hatreds and ignorance so as to avoid extinction and prepare the country for its proper place in an emerging world of change and diversity. Perhaps the best evidence the president gave of his shifting mood, his expanding perspective, came on September 26, 1963, before an avowedly conservative and initially skeptical audience at the Mormon Tabernacle in Salt Lake City, less than two months before his death. "It is little wonder, then," he said, that "in this confusion, we look back to the old days with nostalgia. It is little wonder that there is a desire in the country to go back to the time when our Nation lived alone." But the irreversible tides of science and politics and technology had made that impossible and "in world affairs, as in all other aspects of our lives, the days of the quiet past are gone forever."

If the nation was to survive and prosper, then it had to accept certain realities which would henceforth limit and compress American universalism to a degree never before perceived in the postwar world.

We must first of all recognize that we cannot remake the world simply by our own command. When we cannot even bring all of our own people into full citizenship without acts of violence, we can understand how much harder it is to control events beyond our borders. Every nation has its own traditions, its own values, its own aspirations. Our assistance from time to time can help other nations preserve their independence and advance their growth, but we cannot remake them in our own image.

America had "moved so far into the world" after 1945 out of fear that traditional Soviet expansionism would engulf all of Europe and Asia. But "after some gains in the fifties the Communist offensive, which claimed to be riding the tide of historic inevitability, has been thwarted and turned back in recent months," and the dream of historic inevitability had been "shattered" by the determination of peoples everywhere to shape their own destinies. This very world of emerging diversity insured that no one power, no single ideology, could triumph, and the president warned his listeners that they "must recognize that foreign policy in the modern world does not lend itself to easy, simple, black-and-white solution. If we were to have diplomatic relations only with those countries whose principles we approved of, we would have relations with very few countries in a short time." For the purpose of foreign policy "is not to provide an outlet for our own sentiments of hope or indignation; it is to shape real events in a real world." The president closed with an invitation that his listeners and his countrymen everywhere accept the emerging world of variety and discrepancy and live with it, accept the very fact, indeed, that a diversified world, with all its confusions and fatigues, offered the kind of environment in which America would find itself safest and happiest.[11]

There is sufficient ambiguity in Kennedy's Salt Lake City speech

—and indeed in many of his actions throughout the last year of his life—to generate continued skepticism in the minds of critical scholars. Just how far, for example, would a United States under John Kennedy's leadership have felt it could legitimately go in "assisting" the nations of the "underdeveloped" world to "preserve their independence"? Could such assistance include massive military intervention such as would come in Indochina within two years? As with every other fact of the man's life and work, we shall never know.

And yet when the cold and astringent atmosphere in which he moved is again recalled, it is difficult not to conclude that during the last year of his life John F. Kennedy had begun moving, however haltingly and carefully, beyond his time and place in order to seek new solutions and test out new policies and responses that would better fit the United States into a rapidly changing world. He had obviously begun—rhetorically, if not in terms of hard policy-making—to challenge those traditional notions of American messianism which had been transformed from moral expressions to economic and military policies as a result of cold war tensions. On numerous occasions he stated a rather fervent hope that he would meet and badly defeat Senator Goldwater (whom he personally liked) in the 1964 campaign, because he believed that Goldwater stood for all the outworn orthodoxies of universalism that were most dangerous to American interests in a changing world. He had begun a personal and lonely journey toward new comprehension and fresh perspective, and he was beginning to lead his countrymen away from old verities and old terrors.

In a melancholy way the the impact of his tragically foreshortened quest was not immeasurable. As Kenneth Crawford wrote within hours after the assassination, if a man's greatness can be weighed by the enemies he made, then Kennedy must be accounted a great man. For he was deeply hated at his death by all who, in one way or another, feared and despised the simple adventure of living well and freely, who raged at the ordeal of change especially when it demanded the surrender of privilege and a felt sense of omnipotence, and who were contemptuous of leaders who would risk abandonment of old certainties in order to comprehend new realities.

The Kennedy promise, then—the promise, that is, of the man and not the myth—was an end at last to the grim cluster of habits and values that had seized and defined the national temperament as a result of the Second World War. Entering office as one of the many warriors of the Second World War grown older but scarcely more mature, Kennedy moved during the last year of his life toward an abandonment of the veteran generation's verities and toward the vision of a truly *post*war world of diversity and measurable peace. He promised, in short, to become the last warrior.

His death destroyed the promise. The last warrior had enlisted lieutenants much like himself except in their fundamental inability to sense and move with change. If Tom Wicker is to be believed, Lyndon Johnson's Indochina tragedy began with his first day in office, when, in looking back toward the old world instead of ahead toward the new, he asserted that he would not allow it to be said that he was the one who "lost" Vietnam as Harry Truman had been charged with "losing" China. The entrenched axioms of the veteran generation and of the cold war which sustained and defined it swiftly resumed their dominance over the minds of policymakers and a majority of citizens. But, of course, the spirit changed; the old gaiety of power fled the White House with Kennedy's ghost. Where he had initially been an enthusiastic proponent of veteran-generation verities, his lieutenants and successors, benumbed by the assassination, became dogged defenders of a life-style increasingly besieged by rapid change and mounting dissent. Where he had proved, finally, to be somewhat flexible, they proved to be completely rigid. This very sense of blind, bulldog purpose locked the Johnsons and the MacNamaras and the Bundys and the rest into an increasingly dubious policy of commitment and escalation in Indochina, into a war whose scope and scale of indiscriminate violence rose with every frustration until at last a perfect pitch of horror was achieved.

By this time rejection of the flickering Kennedy promise was so complete among members of the veteran generation that no apparent thought was given either at the White House or, initially, across the country as to whether or not the generation of the sixties might have wittingly or unwittingly sensed and accepted Kennedy's vision of a world of diversity and peace and incorporated that vision into

War and Society 10

IF YOU seek its monuments, look around. More than thirty years later they are with us still: at Auschwitz, Belsen, and a score of other carefully preserved relics of Nazi barbarism; in the still uncompleted revolutions of Asia and Africa; in the weapons cultures and economies of the great nuclear powers who generated and shaped the cold war environment in which the world has lived since the first postwar spring; in the geopolitical configuration of Europe that has remained frozen for over a generation in the pattern of 1945; in the very existence of the state of Israel and the perpetual crises between Arab and Jew, whose ramifications are worldwide and literally world shaking. The list is endless. A score of countries, a hundred thousand cities, towns, and villages, countless individuals, carry the scars of the Second World War. For over three decades, while standing at the brink of fresh calamity, the world has struggled through a massive, emotional hangover induced by that intoxication with mass social violence that so gripped the human race between 1939 and 1945.

To a frightening degree the opponents of nazism have found themselves infected with the very virus they sought to destroy. Seldom before the age of Hitler and Stalin had men so earnestly preached and practiced that the only proper resolution of grievance and dilemma, whether real or fancied, lay in the unlimited application of naked force. This was Hitler's legacy to the world, and it corrupted all too many personalities, as the führer himself knew it would. We have, all of us, been defiled by the holocaust of 1939-

45. That we all recognize this in some deep, instinctive way is apparent in our most casual speech and thought. How often those of us who possess memories of the war years, however dim, begin or end a sentence with the phrase "since the war." There have, of course, been many wars of fearful, if limited, ferocity since 1945, but we all know which war we mean. We all instinctively realize that something so terrible happened to ourselves and our civilization over thirty years ago that it will forever shape and haunt our lives.

Yet in America's case the term "postwar" and the thinking it has engendered has exerted a pernicious influence upon professional and public thinking. Never has the growing tendency of the American historical guild to think and teach and publish and reward on the basis of a sausage-link view of the past been more fatal to comprehension than in the implicit insistence that the Second World War was somehow a discrete event that ended once and for all when MacArthur turned away from the peace table on the *Missouri*'s quarterdeck shortly after nine o'clock on the morning of September 2, 1945. The assumption that somehow the world war and the cold war which followed so hard upon it were separate, if connected, developments has tended to chop up and fatally distort our view of the recent past.

For while it is true that much of the rest of the world has slowly but unmistakably moved out from beneath the long shadow of the Second World War, it is clear that the great victors have not. By the mid-sixties at the very latest, it had become obvious that the vanquished had indeed fashioned new and generous sociopolitical orders. Japan and the Federal Republic of Germany not only no longer constituted threats to world peace; they had become pillars of international stability and responsibility. At the same time a new generation was emerging in a Western Europe that had not known strife for twenty years and had begun to question seriously the apparent commitment of the Great Powers to incessant confrontation. Even broad areas of the non-Western world had begun to achieve a modicum of stability following the peaceful or forceful seizure of their own destinies. Only the Great Powers and their immediate clients seemed unable to shake off a bondage to a violent past.

It is impossible, given the nature of the Soviet regime, to assess fairly and scrupulously the precise effects of the Second World War upon recent Russian life and policy. (It is intriguing to note, however, the enormous emphasis which the regime placed upon the thirtieth anniversary of V-E Day, an event scarcely noted seriously in the West.) But the lingering impact of the war upon the United States was readily observable as late as the mid-seventies.

Watergate was no whim of history. It had been in the making for thirty years. The scandals themselves, the officials who committed or permitted them, and, yes, the women who allowed themselves and their men to be pressed into a corrupt mold: all were products of that rootless, manipulative, cynical, and exploitative life style which the veteran generation had grafted onto so much of postwar American life. As Garry Wills and others have noted, the political atmosphere which eventually produced Watergate first emerged during the earliest years of the postwar era in and around the Los Angeles basin. In the late 1940s tens of thousands of young veterans and their families poured into sunny southern California from the cold and dark cities, towns, and farms of the East and Middle West. The young people sought a new life, new opportunities, and new hopes amid those warm hills and valleys often first glimpsed during confused wartime travels. What they all too often found instead were the inhuman pressures of feverish competition and a frighteningly impersonal social order amid a steadily deteriorating physical environment.

Southern California quickly became a land of unplanned, mushrooming growth. In the next quarter century all of California, but especially that sprawling and previously rather sleepy region stretching from Santa Monica to San Pedro, was transformed into a vast urban and suburban mess of freeways and tracts and shopping centers, ruining once and for all what had been a fragile loveliness. In that atmosphere of feverish growth, civility and services decayed, and public life swiftly became defined by what Wills has felicitously labeled a "politics of resentment," which structured a social order of alienation and anxiety. "Progressive" legislation enacted years before in Sacramento by earnest do-gooders who honestly believed in the inherent corruption of party politics insured political fluidity. The initiative, referendum, and recall, when coupled with crossover voting, guaranteed a weak, comparatively unstructured, and, above all, undisciplined political order in which party organization counted for little and each candidate was essentially on his own to seek and carve out as large an empire as he and his intensely loyal faction could. A premium was thus placed upon a loner style of politics in which the highest principle was all too often the dedicated and reciprocal loyalty of candidate and followers above any abstract notion of or commitment to public service.

To obtain that 51 percent of the vote necessary to gain and maintain power in an atmosphere of frequent anomie and desperation, it was mandatory, as a political analyst named Murray Chotiner quickly perceived, to speak not to people's diffuse hopes and dreams, but rather to their very real and immediate fears and animosities.* Young Richard Nixon, fresh out of the navy in 1946 and ideologically and emotionally rootless, became at once an early beneficiary and an apt disciple both of the politics of resentment and the politics of factionalism.

Nixon was destined to reflect and project the worst of the veteran generation's practices and beliefs precisely because at war's end he remained such an intellectual, moral, and ethical tabula rasa. He was still waiting to become whatever those who could help him most wanted him to become. As Garry Wills was to note prophetically years later: "Nixon is a postwar man. Politically, he does not preexist the year 1946. . . . For Nixon the thirties seem not to have taken place."[1] A style thus forged in the distinct regional caldron that was southern California of the late forties quickly found its chief proponent, and both the man and the style became a national phenomenon as the pace, the values, and the aspirations of

---

* It is interesting to note Joachim C. Fest's comment about Dr. Karl Lueger, mayor of Vienna at the turn of the century, "spokesman for petit bourgeois anti-Semitism," and Adolf Hitler's spiritual idol and tactical guide. "The mass party Lueger formed with the aid of emotional slogans was living proof that anxiety was—as happiness had been a century before—a new idea in Europe, powerful enough to bridge even class interests." Fest, *Hitler* (New York: Vintage Books, 1975), pp. 42-43. Forty-five years separated the discovery and application of anxiety politics in Central Europe and in the far southwestern corner of the United States.

southern California living gradually spread over the rest of the country in the fifties and sixties.

Theodore White is right. The image of Richard Nixon as a loser is simply wrong. For a long time he was a consistent winner. Indeed, prior to 1960 Nixon never lost an election. He became congressman, senator, and then vice-president at astoundingly young ages. While still in his early forties he was, briefly, virtual president of the United States following Eisenhower's heart attack, and he did, from all available accounts, a very creditable job in maintaining the rhythm and flow of the administration until the chief could recover sufficiently to resume power. Even Nixon's 1960 loss to Kennedy was legally narrow and, to many, factually and morally questionable. And in 1968, by a narrow margin and by a plurality, not a majority, it is true, he won the greatest prize of all. The record is clear: a substantial portion of the veteran generation responded favorably, if seldom enthusiastically, to the person and politics of a man who was all too often consumed by personal bitterness, spite, and malice. Nixon's politics of resentment evoked a powerful and consistent surge of support throughout postwar America. Indeed, in examining the public record in the thirty years following Hiroshima, the historian does not claim too much when he argues that this was, preeminently, the age of Nixon, rather than the era of Harry Truman or Dwight Eisenhower or Lyndon Johnson or John Kennedy. Nixon made a greater impact on his countrymen over a longer period of time than any other individual. His ultimate tragedy, his shame, and his crimes, if such they were, must be shared by his countrymen in rueful recognition of their own failings.

But condemnation is no substitute for analysis, though it has often seemed to be so in postwar America. We are still left with haunting questions about the origins of Watergate. Was it a phenomenon wholly explicable in terms of the Second World War era, or do its roots reach back much farther in national life? The answer seems to be that Watergate was only the most recent culmination of a recurrent national cycle of aspiration, triumph, decay, and disillusion, and that, as with many other aspects of national life, the Second World War played midwife to this latest cycle but did not create the cycle itself.

There is a great poignance to the story of America's post-1945 veteran generation. To elaborate upon an earlier observation, this generation has, without fully realizing it, been condemned to play out a familiar drama, to reenact a recurrent tragedy, that has been part of the very fabric of American life from the start. The tragic dilemma of failure through, by, and because of success can be traced back to seventeenth-century Massachusetts Bay and then all the way to the present. Throughout our past, countless groups have succeeded in fulfilling specific dreams beyond all bounds of logical expectation. Cherished objectives have been achieved to apparent perfection. Then each group discovered that life went on, that triumph could not be eternally frozen, that the children and the children's children had developed new drives, new perspectives, fresh needs that clashed or were directly at odds with the prevailing atmosphere.

What remains to be explored is the peculiarly consistent reaction of the achievers to the inevitable decay of their achievements. Perceiving and decrying the decline of the covenant theology and spirit in late-seventeenth-century New England, Puritan divines resorted to hypocrisy, fraud, and finally outright terror (in the case of the Salem witch trials) to defend their theocracy. The Puritan spirit was ebbing under the impact of material attractions, social development, population diffusion, and the simple passage of time. There was no feasible way to retrieve it. Yet for a brief time power remained in the hands of those wedded to an older ideal, to an outworn social concept, to an exhausted religious vision. And they determined to resist the changing order, to revive the old ways through a rhetoric of fear where possible and a policy of repression where and when necessary. Eventually they were not defeated so much as discredited; they were not overthrown so much as simply submerged by the irresistible flood of immigration and change that constituted the basis of the rapidly evolving social order that was colonial America.

A century later a similar behavioral pattern developed in the politics of the Federalist faction, most of whose members had more or less supported the Revolution and the quest for a strong, central government. Stout defenders, for the most part, of the still prevailing but decaying, elitist sociopolitical order of colonial times, these self-styled "friends of government" were able to staff and dominate the administrations of George Washington and John Adams. From positions of national power, they righteously resisted all interpretations of the revolutionary and Constitutional achievements that would expand real political power beyond the bounds of the entrenched orders in each locale. In time the Federalists took their very identity from their resistance to those seeking, in Paul Goodman's phrase, an equal access to power. But their own power bases in the states and cities of late-eighteenth- and early-nineteenth-century America proved too narrow and too ephemeral to sustain their pretensions. Although the Revolution had given birth to countless and contradictory streams of thought and aspiration, the notion of democracy had taken strong and deep hold in a citizenry politically aroused by the vast drama of its time.

Jefferson, Madison, and their Democratic-Republican colleagues increasingly resisted the assumptions and policies of their temperamental antagonists. They first broke with the Washington administration and thereafter resisted both the Adams and "high" wings of the Federalist formation. And as Republican resistance grew and popular animosity developed, both moderate and extreme Federalists resorted, as had their Puritan grandfathers, to terror and repression. Though no political witches were condemned or burned to death, the Alien and Sedition Acts represented, as John Miller has noted, a very real crisis in freedom.

Criticism of the president became a high crime; criticism of the government was declared equally illegal; fear of and hostility toward newly arrived immigrants, newly enfranchised citizens, was written into a law which stipulated a generation's wait before the "alien" could achieve the full blessings of liberty and decision making. Politics in and out of Congress became charged with venom; the first full decade of the national experience became, in Marshall Smelser's phrase, an age of nearly unrestrained passion and division. Never again prior to 1850 would the republic be in such peril of dissolution as it was in 1798-1800. All that saved the new nation from collapse was a hastily and almost inadvertently contrived two-party system that barely managed to contain and compress political violence within an institutional framework in which competition and animosity were focused upon the ballot box rather than the bayonet.

Two centuries later the republic again experienced, for the first time in a hundred years, a Constitutional and administrative crisis of the gravest proportions. That crisis originated in a measurable, long-developing public mood of frustration and anger, not with things as they were but with things as they threatened to become. A veteran generation that had defined itself by the stupendous achievement of winning a war discovered that after "unconditional" triumph life went on. Wartime comrades quickly became peacetime antagonists, and wartime enemies just as quickly had to be accepted as reliable peacetime friends. A generation that had dreamed of and slaved for personal, familial, and national affluence and security and had gotten it all found its achievements and indeed its values all too quickly mocked by its children, who, in their own apparently perfect security and perfect arrogance, never dreamed (and certainly never knew) what it was like to go to bed hungry and lonely and frightened of tomorrow. A sour, sullen, despairing, almost nihilistic mood gripped many members of the veteran generation by the mid-sixties. Nothing they had done, from making money and remaking the nation to measurably improving the lot of Catholics, Jews, blacks, and poor people in general, seemed to have any meaning, any permanence. Consistently generous efforts to remake the world in a nobler, stabler, more affluent cast had seemingly gone for naught.

It was to and for these disheartened and despairing millions that Nixon increasingly spoke in the two decades following the Second World War. By the late sixties, if not long before, Nixon had become the quintessential man of his time and place. As with the radical young whom he so deeply and publicly despised, he defined himself and his world by his own grievances. Millions of his fellow countrymen accepted him, supported him, and ultimately promoted him to the highest office because they saw in him a portion—and a respected portion—of themselves. In 1968 the politics of resentment at last reached the center of national life.

Once in power, Nixon acted no differently than could have been expected. America, his America of the "silent majority," had to be walled in and defended against the bums, the foolish liberals, the dangerous radicals, the legitimate political opponents, and all the other forces of opposition that threatened the power, the will, the autonomy of the man, his administration, and his followers. In his lust for perfect security, perfect comfort, perfect power, Richard Nixon became the perfect symbol of the veteran generation.

Upon reaching the White House, Nixon added to his bedrock politics of resentment an already existing obsession in many areas of government with "credibility," an obsession derived, as Jonathan Schell has stressed, from agonizing recollections of the failure of appeasement in the thirties on the one hand and an equally anguished recognition of the need to resolve the paradox of nuclear weapons possession and military paralysis on the other. Under the enormous pressures of governance, particularly governance exercised by men with little or no prior experience, the politics of resentment and credibility shaded all too often into a politics of revenge and attempted suppression whenever and wherever the presidential will seemed thwarted or questioned.

The president and many, if by no means all, of his men began, wittingly or not, to build the actual foundations of a modern totalitarian police state in America whose faint outlines began to resemble those of Nazi Germany. The historian, himself a product of the postwar era with all its complex pressures, must constantly work to avoid hysteria of his own. Richard Nixon's America cannot be equated with Adolf Hitler's Germany. Nor did the Nixon administration represent a complete break with traditional practice and behavior; it intensified to an unprecedented degree existing postwar American trends. But what is so terrifying to the advocate of democratic republicanism was the unmistakable presence of Nazilike elements, however embryonic.

True, there were no political murders in America between 1969 and 1974, but there was much attempted and some successful character assassination, whose techniques young Richard Nixon had learned long before in the Alger Hiss case. True, there were no bands of thugs beating up opponents on the street, although the "goon squad," which at one point, before being turned back by the police, was poised to rush the Capitol, might well have been a promise of things to come. There was no Reichstag fire, although a proposal to firebomb the Brookings Institution to cover a theft is rather hauntingly reminiscent. There surely were no Treblinkas or Mauthausens or Dachaus, or any concrete suggestions thereof. But President Nixon's own recorded anti-Semitism was of a depth and intensity sufficient to appall those who could recall the moment in their lives when the films from the Germany of 1945 were first flashed on American screens.

To be sure, the Nixon administration had no monopoly on Fascist behavior in the late sixties and early seventies. Nazilike tactics on the part of students and radicals—including the blowing to bits of innocents—was frighteningly widespread in those years. But as others have stressed, the radicals and terrorists did not hold the power of national government in their hands. The president and his men did, and the record indicates beyond question that such power was employed directly to obstruct justice, suppress evidence, cover up crime, subvert institutions, taint an independent court system, destroy careers, attack a free press, and make general war on those citizens whose ideas or deportment they disapproved. How far some of the more paranoid, irresponsible, or simply foolish members of the Nixon White House might have been *tempted* to go, had there not existed to thwart them a vast bureaucracy and numerous sources of responsible power beyond their immediate control, is an interesting, if terrifying, question. The existing public record does not support a supposition of restraint.

Yet again, it needs to be stressed that Nixon and his fellow Watergate conspirators *were* men of their time. The very atmosphere in which they developed and worked was congenial to warped ideas of political power. Would the Nixon White House have been tempted to use the Internal Revenue Service, FBI, and CIA to spy upon and ruin individuals had not such domestic espionage been carried on in the past in obvious violation of the spirit, if not the letter, of the law? Would the Nixon White House have considered use of the CIA at all in such matters had not the CIA been employed with gross abuse by earlier administrations? Would the Watergate conspirators have been so tempted to use the powers of government to subvert outside institutions had not governmental power been used before, on both state and national levels, to coerce universities into forcing loyalty oaths upon faculties, often firing those who would not sign? Would certain members of the Nixon White House have been so eager to "screw" their "political enemies" if the country had not been so hospitable to the destructive tactics and crude rhetoric of Joseph R. McCarthy? Would the extremists within the Nixon entourage have been so eager to purge the bureaucracy of all those who in any way might obstruct or dispute the White House will if there had not existed the example of the State Department purge of the early fifties in which first-rate minds and personalities were expelled, not because of subversive views, but because of unpopular ones? Would Nixon himself have been tempted to increase his personal fortune by highly questionable means had not the presidency become an obvious source of personal enrichment to two of his three immediate predecessors?

By all accounts Richard Nixon had become not only a bitter, but a bewildered, man even before he abandoned his shattered presidency for the cloister of San Clemente. And for all his grievous misdeeds he has a certain right to feel betrayed. Nothing that the man did or had done or permitted to be done in 1969, 1971, 1972, or 1973 was out of character with what he had done or permitted to be done earlier in his career. And that career was, whether it will be admitted or not, firmly in the mainstream of postwar American life. As president, Richard Nixon went further, it is true, than he had ever done before; after all, he had the power to do so. But the potentiality for a gross abuse of presidential power had long been evident in his career. Yet that career had, with one egregious exception, prospered. It prospered because Nixon the political man, Nixon the political stylist, Nixon the political technician, struck a powerfully responsive chord in a veteran generation that had come out of the Second World War prizing more than anything else power and toughness (the football metaphors are pervasive in Richard Nixon's America) and a certain blind righteousness leaning toward revenge.

Watergate thus represented the final expression and ultimate bankruptcy of the worst of the veteran generation's values and assumptions: the belief in force, the acceptance of expediency, the easy surrender to bitterness and malice—abroad as well as at

Notes

Introduction

1. Quoted in Philip Rieff, "The Meaning of History and Religion in Freud's Thought," in Bruce Mazlish, ed., *Psychoanalysis and History* (Englewood Cliffs, N.J.: Prentice-Hall, 1963), p. 44.

2. Bertram D. Wolfe, *Three Who Made a Revolution: A Biographic History* (Boston: Beacon Press, 1948).

3. Murray Kempton, *Part of our Time: Some Monuments and Ruins of the Thirties* (New York: Delta, 1967), p. 1.

4. William Sheridan Allen, *The Nazi Seizure of Power: The Experience of a Single German Town, 1930-1935* (Chicago: Quadrangle Books, 1965), p. 278.

Chapter 1

1. Quoted in Harry Bayard Price, *The Marshall Plan and Its Meaning* (Ithaca, N.Y.: Cornell University Press, 1955), p. 294.

2. Walter Laquer, *Europe since Hitler* (Baltimore: Penguin Books, 1972), p. 280.

Chapter 2

1. Angus Calder, *The People's War* (New York: Ace Books, 1972), pp. 382-87. An exception to this rule seems to have been set in those

Continental countries where the wartime resistance was at once comparatively effective and unsparing in its use of woman power. The resistance experience in France especially seems to have had a direct bearing on the enhanced postwar status of women and their demands for even greater participation in the public life of the republic. See Henri Michel, *The Shadow War: European Resistance, 1939-1945*, trans. Richard Barry (New York: Harper & Row, 1972), pp. 191-94.

2. Nazi efforts to portray their seizure and use of power as a deliberately contrived social revolution in which traditionally rigid class distinctions were swept away in a tide of bourgeois folk egalitarianism have been sharply challenged by the findings of Richard Grunberger and David Schoenbaum. Grunberger has argued with considerable effect that the Nazi movement was at best a "pseudo-revolution" that left older distinctions, differences, and privileges practically intact, at least through the days of the Officers' Plot of July 1944. In Schoenbaum's memorable words, "Destruction alone was a common goal after all others—'Beamtenstaat' and Volksgemeinschaft, 'back to the land' and back to the boundaries of 1918, the salvation of private property and the achievement of 'national socialism'—had eliminated one another in a process of mutual cancellation. In the end, with the achievement of each partial goal, the destruction of unions and aristocracy, of Jews, of the Rights of Man and of bourgeois society, destruction was all that was left." Richard Grunberger, *The Twelve-Year Reich: A Social History of Nazi Germany, 1933-1945* (New York: Ballantine Books, 1971); David Schoenbaum, *Hitler's Social Revolution* (New York: Doubleday Anchor Books, 1967), p. 288.

3. F[rancis] C. Jones, *Japan's New Order in East Asia: Its Rise and Fall, 1937-1945* (New York: Oxford University Press, 1954), p. 3.

Chapter 3

1. General Heinz Guderian, *Panzer Leader*, abridged ed. (New York: Ballantine Books, 1967), pp. 115-17.

2. Quoted in Alan Clark, *Barbarossa: The Russian-German Conflict, 1941-45* (New York: Signet Books, 1965), p. 64.

3. *Hitler's Secret Conversations, 1941-1944*, introduction by H. R. Trevor-Roper (New York: Signet Books, 1961), pp. 58-60.

4. William J. Newman, *The Balance of Power in the Interwar Years, 1919-1939* (New York: Random House, 1968), pp. 147-48.

5. Clark, *Barbarossa*, p. 102; Guderian, *Panzer Leader*, p. 176.

6. Clark, *Barbarossa*, p. 208. For a contrary view, see Rudolf Hofmann's lengthy essay, "The Battle for Moscow, 1941," in H. A. Jacobsen and J. Rohwer, eds., *Decisive Battles of World War II: The German View* (New York: G. P. Putnam's Sons, 1965), pp. 137-78, esp. p. 177.

7. American accounts of Pearl Harbor "treachery" are legion; for a similar Japanese view, see Masanori Ito, *The End of the Imperial Japanese Navy* (New York: McFadden Books, 1965), pp. 32-34.

8. Bruce M. Russett, *No Clear and Present Danger: A Skeptical View of the U. S. Entry into World War II* (New York: Harper & Row, 1972).

9. Paul W. Schroeder, *The Axis Alliance and Japanese-American Relations, 1941* (Ithaca, N.Y.: Cornell University Press, 1958), p. 203.

10. Barbara Tuchman, *Stilwell and the American Experience in China, 1911-1945* (New York: Bantam Books, 1972), pp. 212, 214, 225.

11. Quoted in Ito, *End of the Imperial Japanese Navy*, pp. 14-15.

Chapter 4

1. Peter Calvocoressi and Guy Wint, *Total War: Causes and Courses of the Second World War* (London: Allen Lane, Penguin Press, 1972), p. 479.

2. C. P. Snow, *Science and Government* (New York: Mentor Books, 1962), p. 47.

3. Ibid., pp. 48-49, 111.

4. Ibid., p. 47.

5. Calvocoressi and Wint, *Total War*, p. 538.

Chapter 5

1. Robert Jay Lifton, *History and Human Survival* (New York: Vintage Books, 1971), esp. pp. 195-207.

2. Herbert London, "The Crumbling of One Man's World," *Washington Post*, March 16, 1975.

3. John W. Aldridge, "In the Country of the Young," *Harper's Magazine* 239 (October 1969):49-50.

4. Joan Didion, "A Generation Not for Barricades," *Life* 68 (June 5, 1970):26.

5. Albert Goldman, *Ladies and Gentlemen, Lenny Bruce!!* (New York: Ballantine Books, 1974), p. 261. Italics in the quotation are Goldman's.

6. William H. Whyte, *The Organization Man* (New York: Simon and Schuster, 1956).

7. Ralph Waldo Emerson, "Historic Notes of Life and Letters in New England," in Perry Miller, ed., *The American Transcendentalists: Their Prose and Poetry* (Garden City, N.Y.: Doubleday Anchor Books, 1957), pp. 5-6.

8. The shattering impact of the Manson murders upon radical youth is summarized by the editors of *Rolling Stone* in their compendium, *The Age of Paranoia: How the Sixties Ended* (New York: Pocket Books, 1972), pp. xvii-xviii, 331-402.

Chapter 6

1. Adam B. Ulam, *Stalin: The Man and His Era* (New York: Viking Press, 1973), pp. 652-53.

2. Ibid., p. 643.

3. Ibid., pp. 659-60.

Chapter 9

1. Henry Fairlie, *The Kennedy Promise: The Politics of Expectation* (New York: Dell Books, 1974).

2. Benjamin Bradlee, "He Had that Special Grace," *Newsweek*, December 2, 1963, p. 38.

3. Christopher Lasch, *The New Radicalism in America* (New York: Alfred A. Knopf, 1965), p. 321.

4. Quoted in ibid., p. 312.

5. See *Washington Post,* October 30, 1972, p. A-8 and May 24, 1973, p. 12.

6. James Tracy Crown and George P. Penty, *Kennedy in Power* (New York: Ballantine Books, 1961), pp. 169-70, 191.

7. Shannon, "The Kennedy Administration: The Early Months," *American Scholar* 30 (Autumn 1961):481.

8. Butler, "An Englishman's Reflections on the Change of Administration," *American Scholar* 30 (Autumn 1961):527.

9. May, "In a Time of Unmanifest Destiny," *American Scholar* 30 (Autumn 1961):552-53.

10. Henry Fairlie, "We Knew What We Were Doing When We Went into Vietnam," *Washington Monthly* 5 (May 1973):7-26.

11. *Public Papers of the Presidents: John F. Kennedy, 1963* (Washington, D.C.: U.S. Government Printing Office, 1964), pp. 733-38.

Chapter 10

1. Garry Wills, *Nixon Agonistes: The Crisis of the Self-Made Man* (New York: Signet Books, 1971), p. 83.

Bibliographic Essay

The Second World War era has generated far more literature and documentation than even the most assiduous scholar can know or master. A few of the thousands of monographs, biographies, memoirs, and speculative essays which have contributed most to my thinking about this period over the past quarter century or so have already been cited in the text and do not need further recognition. The manuscript sources from which many of my ideas have developed are cited in my three previous works in this field: *Dubious Victory: The United States and the End of World War II* (Kent, Ohio: Kent State University Press, 1973); *After Yalta: America and the Origins of the Cold War* (New York: Charles Scribner's Sons, 1973); and *Roots of Tragedy: The United States and the Struggle for Asia, 1945-1953* (Westport, Conn.: Greenwood Press, 1976). Other published writings from which I have derived much factual and speculative enrichment include the following:

General Works

Hanson W. Baldwin, *Battles Lost and Won: Great Campaigns of World War II* (New York: Harper & Row, 1966); B. H. Liddell Hart, ed., *The German Generals Talk* (New York: Berkley Publishing, 1958, originally published in England as *The Other Side of the Hill*, 1948); idem, *History of the Second World War* (New York: G. P. Putnam's Sons, 1971); Hans-Adolf Jacobsen and Jurgen Rohwer, *Decisive Battles of World War II: The German View*, Edward Fitzgerald, trans. (New York: G. P. Putnam's Sons, 1965); Louis L. Snyder, *The War: A Concise History, 1939-1945* (New York: Julian Messner, 1961); A. J. P.

Taylor, *The Origins of the Second World War* (New York: Atheneum, 1961); Chester Wilmot, *The Struggle for Europe* (London: Fontana Books, 1959); and Gordon Wright, *The Ordeal of Total War, 1939-1945* (New York: Harper & Row, 1968). William L. Langer and S. Everett Gleason's works, *The Challenge to Isolation, 1937-1940* and *The Undeclared War, 1940-1941* (New York: Harper and Brothers, 1952, 1953), fully justify their comprehensive general title *The World Crisis and American Foreign Policy;* after twenty-five years these huge volumes remain surprisingly fresh, detailed, and authoritative. Winston Churchill's six-volume history-reminiscences continue to be the single most compelling commentary not only on the war years, but on the decade of depression and appeasement which preceded them. The fact that recent scholarship has rendered many of Churchill's assertions and judgments suspect lessens neither their importance nor their fascination. The recognized prologue to the Second World War is masterfully treated by Hugh Thomas in *The Spanish Civil War* (New York: Harper & Brothers, 1961).

Hitler and the Problem of Totalitarianism

I am uncertain of my debt to the fledgling field of psychohistory, and I am even less sure of the extent to which my perspectives have been shaped by an unsystematic reading in the history of psychiatry and of the philosophy of modern science. However, the following works have had an undeniable impact upon my thinking: Jacques Barzun, *Darwin, Marx, Wagner: Critique of a Heritage* (Garden City, N.Y.: Doubleday Anchor Books, 1958); idem, *Classic, Romantic, and Modern* (Garden City, N.Y.: Doubleday Anchor Books, 1961); Loren Eisley, *Darwin's Century: Evolution and the Men Who Discovered It* (Garden City, N.Y.: Doubleday Anchor Books, 1961); Sigmund Freud, *A General Introduction to Psychoanalysis,* trans. Joan Riviere (New York: Permabooks, 1953) and *Civilization and Its Discontents,* trans. and ed. James Strachey (New York: W. W. Norton, 1962); John C. Greene, *The Death of Adam: Evolution and Its Impact on Western Thought* (New York: Mentor Books, 1961); Gertrude Himmelfarb, *Darwin and the Darwinian Revolution* (Garden City, N.Y.: Doubleday Anchor Books, 1962); Richard Hofstadter, *Social Darwinism in American Thought* (Philadelphia: University of Pennsylvania Press, 1944); Bruce Mazlish, ed., *Psychoanalysis and History* (Englewood Cliffs, N.J.: Prentice-Hall, 1963); and R. J. Wilson, ed., *Darwinism and the American Intellectual* (Homewood, Ill.: Dorsey Press, 1967). Konrad Lorenz's *On*

Aggression (New York: Harcourt, Brace and World, 1966) is brilliantly suggestive, yet disturbingly cold and repellent in its insistence upon the animal nature of all life. Two works which seek to relate modern psychiatric philosophy and practice directly to the holocaust and the Nazi concentration camps are Bruno Bettelheim, *The Informed Heart: Autonomy in a Mass Age* (New York: Avon Books, 1971) and Viktor Frankl, *Man's Search for Meaning* (Boston: Beacon Press, 1962, originally published as *From Death Camp to Existentialism*).

I have read most of the leading works in English on the Nazi death camps and the "final solution." The best among these are Lucy S. Dawidowicz, *The War Against the Jews* (New York: Bantam Books, 1976) and Eugen Kogon, *Theory and Practice of Hell* (New York: Octagon Books, 1973). As for the great totalitarian himself, I find Alan Bullock's *Hitler: A Study in Tyranny* (New York: Harper and Brothers, 1953) still insightful though it needs to be supplemented with Joachim C. Fest's more recent and superlative *Hitler* (New York: Harcourt, Brace and Jovanovich, 1974) and even John Toland's often disappointing *Adolf Hitler* (Garden City, N.Y.: Doubleday, 1976). Among the flood of memoirs by survivors of the Nazi years, the most significant recollections of Hitler have been written by Albert Speer, though Speer's character and motives remain often obscure and suspect. Three contemporary works about Hitler and nazism are indispensable: G. M. Gilbert, *Nuremberg Diary* (New York: Farrar, Straus and Cudahy, 1947); *Hitler's Secret Conversations, 1941-1944* (New York: New American Library, 1953); and Louis P. Lochner, ed. and trans., *The Goebbels Diaries* (New York: Popular Library, 1948).

Among the many efforts to describe or understand the Nazi movement either by itself or as part of a wider phenomenon are these: Hannah Arendt, *The Origins of Totalitarianism* (New York: Harcourt, Brace, 1951), an immense, turgid, but ultimately enlightening effort; portions of Seymour Martin Lipset, *Political Man: The Social Bases of Politics* (Garden City, N.Y.: Doubleday Anchor Books, 1963); the works of Schoenbaum, Grunberger, and William Sheridan Allen cited in the text; Telford Taylor, *Sword and Swastika* (New York: Simon and Schuster, 1952), an early and satisfactory effort to explain as fully as possible the subversion of the German officer corps to the Nazi movement; and William L. Shirer, *The Rise and Fall of the Third Reich* (New York: Simon and Schuster, 1960), a far better and more informative work (especially on Berlin and Germany in the 1930s) than the historical guild would acknowledge, despite its many analytical and conceptual flaws. Edward L. Homze's *Foreign Labor in Nazi Germany*

(Princeton: Princeton University Press, 1967) is a particularly chilling account of what happened when Nazi ideology, the Nazi bureaucracy, and German war needs all blended to produce a new form of slavery in modern Europe. Jacques Delarue's *The Gestapo: A History of Horror* (New York: Dell Publishing, 1964) is self-explanatory. The book won the Prix de la Résistance.

The peculiar mix of bourgeois striving and respectability, architectural and artistic grandiosity and corruption, and political hysteria and hatred that was nazism can never be adequately grasped from the printed word alone. Film is the greatest teacher. Fortunately, the Nazis were great recorders of their own debased achievements, and their enemies were equally great recorders of their eventual collapse. Documentary films about Nazi Germany have abounded in the past forty years, and there is no sign that celluloid biographies of Adolf Hitler and celluloid histories of nazism and of the Second World War have reached an end. Among the greatest classic studies of nazism in all its guises are the two monumental works by Leni Riefenstahl, *The Triumph of the Will*, a four-hour paean of praise to the annual Nazi party rally at Nuremberg in 1934, and *Olympiad,* her equally long and highly impressionistic record of the "Nazi Olympics" at Berlin in August of 1936. Two other films of much more recent vintage deserve mention: *Swastika,* a record of life in Nazi Germany in the 1930s—including life at the very top among the Hitler entourage at Berchtesgaden—contrasted at the end with some of the more ghastly scenes from the liberated death camps of 1945. The film can be profitably (if that is the word) viewed in conjunction with a careful reading of Grunberger and one of the better general histories of the Third Reich. Various portions of the Thames production of *World at War* contain important scenes and commentary on Nazi Germany, though the book written from that series (and carrying the same title) by Mark Arnold-Forster (New York: New American Library, 1974) is most disappointing.

I have supplemented reading about Nazi Germany over the past twenty-five years or so with complementary studies of some other contemporary totalitarian regimes. Among the most important of these are the following: Robert Conquest, *The Great Terror* (New York: Harper & Row, 1968), still, despite Solzhenitsyn, a great history of the Stalin purges of the 1930s; Solzhenitsyn's own factual and fictionalized accounts of the Gulag; Isaac Deutscher, *Stalin: A Political Biography* (New York: Oxford University Press, 1949); Ivone Kirkpatrick, *Mussolini: A Study in Power* (New York: Avon Books, 1964); Leonard Mosley, *Hirohito, Emperor of Japan* (New York: Avon Books, 1967);

Edwin O. Reischauer, *Japan Past and Present*, 3d ed. (New York: Alfred A. Knopf, 1964); John Toland, *The Rising Sun: The Decline and Fall of the Japanese Empire, 1936-1945* (New York: Random House, 1970); and Adam B. Ulam, *Stalin* (New York: Viking Press, 1973).

Grand Strategy

Grand strategy was fashioned in equal measure from the imperatives of the Grand Alliance, the relative strengths of each of the three great partners, and the Allied reaction to Axis policies, plans, and capabilities. The most stimulating discussions of this topic from the Allied side are Kent Roberts Greenfield, *American Strategy in World War II* (Baltimore: Johns Hopkins Press, 1963) and Samuel Eliot Morison, *Strategy and Compromise* (Boston: Little, Brown, 1958). From the Axis perspective see Jacobsen and Rohwer, op. cit., as well as the various studies cited in the text. Stimulating and knowledgeable discussions of both Axis and Allied grand strategy and tactics—and their frequent limitations—can also be found throughout Morison's magisterial, fifteen-volume *History of United States Naval Operations in World War II* (Boston: Little, Brown, 1947-60) and in Liddell Hart's *History of the Second World War*, as well as in portions of the over-one-hundred-volume *History of the United States Army in World War II*, the famous "green back" series produced by the Office of the Chief of Military History (Washington, D.C.: U.S. Government Printing Office, 1955-19—).

Since Allied strategy ultimately depended upon the diplomacy of the Grand Alliance, an understanding of how that alliance came into existence and how it functioned is essential. The two best single-volume works on the subject remain Herbert Feis, *Churchill, Roosevelt, Stalin: The War They Waged and the Peace They Sought* (Princeton: Princeton University Press, 1957) and William Hardy McNeill, *America, Britain, and Russia: Their Cooperation and Conflict, 1941-1946* (London: Oxford University Press, 1953). Three recent studies which emphasize the ever-precarious nature of the Grand Alliance, not excluding its Anglo-American component, are Stephen E. Ambrose, *Eisenhower and Berlin, 1945: The Decision to Halt at the Elbe* (New York: W. W. Norton, 1967); Robert Beitzell, *The Uneasy Alliance: America, Britain and Russia, 1941-1943* (New York: Alfred A. Knopf, 1972); and Warren F. Kimball, *The Most Unsordid Act: Lend-Lease, 1939-1941* (Baltimore: Johns Hopkins Press, 1969).

Leading participants in or witnesses to Grand Alliance diplomacy have set down their impressions in a flood of memoirs and histories. Among the best of these are Churchill's six-volume work already mentioned; John R. Deane, *The Strange Alliance: The Story of Our Wartime Cooperation with the Russians* (New York: Viking Press, 1947); Anthony Eden, *The Reckoning: Memoirs of the Earl of Avon* (Boston: Houghton Mifflin, 1967); Joseph C. Grew, *Turbulent Era: A Diplomatic Record of Forty Years,* 2 vols. (Boston: Houghton Mifflin, 1952); George F. Kennan, *Memoirs, 1925-1950* (Boston: Little, Brown, 1967); William D. Leahy, *I Was There* (New York: Whittlesey House, 1950); Robert E. Sherwood, *Roosevelt and Hopkins: An Intimate History* (New York: Bantam Books, 1950); Edward R. Stettinius, Jr., *Roosevelt and the Russians: The Yalta Conference* (Garden City, N.Y.: Doubleday, 1949); and Harry S. Truman, *Memoirs: 1945, Year of Decisions* (New York: Signet Books, 1965). The official American record of the Grand Alliance insofar as it was made in conferences and exchanges among the Big Three and their many military and diplomatic subordinates from 1941 to 1945 has now been published in the many conference and topical volumes of the ongoing series, *Foreign Relations of the United States,* produced by the Historical Office of the U.S. Department of State and published by the U.S. Government Printing Office. A partial Soviet record covering the three great wartime conferences has been published in Robert Beitzell, ed., *Tehran, Yalta, Potsdam: The Soviet Protocols* (Hattiesburg, Miss.: Academic International Press, 1970).

The Origins and Development of the Cold War

The literature on this topic is as vast, as varied, and as controversial as any in American historiography today. Since a substantial proportion of the preceding essays has been devoted to a refutation of revisionist historiography, it is only fair that the reader sample as wide a selection of New Left writing as possible. The best, most complete, and most recent bibliography is found in Thomas G. Paterson, ed., *The Origins of the Cold War,* 2d ed. (Lexington, Mass.: D. C. Heath, 1974). Leading revisionist works include the following: Gar Alperovitz, *Atomic Diplomacy: Potsdam and Hiroshima* (New York: Simon and Schuster, 1965); Stephen E. Ambrose, *Rise to Globalism* (Baltimore: Penguin Books, 1971); Richard J. Barnet, *Roots of War* (New York: Atheneum, 1972); Diane Shaver Clemens, *Yalta* (New York: Oxford University Press, 1970); Richard J. Freeland, *The Truman Doctrine and the Origins of McCarthyism* (New York: Alfred A. Knopf, 1971); Lloyd C. Gardner, *Architects of Illusion: Men and Ideas in American Foreign Policy, 1941-1949* (Chicago: Quadrangle Books, 1970); Gabriel Kolko, *The Politics of War: The World and United States Foreign Policy, 1943-1945* (New York: Random House, 1969); Joyce and Gabriel Kolko, *The Limits of Power: The World and United States Foreign Policy, 1945-1954* (New York: Harper & Row, 1972); Thomas G. Paterson, *Soviet-American Confrontation: Postwar Reconstruction and the Origins of the Cold War* (Baltimore: Johns Hopkins Press, 1973); Athan G. Theoharis, *Seeds of Repression: Harry S. Truman and the Origins of McCarthyism* (Chicago: Quadrangle Books, 1971); and William Appleman Williams, *The Tragedy of American Diplomacy* (New York: Dell Publishing, 1962). The standard cold war text from this perspective is Walter LaFeber's excellent *America, Russia and the Cold War, 1945-1975* (New York: John Wiley & Sons, 1976).

Two cogent and critical studies of New Left historiography are Robert James Maddox, *The New Left and the Origins of the Cold War* (Princeton: Princeton University Press, 1973), which emphasizes scholarly and methodological weaknesses, and Joseph Siracusa, *New Left Histories and Historians* (Port Washington, N.Y.: Kennikat Press, 1973), which lays greater stress upon philosophical and conceptual shortcomings.

Early efforts to view the cold war from a postrevisionist perspective include Lynn Ethridge Davis, *The Cold War Begins: Soviet-American Conflict over Eastern Europe* (Princeton: Princeton University Press, 1974); John Lewis Gaddis, *The United States and the Origins of the Cold War, 1941-1947* (New York: Columbia University Press, 1972); and my own *After Yalta* and *Roots of Tragedy*.

The more intrepid and intrigued readers may test this paroxysm of scholarship against the official American record. The *Foreign Relations* series has reached some sixty published volumes for the period 1945-50, embracing nearly the entire foreign-policy record for the years between the end of the Second World War and the beginning of the Korean conflict.

Postwar America

Here again the literature is so immense and complex as to defy true mastery. For background the reader should begin with three works on the domestic history of the war years that merit more than passing interest: Richard R. Lingeman, *Don't You Know There's a War On? The*

American Home Front, 1941-1945 (New York: Paperback Library, 1971); Geoffrey Perrett, *Days of Sadness, Years of Triumph: The American People, 1939-1945* (New York: Coward, McCann & Geoghegan, 1973), a truly superlative account; and Richard Polenberg, *War and Society: The United States, 1941-1945* (Philadelphia: J. B. Lippincott, 1972).

A number of brief surveys of the post-1945 period have been written; one of the most recent and best is Carl N. Degler's *Affluence and Anxiety* (Glenview, Ill.: Scott, Foresman, 1968), which contains an excellent critical bibliography. John Brooks, *The Great Leap: The Past Twenty-five Years in America* (New York: Harper & Row, 1966) is most stimulating and provocative, as is Philip Slater's *The Pursuit of Loneliness: American Culture at the Breaking Point* (Boston: Beacon Press, 1970), which should be read in conjunction with David Reisman et al., *The Lonely Crowd* (Garden City, N.Y.: Doubleday, 1950), the classic contemporary comment on the national character. A far smaller classic, but a jewel of its kind, is Robert Douglas Mead's *Reunion: Twenty-five Years out of School, A Personal History of the Middle Generation* (New York: Saturday Review Press, 1973). John Kenneth Galbraith's social criticisms parading as economic verities have become essential commentaries upon the sources and nature of contemporary American excess; see his *American Capitalism: The Theory of Countervailing Power* (Boston: Houghton Mifflin, 1952); *The Affluent Society* (Boston: Houghton Mifflin, 1958); and *The New Industrial State* (Boston: Houghton Mifflin, 1967). William O'Neill sought to write a durable and compelling instant history of the 1960s and sometimes succeeded remarkably well. The bibliography in his *Coming Apart: An Informal History of America in the 1960s* (New York: Quadrangle-New York Times Books, 1971) is a valuable study in itself. Other works of general interest on postwar America include these: Henry Brandon, *As We Are* (New York: Popular Library, 1962); Alexander Kendrick, *The Wound Within: America in the Vietnam Years, 1945-1974* (Boston: Little, Brown, 1974); Bill Moyers, *Listening to America* (New York: Dell Books, 1972); William L. Shirer, *Midcentury Journey* (New York: Farrar, Straus and Young, 1952); and Dan Wakefield, *Supernation at Peace and War* (Boston: Little, Brown, 1968). Ralph G. Martin's anthology, *The G.I. War, 1941-1945* (New York: Avon Books, 1967), contains a lengthy epilogue on the veteran generation's often frustrating and unhappy adjustment to postwar life in the America of the late forties.

The shortcomings and eventual "militarization" of American education at all levels can be gleaned from many sources, some of which I have already indicated above. Among the most important for this author were Arthur E. Bestor, *Educational Wastelands* (Urbana, Ill.: University of Illinois Press, 1953); Edgar Z. Friedenberg, *Coming of Age in America: Growth and Acquiescence* (New York: Random House, 1965); Paul Goodman, *Growing up Absurd: Problems of Youth in the Organized Society* (New York: Vintage Books, 1960); Clark Kerr, *The Uses of the University* (Cambridge: Harvard University Press, 1963); Seymour Martin Lipset and Sheldon S. Wolin, eds., *The Berkeley Student Revolt: Facts and Interpretations* (Garden City, N.Y.: Doubleday, 1965); and Michael V. Miller and Susan Gilmore, eds., *Revolution at Berkeley: The Crisis in American Education* (New York: Dell Publishing, 1965).

The flavor, fever, and frequent malevolence of postwar American politics is reflected and commented upon in many works. Despite grave flaws, the best place to start a review of recent American political development is in the pages of Theodore White's series, *The Making of the President* (New York: Atheneum, 1961, 1965, 1969, and 1973), which has become a quadrennial event in American publishing and popular culture ever since White worshipfully told of John Kennedy's triumph in 1960. The later volumes, particularly those dealing with 1968 and 1972, began to suffer very badly from White's endemic and unbiased reverence for the winner as winner (Richard Nixon in both cases). The writer tried to efface this blemish as gracefully as possible in his *Breach of Faith: The Fall of Richard Nixon* (New York: Atheneum, 1975).

Two other general works deserve special note: Daniel Bell, ed., *The Radical Right* (Garden City, N.Y.: Doubleday Anchor Books, 1964) and John H. Bunzel, *Anti-Politics in America* (New York: Alfred A. Knopf, 1967). Two excellent studies of McCarthyism are Robert Griffin, *The Politics of Fear: Joseph R. McCarthy and the Senate* (Lexington, Ky.: University of Kentucky Press, 1970) and Richard H. Rovere, *Senator Joe McCarthy* (New York: World Publishing, 1959). The best study of the Truman presidency to date is Alonzo Hamby, *Harry Truman and American Liberalism* (New York: Columbia University Press, 1974). The Eisenhower years are examined in Charles C. Alexander, *Holding the Line: The Eisenhower Era, 1952-1961* (Bloomington, Ind.: Indiana University Press, 1975) and Herbert S. Parmet, *Eisenhower and the American Crusades* (New York: Macmillan, 1972). An exhaustive but never exhausting study of the presidential campaigns and the country as a whole in 1968 is Lewis Chester, Godfrey Hodgson, and Bruce Page, *An American Melodrama* (New York: Viking Press, 1969). A spirited, leftist critique of recent American domestic as well as foreign policy that is both compelling and intriguing is Howard Zinn, *Postwar America, 1945-1971* (Indianapolis: Bobbs-Merrill, 1973).

The Kennedy family and the "one, brief shining moment" that was Camelot have kept many a writer in business. The public seems never to tire of the Kennedys—or of books about them—so it is unnecessary to list in scholarly order all of the countless volumes and articles on both John and Robert Kennedy which I have read or consulted. Suffice it to say that the "standard" works, both worshipful and critical, have provided me with the balance I tried to project in Chapter 9. Chief among these are the books by Burns, Fairlie, Galbraith, Hilsman, Lasch, Powers and O'Donnell (in which JFK comes off as surprisingly cold and humorless), Salinger, Schlesinger, Sidey, Sorenson, Walton, and Whalen.

As for Richard Nixon, it should be clear to anyone who lived through the Watergate years as a reasonably perceptive individual that more words and attention were lavished on this personality than on anyone else in living memory. Nixon himself, despite an ostensible penchant for secrecy and privacy, had spoken of himself often and at great length, particularly of his early years of poverty. My final evaluation of Nixon the man and politician was forged after reading the unfolding Watergate tale in the pages of the *Washington Post* and (less frequently) the *New York Times* each morning between October 1972 and August 1974. I have also tried to read most of the so-called White House Transcripts which the president released, and I reread Theodore White's assessments and evaluations of the man in the relevant volumes of the *Making of the President* series. Both of the Woodward and Bernstein books, *All the President's Men* and *The Final Days* (New York: Simon and Schuster, 1974 and 1976), have influenced my views as has Garry Wills, *Nixon Agonistes: The Crisis of the Self-Made Man* (New York: Signet Books, 1971), a classic study not only of the chief product of the contemporary American political system, but of that system itself with all its flaws and failures.

Index

About the Author

Lisle A. Rose has written extensively on aspects of diplomatic history. Among his earlier works are *Prologue to Democracy, After Yalta, Dubious Victory,* and *Roots of Tragedy: The United States and the Struggle for Asia, 1945-1953* (Greenwood Press, 1976).